# The United Nations and Transnational Organized Crime

# The United Nations and Transnational Organized Crime

Edited by
Phil Williams and Ernesto U. Savona

FRANK CASS
LONDON • PORTLAND, OR

*First published in Great Britain by*
FRANK CASS & CO LTD
Newbury House, 900 Eastern Avenue
London IG2 7HH, England

*and in the United States by*
FRANK CASS
c/o ISBS
5804 N.E. Hassalo Street, Portland, Oregon 97213-3644

Copyright © 1996 Frank Cass & Co. Ltd.

**Library of Congress Cataloging-in-Publication Data**
A catalog record of this book is available from
the Library of Congress.

**British Library Cataloguing in Publication Data**
A catalogue record of this book is available
from the British Library.

ISBN 0-7146-4733-0 (hb)
ISBN 0-7146-4283-5

Printed in Great Britain by Antony Rowe Ltd.

This group of studies first appeared in a Special Issue on 'The United Nations and Transnational Organized Crime' in *Transnational Organized Crime*, Vol.1, No.3, published by Frank Cass & Co. Ltd.

All rights reserved. No part of this publication may be reproduced, stored in a retrieval system, or transmitted in any form, or by any means, electronic, mechanical, photocopying, recording, or otherwise, without the prior permission of Frank Cass and Company Limited.

# Contents

| | | |
|---|---|---|
| Introduction | **Phil Williams** and **Ernesto U. Savona** | vii |

| | |
|---|---|
| Problems and Dangers Posed by Organized Transnational Crime in the Various Regions of the World | 1 |
| National Legislation and its Adequacy to Deal with the Various Forms of Organized Transnational Crime: Appropriate Guidelines for Legislative and Other Measures to be Taken at the National Level | 43 |
| Most Effective Forms of International Cooperation for the Prevention and Control of Organized Transnational Crime at the Investigative, Prosecutorial and Judicial Levels | 80 |
| Appropriate Modalities and Guidelines for the Prevention and Control of Organized Transnational Crime at the Regional and International Levels | 108 |
| The Feasibility of Elaborating International Instruments, including Conventions, against Organized Transnational Crime | 141 |
| Conclusions and Recommendations of the International Conference on Preventing and Controlling Money Laundering and the Use of the Proceeds of Crime: A Global Approach | 161 |
| Report of the Secretary-General: Implementation of General Assembly Resolution 49/150 on the Naples Political Declaration and Global Action Plan against Organized Transnational Crime | 169 |

# Introduction

## PHIL WILLIAMS and ERNESTO U. SAVONA

Threats to international security in the 1990s are less direct and apocalyptic than they were during the Cold War, but they are also more diffuse and insidious. The international community through the remainder of the 1990s and into the next millennium faces a set of challenges or threats that is as complex as it is novel. One of the most serious of these threats is that posed by transnational organized crime. Unlike most other transnational problems, such as AIDS, the spread of exotic diseases, population growth, and environmental degradation, transnational organized crime involves malevolence. The threat it poses to national and international security, although subtle and indirect, is not the inadvertent by-product of long-term trends but is rather an inevitable consequence of the activities of organizations that deny the state its legitimate monopoly of violence, that corrupt state institutions, that threaten the integrity of financial and commercial sectors of society, and that routinely disregard or contravene legal and social norms and conventions at both the domestic and international levels. What makes these forms of behaviour even more disquieting is that they allow criminal organizations to accumulate a degree of power and wealth that rivals and in some cases surpasses that possessed by governments. As these organizations become more deeply entrenched in their respective societies, they pose a threat to both democracy and the rule of law. The scale of the challenge is exemplified by comparing contemporary criminal organizations such as the Colombian drug cartels with those of the prohibition era in the United States. From today's perspective, Al Capone, the pre-eminent organized crime figure of his era, was a small time gangster with limited ambitions and constricted horizons, his empire no more than a local fiefdom. And the fact that he was jailed for tax evasion would be almost incomprehensible to criminal entrepreneurs who employ specialists to hide, transmit and legitimize the money they earn from their criminal activities.

To some extent, of course, this is simply the result of the changed context within which organized crime now operates. New opportunities have been grasped eagerly and effectively, leaving law enforcement trailing behind and working to match the inventiveness, adaptability and resilience of criminal organizations that have become transnational in both thought and deed while operating from safe home bases or 'sanctuaries'. Criminal organizations carry on their activities in what for them is, in effect, a borderless world, while law enforcement is significantly constrained by having to operate in what is still a bordered world. Both criminal personnel and 'hot money' have unprecedented mobility and are able to find cover and recruits in transnational ethnic networks created by migration and diasporas and that are difficult for domestic law enforcement to penetrate. Moreover, the technological sophistication of post-industrial states is increasingly becoming a source of vulnerability as well as a source of power. As such, it is something that could be exploited either by ruthless criminal organizations that are willing and able to grasp new opportunities to extend their influence and to augment their wealth or by desperate organizations that feel they are being pushed into a corner where an attack on the technological infra-structure of the threatening state looks attractive whether for defense or retaliation. The combination of the criminal organization and the skilled computer hacker is a frightening one.

The international community, preoccupied as it was with East-West competition and with regional conflicts, has been slow to come to terms with the new challenge posed by transnational criminal organizations. One major initiative in bringing the threat to public attention, however, was the World Ministerial Conference on transnational organized crime held in Naples from 21 to 23 November 1994. Convened by the United Nations to discuss the dangers posed by transnational organized crime and to identify various forms of international cooperation for its prevention and control, the Conference brought together Ministers of Justice and Ministers of the Interior from 142 states. It concluded with a Political Declaration and Action Plan designed to initiate more effective measures to prevent and control cross-border criminal activities. The Political Declaration and Action Plan were reproduced in Issue 1 of the journal *Transnational Organized Crime*. We thought it might be appropriate and helpful for the readership of the journal, however, to present a special issue making available the background papers that were prepared for the Conference, as well as the report of a UN Conference on money laundering, and a follow up report on implementation of the Political Declaration and Action Plan that, on 18 September 1995, was submitted by the Secretary-General to the UN General Assembly.

The background papers were translated into six languages and were made available to all the delegates at the Conference. Prior to this they underwent a process of gestation based on draft reports completed by the two editors of this volume and that included some amendment and refinement by the Secretariat of the UN Crime Prevention Branch. This second stage was important in locating the documents within the overall context of previous UN activities in this area and in relating the policy recommendations to the agenda of the Naples Conference. The result can be seen in the first five papers contained in this volume. The papers provide not only an overview of the challenge posed by transnational organized crime but also a series of recommendations of the kind of measures that can be initiated in response at the national, regional, and global levels. The first essay deals with the threat and highlights the reasons why organized crime has taken on a transnational character as well as the kinds of challenges it poses to national and international security. The second essay looks at one element of the response - those components of national policy that are particularly useful in combating organized crime. Arguing that national strategies to counter organized crime have to encompass both prevention and control activities, this paper draws on the substantive and procedural legislation of a variety of countries including the United States, Italy, Jamaica, Britain and Germany, to identify particular measures that tend to be most effective against organized crime. It suggests that emphasis should be placed on criminalization of participation in criminal organizations, prohibition of the laundering of the proceeds of crime, and seizures of the assets obtained through criminal activities. As far as law enforcement efforts go, the paper argues that emphasis should be placed on intelligence and on methods to penetrate criminal organizations. Emphasis is also placed on preventive strategies, including those that would lead to greater transparency of banking and financial sectors.

The third paper moves from the domestic realm to that of international cooperation. It outlines the rationale for inter-state cooperation against transnational organized crime, but also identifies the impediments to cooperation, many of which come down to concerns over sovereignty. One of the suggestions is for personnel exchanges that would help to create the law enforcement networks that are necessary to combat the sophisticated criminal networks that have developed and become increasingly transnational in scope. In addition, initiatives in this area should be supplemented by further efforts at information sharing. Perhaps most important of all, however, the paper argues that strenuous efforts should be made to build up the criminal justice systems in developing states and states in transition, many of whom inadvertently provide sanctuaries for criminal organizations. More formal cooperative ventures such as extradition treaties and mutual legal assistance are also discussed. Building on this discussion, the fourth paper considers appropriate modalities and guidelines for the prevention and control of transnational organized crime at the regional and international levels. As well as looking at previous initiatives in the struggle against transnational organized crime, it argues that the aims of law enforcement must be to increase and distribute more evenly the risks faced by transnational criminal organizations - and that one of the main ways to achieve this is through greater harmonization of national policies. Paper five picks up this issue of concerted action and considers the strengths and weaknesses of different forms of international cooperation against transnational organized crime. It suggests that bilateral, regional and multilateral forms of cooperation all have certain advantages and that they should be regarded as complementary. Particular attention is also given to the arguments for the elaboration of an international convention against transnational organized crime as well as some of the associated difficulties.

Also on the agenda at Naples was a report of a conference held at Coumayeur earlier in 1994 and dealing with ways of preventing and controlling money laundering and the use of the proceeds of crime. Prepared by one of the editors, this report highlights trends in global money laundering and identifies gaps in the anti-money-laundering net. It argues that laundering of non-drug related criminal proceeds should be as much of a crime as the laundering of drug profits, and should be equally subject to asset forfeiture. Recognizing that a really effective anti- money-laundering regime has to be truly global if it is to do more than force the relocation of laundering, the participants also identified several cooperative mechanisms and common strategies that could contribute significantly towards the achievement of such a goal.

All these documents were prepared for Naples. The final paper in this issue, however, offers a progress report on the Political Declaration and Action Plan adopted at the Naples Conference. As well as emphasizing the importance of collective action, the paper reiterates the value of an international convention against transnational organized crime. It also emphasizes the need for efforts to achieve a more reliable knowledge base about transnational criminal organizations and those methods that are most effective in combating them. Such measures include substantive legislation at the national level imposing penalties for participating in criminal associations and conspiracies, and the development of better evidence gathering and witness protection schemes. At the international level, bilateral and multilateral cooperative arrangements including more extensive provision for extradition and mutual legal assistance treaties, and greater efforts to control money laundering and to confiscate the proceeds of crime, are essential.

It is clear from this document that the World Ministerial Conference helped both to symbolize and to crystallize the response of the international community to the challenge posed by transnational organized crime.It was a major step forward in recognizing that transnational organized crime had become a global problem that jeopardizes international security and stability. It is equally clear, however, that recognizing the problem is still a long way from dealing with it. There are no quick fixes or soft options in the struggle against transnational organized crime. Moreover, success should not be seen in terms of eradication of the phenomenon; perhaps the most that can be achieved is the reduction and subsequent containment of transnational organized crime. And even this requires not only that governments recognize the seriousness of the challenge posed by transnational criminal organizations but also that they allocate resources commensurate with this challenge. Should the members of international community fail to do this then the long term consequences for 'democratic governance' and the rule of law are dismal. The Naples Conference was clearly an important step in avoiding such an outcome, but much more remains to be done.

# Problems and Dangers Posed by Organized Transnational Crime in the Various Regions of the World

**Introduction**

During the last few years, the international community has experienced an increasing number of political upheavals, geopolitical changes and technological restructuring, which have led countries to confront a diversity of challenges. No doubt, organized transnational crime, a new dimension of more 'traditional' forms of organized crime, has emerged as one of the most alarming of these challenges. Organized transnational crime, with the capacity to expand its activities and to target the security and the economies of countries, in particular developing ones and those in transition, represents one of the major threats that governments have to deal with in order to ensure their stability, the safety of their people, the preservation of the whole fabric of society and the viability and further development of their economies.

Responding adequately to the social, political, and economic problems posed by organized crime requires a clear understanding of their roots, their nature and the probability of success of particular kinds of countervailing efforts. Policy made without such an understanding is both fundamentally flawed and doomed to failure. Without insight there can be no solutions. Accordingly, it is necessary to analyse comprehensively the threat posed by transnational criminal organizations. A threat assessment of this kind has to focus on the steps to be taken to reduce the opportunities available to criminal organizations, to disrupt their operations and indict and punish their operatives, and to limit and if possible remove their profits. Furthermore, any society that aspires to a broad knowledge of organized crime must not underestimate the capabilities of the adversary if it wishes to comprehend and thoroughly evaluate that adversary's strengths and weaknesses.

The status of knowledge about organized crime allows key issues to be identified through which all of its features may be investigated. First of all, although there is no single monolithic criminal organization, it is clear that the problem is a global one and that no state or region is immune. Investigations have revealed that the various organizations have different structures, varying criminal emphases and distinct *modi operandi* but, at the same time, there are increasing linkages and cooperative enterprises among these groups. It is critically important, therefore, that governments and the public should be made aware of the threat posed by organized crime groups that cross national borders with speed, ease, and a complete disregard for national laws and regulations. Transnational organized crime has developed in ways that pose a serious challenge for governments and needs to be dealt with as a matter of urgency. The longer the problem is left untreated, the more entrenched and pervasive these groups will become, and the more difficult will it be to disrupt their activities, incarcerate their members and dismantle their organizational structures.

Second, it would be a grave mistake to underestimate the capabilities of these organizations. Traditionally, organized crime has been seen largely as a law and order problem rather than as something that can threaten the viability of societies, the independence of governments, the integrity of financial institutions, and the functioning of democracy. The fact that a particular problem has always been conceptualized and understood within certain parameters does not prevent it from taking on new forms that pose a novel and much more formidable challenge. Organized crime has undergone a transformation of this kind and can no longer be understood as simply a local or national phenomenon. The difficulty is that many policy makers tend to focus only on the local or domestic scene and have been slow to recognize the increasingly transnational nature of the problems they are examining. This has happened, for instance, in countries where the rejection of the 'alien conspiracy model' of organized crime has led to a preoccupation with local, regional and national aspects rather than the international dimensions of the problem.[1]

Third, organized crime groups can vary considerably. While each group has to be understood on its own terms with its own strengths and weaknesses, and not thought of as fitting into a single model, the study of the problem and the elaboration of policies and strategies should always take into account common characteristics and, more importantly, the links between groups in their operations across borders. A failure to consider these issues may lead to generic countermeasures being drawn up for the use of national and international law enforcement agencies, whereas countermeasures in fact need to be tailored carefully to specific organizational characteristics, to the political, economic and cultural contexts within which groups operate, and to the nature and extent of their operations.

A last preliminary remark concerns the reach of transnational organized crime. It is essential to recognize that, in dealing with transnational criminal organizations, criminals must ultimately be sought out in their home base, even though their activities may be geographically very widespread, rather than focusing on specific regions when the real problem is not region specific. This is not to ignore the potential for regional countermeasures as one form of international cooperation to deal with the threat. Regional initiatives provide an important link in a panoply of countermeasures that ideally should encompass local, national, regional, and global levels.

The identification and evaluation of policy responses by the international community need to be based on knowledge. An understanding of the opposition and its activities, aims and *modus operandi* remains crucial to any effort to maintain the rule of law and to promote justice, democracy and peace.

## Key Concepts

### Organized crime

The term 'organized crime' has long been a source of controversy and contention, probably because of differences in the ways of approaching various features of the problem. A broad consensus has nevertheless emerged on several conditions that have to be met before the term may be considered applicable.

Participants in criminal organizations are considered to be persons associated for the purpose of engaging in criminal activity on a more or less sustained basis. They usually engage in enterprise crime, namely the provision of illicit goods and services, or of licit goods that have been acquired through illicit means, such as theft or fraud. Organized crime 'represents in virtually every instance an extension of a legitimate market spectrum into areas normally proscribed. Their separate strengths derive from the same fundamental considerations that govern entrepreneurship in the legitimate market place: a necessity to maintain and extend one's share of the market'.[2]

The activities of organized crime groups require a significant degree of cooperation and organization to provide the illicit goods and services. Like any business, the business of crime requires entrepreneurial skill, considerable specialization, and a capacity for coordination, and this in addition to using violence and corruption to facilitate the conduct of activities. Corruption can range from payoffs to law enforcement officials to the infiltration or co-option of political authorities. Although it has been suggested that, in some instances of organized crime, the use of violence and corruption is not as widespread as it is presumed to be, in other cases it is very much in evidence.[3] Furthermore, both violence and corruption are tactics that organized crime groups tend to resort to for self-protection, the settlement of disputes and the facilitation of illicit business activities.

Experts are also concerned, however, with more controversial issues, such as the size, structure and cohesion of criminal organizations. At one end of the spectrum are those who see organized crime in terms of large hierarchical organizations that are structured rather like traditional corporations. At the other end are those who contend that 'for the most part, organized crime groups tend to be loosely structured, flexible, and highly adaptable. In fact ... the real power and effectiveness of organized crime is found in these amorphous qualities. Rather than resembling a formal corporate structure, organized crime more closely resembles a social exchange network in the community'.[4] Moreover, it is argued, these groups tend to be relatively small in size, fluid in nature and characterized by considerable opportunism.[5] Rather than being seen in terms of dichotomies between small or large organizations and formal structures or informal networks, however, these dimensions can be best understood in terms of a continuum from small to large and from fluid network organizations to bureaucratic structures. In addition, it is important to consider the elements of continuity and evolution that characterize organized criminal groups. Moreover, some groups may combine elements of the formal hierarchical structure at certain levels, with a more amorphous fluid network at the lower levels.

Size and degree of formal structure provide two dimensions along which groups can be identified and compared, as a preliminary to identifying their strengths and vulnerability and devising appropriate countermeasures by governmental and law enforcement agencies.

A third important variation concerns the scope of criminal activities. Some groups are highly specialized and focus upon one kind of activity, such as prostitution or drugs; others engage in a broader range of criminal activities, such as credit card fraud and various financial 'scams'.

The discussion of organized crime has thus far concentrated on the traditional aspects of the subject. There has been, however, a major transformation, whereby what had traditionally been a domestic, local or national problem, was transformed into a major regional and global problem, with pervasive and far-reaching consequences not only for individual states but also for the international community of states.

*Transnational criminal organizations*

The term 'transnational' is generally used to refer to the movement of information, money, physical objects, people, or other tangible or intangible items across state boundaries, when at least one of the actors involved in this movement is non-governmental.[6] Terrorist groups are similar in nature to many corporations. Criminal organizations are also increasingly engaged in activities that tend to cross national borders.

Virtually any tangible item involved in transnational transactions is likely to have a significant economic dimension, in that it can be treated as a commodity or service to which monetary value can be attached.[7] Since the crime industry is about the criminal exploitation of business opportunities and is dominated by supply organizations, it is no surprise to see organizations springing up that transport illicit commodities across national jurisdictions.[8]

The globalization of trade and of consumer demand for leisure products made it natural for criminal organizations to move from national activity to transnational operations. Of course, not all those involved in organized crime operate at this level, but there are inextricable connections between the local and the global, and the transnational dimension of crime has taken on unprecedented importance. Furthermore, it is likely that organized crime groups that are still predominantly national in scope will increasingly operate across borders in the future, in order to exploit market opportunities in other states.

The provision of illicit goods and services has never been completely inhibited by national boundaries. Indeed, 'smuggling has often been called the world's second oldest profession'.[9] The scale of smuggling activity, however, has grown well beyond efforts to avoid tariffs or taxes on licit products, and to a growing extent involves trafficking in illicit products.

Criminals and criminal organizations have increasingly engaged in cross-border activity, both in response to market opportunities and as a means of reducing their vulnerability to law enforcement efforts. Uneven criminal justice and law enforcement capabilities mean that the degree of risk varies considerably according to the location of the organization. Consequently, criminal organizations tend to have a home base in areas where the risks are low and engage in providing illicit goods and services to markets where the profits are very high.

By acting transnationally, criminal organizations are able to obtain access to lucrative markets and to find points of vulnerability that they can infiltrate, while still operating from areas where they are relatively immune to law enforcement efforts. They also channel the proceeds from illicit activities through the global financial system, often using tax havens and relatively unregulated banking centres as major points of access.

These activities have become sufficiently important to suggest the emergence of what have been termed 'transnational criminal organizations', that is, organized crime groups that have a home base in one state but operate in one or more host states where there are favourable market opportunities.[10] These organizations have become major players in global economic activity and are the key players in illicit industries, such as drug production and trafficking, that are global in scope and yield profits higher than the gross national products of some developing and developed states.

They bear many similarities to transnational corporations and, like transnational corporations, they vary considerably in structure, strength, size, geographical range and the scope or diversity of their operations. Some are global in reach and organized hierarchically; others are more limited in the scope of their operations and more fluid in structure. Their common feature is that they engage in unregulated forms of enterprise, involving illicit products and services, the illicit smuggling of licit products, the theft of licit products, or all three kinds of activity.

In trying to understand these organizations, a useful starting point is to view them as a blend of the corporate and the criminal and, for the purposes of analysis and, in certain respects only, as a mirror of transnational corporations. Like transnational corporations, their major concern is the pursuit of profit, and in this pursuit they engage in far-flung economic activities that readily cross national borders. Moreover, both transnational criminal organizations and transnational corporations share a desire to maximize their freedom of action and to minimize the effects of both national and international control over their activities. While this is a useful starting point, however, transnational criminal organizations differ from transnational corporations in several important respects.

First of all, transnational corporations may use economic incentives and sometimes act ruthlessly in order to achieve their economic objectives; but, when licit corporations break the law, it is the exception rather than the rule. With transnational criminal organizations, in contrast, law-breaking is the norm and a key element of their very identity. Although these organizations may invest in licit enterprise or engage in licit business, these enterprises are usually subordinate to their illicit activities. Transnational crime can thus be described as a 'form of economic commerce by illegal means, involving the threat and use of physical force, extortion, corruption, blackmail and other methods, and the use of illicit goods and services'.[11]

There are crucial differences in the means whereby the two kinds of organization obtain market access. In the search for global markets, their antipathy towards national boundaries and their quest for autonomy, transnational criminal organizations are at variance in degree, but not in kind, from transnational corporations. The means they use, however, vary considerably. While licit corporations negotiate with governments for permission to conduct operations on sovereign territory, the criminal organizations obtain access through circumvention rather than consent, and systematically evade efforts to detect, monitor, intercept and disrupt their activities.[12]

Another important element is the use of corruption and violence. While corporate use of violence or bribery is not completely unknown, it is not the norm, whereas criminal organizations use both violence and corruption as a matter of course. Violence is used to intimidate or eliminate business rivals or even government and law enforcement authorities that attempt to inhibit the activities of transnational criminal organizations. Violence is also a means of maintaining internal order and discipline.[13]

Corruption is used to provide a congenial environment in which the criminal organizations can carry on their activities with impunity. It can range from the bribery of low-level law enforcement officials to ignore particular criminal activities to the offering of inducements to high-ranking government officials to acquiesce in the group's activities and to provide information about countermeasures by the government. Corruption can be used to neutralize both individuals and institutions and can have deleterious effects on political culture and on the social fabric.

Criminal organizations not only supply illicit products but also steal licit products. The widespread use of theft is another factor differentiating transnational criminal organizations and licit transnational corporations. The notion that transnational criminal organizations are concerned with minimizing risk and maximizing profit is very much in accord with licit business. The difference is that the risks the criminal organizations are prepared to take are much greater than those contemplated by corporations in licit business. Moreover, the risk-reduction activities are themselves aimed at the institutions of government.

## Explaining the Rise of Transnational Criminal Organizations

### Transnational opportunities

The nature of crime reflects many features of society. With the vast increase in the number of economic and social transactions across national borders and the increasing porousness of the nation state, it is natural and inevitable that organized criminal activity should also move from the national to the transnational level. Alongside the new opportunities that have opened up for legitimate entrepreneurs, new opportunities for illicit enterprise have also manifested themselves.

Opportunities at the global level stem from long-term secular trends in global politics and economics that have encouraged the development of a myriad of transnational organizations. The evolution of the 'global village' has fundamentally changed the context in which both legitimate and illegitimate businesses operate and has opened up unprecedented opportunities for transnational crime. Increased interdependence among nations, the ease of international travel and communications, the permeability of national boundaries and the globalization of financial networks have created global markets for both licit and illicit commodities. The scale of these activities can be understood in large part as a reflection of opportunities presented by changes both in international relations and within states. Transnational criminal organizations are both contributors to and beneficiaries of several major changes in global politics and economics. The following data may shed some light on the speed with which the world market has evolved:

(a) The speed and ease of international transport has greatly increased the ability of people and products to cross national boundaries. 'Between 1960 and 1974 ..., passenger volume on international commercial flights rose from 26 billion passenger miles to 152 billion'.[14] By 1992 the figure had increased to between 600 and 700 billion passenger miles;[15]

(b) The growth of international trade, facilitated by the free trade system of the postwar period, has involved a vast increase in the import and export of goods and services. In 1970 global imports totalled 330,940 million United States dollars. By 1980 the figure had reached $2,047,303 million and by 1990 had increased to $3,533,383 million.[16] Moreover, as the use of containerized shipments has grown, so has their use to smuggle large volumes of illicit products, including drugs, across borders, a development that illustrates the ability of transnational criminal organizations to exploit licit trade in a parasitical fashion.

The growth of global trade has been accompanied by the evolution of global financial networks. The reliance on a few hard currencies as a global mechanism of exchange has facilitated the growth of transnational economic transactions. The scale and complexity of these transactions, however, have made it enormously difficult for governments to regulate and control monetary movements across national boundaries. This is not surprising: money is 'the most fungible of all commodities. It can be transmitted instantaneously ... It can change its identity easily and can be traced only with great effort'.[17]

The world has also witnessed the rise of cosmopolitan world cities, which act as the key nodes in the global economic system, as the repositories of capital and wealth, and also as major facilitators of cross-border transactions. Such cities are the successors to the port cities that, in the past, were often the major incubators for the development of criminal organizations.[18] As such they provide bases from which these organizations can operate. Entrepreneurial centers that have played a crucial role in transshipment of licit goods also tend to be used as transshipment centers for illicit goods. The uncontrolled development of industrial and post-industrial societies, which have become 'mass consumption' societies, has had its schizophrenic side-effect. Surplus wealth has created new opportunities for recreation and leisure and a demand for illicit goods and services.

The communication revolution has created a degree of global transparency that has highlighted inequalities among societies and encouraged the desire to emulate the patterns of consumption of economically advanced societies. A global market place has emerged in which consumers 'have access to information about goods and services from around the world' and entrepreneurs have recognized the opportunities for global marketing.[19] The best example of a global illicit market can be seen in the emergence of illegal drugs as a global commodity of immense significance. Although the drug of choice differs from region to region, illicit drugs have become a truly global product. Some estimates have suggested that the global trade in drugs is larger than the global trade in oil and place the figure as high as $500 billion a year.[20]

The end of the cold war and the triumph of capitalism and liberal democracy have facilitated the introduction of entrepreneurial capitalism into Eastern Europe and the former Soviet Union. At the same time, these states have yet to develop anything more than the most rudimentary mechanisms for regulating the kinds of economic enterprises that are emerging. The turbulence that has arisen, the decline of existing structures of authority and legitimacy, the resurgence of ethnic and regional conflicts and the rise of subnational groups have provided new opportunities and pressures for criminal activity, in some cases as a source of funding for weapons for ethnic conflict.

Another worrying feature of global integration in a shrinking world is the increase in migration and the growth of ethnic networks, which have been of enormous value to the operations of criminal organizations. While it is clear that most immigrants are law-abiding citizens, migration has greatly facilitated the creation of network structures for the supply of illicit goods. Ethnic enclaves provide a basis for recruitment by transnational criminal organizations that have a national base and can evoke ethnic loyalties, especially when the immigrant groups have not been fully integrated into their adopted society. Even casual participation or marginal involvement can yield greater rewards than those to be obtained through the licit economy. Moreover, ethnic networks are very difficult to penetrate. The barriers of language and culture provide built-in defence mechanisms that are strengthened by ties of kinship and inherent suspicion of authority.

All these developments present new opportunities for transnational crime. The scale of global economic activity, for example, makes it possible to hide illicit transactions, products and movements within licit transactions, products and movements. At the same time, the growth of a global financial system allows criminal organizations to move the profits from their illegal transactions with speed, ease and relative impunity. Money-laundering is simply one sub-set of the much larger problem facing states in their efforts to restore control over a global financial network that operates according to the logic of the market and is not readily amenable to national preferences or the efforts of central or even coordinated management. As one commentator has noted, 'the world in which the new economy functions is more akin to an electronic commons than it is to an economy. And like any commons - a grazing commons in an ancient English town, for example - this new electronic space is owned not by governments but by the people who use it'.[21] The sheer volume of money in the financial system and the ease with which it can be moved electronically have also made it much easier to obscure, move, and 'clean' the profits from illicit activities. The system itself has outrun the development of rules and regulations. There are also so many points of access to the global financial system that making access in some areas more difficult for money earned through illicit activities does not eliminate laundering, it simply encourages its relocation.

Against this background, it is not surprising that transnational criminal organizations display considerable entrepreneurial flair, rivaling transnational corporations in the scale and sophistication of their efforts to create and exploit global markets.

*National sanctuaries*[22]

At the national level, criminal organizations with the capacity for cross-border activities have flourished where the state has been weak or acquiescent, and where its apparatus has been corrupt or collusive. Governments that are lacking in legitimacy and authority or are not fully in control of the territory under their jurisdiction provide congenial environments for the emergence of transnational criminal organizations. For example, two factors have been identified as crucial to the establishment of a corporate headquarters and processing centre for the cocaine industry: first, the attack on government legitimacy by 'narco-traficantes' and the consequent weakening of the state, and secondly, the existence of geographical features that have allowed many regions of a particular country such a high degree of autonomy from the government that the drug 'barons' can freely dominate those regions.[23] From this standpoint, it can be argued that the failure of the international community to realize the danger has allowed the situation to flourish, with the country having come to be dominated by the illicit drug industry.

Perhaps the most striking recent example of the way in which transnational criminal organizations can thrive in an environment of political, social and economic upheaval can be seen in the states of the former Soviet Union. Russian criminal organizations are not new, but the demise of the Communist Party, the disintegration of the Soviet Union, and the collapse of the criminal justice system clearly produced conditions that were highly conducive to the consolidation of existing criminal organizations and the emergence of new ones. Groups that had been limited in the scope and impact of their operations by the intrusiveness of the Communist Party have become much more active and successful. The implication of the Russian example, which reflects the situation elsewhere, is that organized crime thrives amidst political and economic turbulence. Weak government, though, is only one of the several forms of government that allow transnational criminal organizations to operate with impunity. There are also acquiescent governments that are unwilling, rather than unable, to take counteraction, either because they fear the disruptive consequences of such action or because they regard the net effect of transnational criminal activity as beneficial to society. This type of permissive environment makes an ideal home base for transnational criminal organizations.

Corruption among government officials is another factor; they derive so much direct benefit from criminal activity that they are unwilling to do anything to reduce or contain it. There is also what might be termed the 'collusive' factor, when those in power are themselves deeply involved in some form of criminal activity. Perhaps the best example of this occurred in the early 1980s in a Latin-American country where the linkages between drug traffickers and high government officials were so strong that it was impossible to disentangle the military government from the narco-traffickers; so much so that the country came to be described as a 'narcocracy'. The difference between collusive and corrupt practices lies in the degree of direct involvement in the organized crime industry.

Some areas, of course, might be characterized by both weakness and corruption. In these circumstances, the organs of state, the criminal and the commercial spheres tend to become increasingly enmeshed and entangled. The greater the symbiosis, the more the transnational criminal organization is able to function without hindrance or impediment. Establishing what is, in effect, an autonomous base, the transnational criminal organization can then engage in its illicit business on a regional or global scale, knowing that, although some of its activities may be disrupted by foreign law enforcement efforts, the core of the organization is unlikely to be seriously threatened.

Symbiotic relationships could also be established with governments outside the home state of the organization. Transnational criminal organizations have a substantial capacity to corrupt governments and infiltrate commercial institutions. There is also a highly dynamic quality to these organizations. As the Secretary-General noted in his report on the control and proceeds of crime, submitted to the Commission on Crime Prevention and Criminal Justice at its second session, 'Consonant with the modern corporate structure of organized and transnational criminal groups, profits are systematically 'reinvested' to ensure smooth operations and finance the expansion which often has become the long-term strategic objective.'[24] Against this background, some of the major transnational criminal organizations are analysed below.

**Major Transnational Criminal Organizations**

There is no single model of transnational criminal organization. The groups vary in shape and size and in skills and specializations. They operate in different geographical domains and different product markets and use a variety of tactics and mechanisms for circumventing restrictions and avoiding law enforcement. Transnational criminal organizations range from highly structured organizations to more fluid and dynamic networks. In business terms, they extend from corporations to local franchises. For example, the drug trafficking cartel based in the city of Cali, in Colombia, is perhaps the nearest to a formal corporate structure based on a clear hierarchy, functional specialization and forward integration of activities. It is also a fairly large organization - albeit involving many separate and distinct sub-groups - with extensive global operations. At the wholesale and retail levels, it is divided into small cells that operate locally, keep meticulous financial records, and return the proceeds of their drug sales to their corporate executives. At the other end of the spectrum are the small, highly fluid Nigerian organizations, which act as couriers and engage in only the trafficking stages of the drug industry.

Another way in which transnational criminal organizations differ is in the scope of their activities. Nigerian organizations, for example, engage in an extensive range of criminal activities, including credit card fraud and business swindle. Russian criminal organizations have an even wider repertoire of operations and seem indifferent to whether the product they traffic in is drugs, arms, industrial metals or nuclear material. Their activities also include bank fraud and embezzlement, extortion, prostitution, car theft and kidnapping. Asian criminal organizations, such as the Yakuza and the Chinese Triads, also operate across the whole spectrum of illegal activities. The Colombian cartels, in contrast, are in the drug industry and everything else is subordinate to that. They engage in corruption, violence and money-laundering only to promote their business.

Although transnational criminal organizations are the quintessential 'sovereign free' actors, they do make alliances with other criminal organizations, with terrorist and insurgency groups, and sometimes even with governments.[25] The nature, purpose, scope and robustness of these alliances are not well understood. Nevertheless, they reflect the fact that the organizations have become sophisticated in their operations and behave as rational actors to enhance their business opportunities and to minimize their vulnerability. Moreover, the organizations are often characterized by a very good business sense, by an efficient and effective management system based on generous financial inducements and severe penalties, by effective intelligence and counter-intelligence capabilities, and by considerable resilience.

*The Italian Mafia*

In considering transnational criminal organizations, the Sicilian and Italian Mafias stand out as among the most complex and intriguing of these organizations. The Mafia has been variously defined as 'a type of criminal association; a historical reality; a cultural code, albeit one that is exploited; or a power structure which interacts with the legal system in all the multiplicity of its forms'.[26] As used in Italy, it generally refers to the Sicilian Mafia or 'Cosa Nostra', the Neapolitan Camorra, predominantly formed by local organizations, the Calabrian 'Ndrangheta, with a family-based structure that deals in contraband tobacco, drugs and kidnapping, and the Sacra Corona Unita in Apulia, established by Cosa Nostra to exploit the seaboard of the region for drug trafficking. The most important of these, however, is clearly the Cosa Nostra. Like the other Italian groups, the Cosa Nostra is based upon the law of silence and close associations that are partly functional, partly personal and familial, and partly based on fear. If the

Sicilian Mafia retains many of its traditions, however, it has also proved to be both dynamic and adaptive. Stemming from the imposition of its authority on citizens when the state was weak, the Sicilian Mafia has successfully moved from rural to industrial and business cultures, and from a local and national force to a transnational one.[27] Although many of its activities are still regional and its power remains based in southern Italy, where it has sought to nullify competition in legal business by illegal action, the Cosa Nostra has increasingly become a transnational enterprise. This development has been facilitated by migration flows. Sicilian migration to the United States facilitated a Sicilian share of the American heroin market. The same thing occurred in Germany, where it was recently disclosed that 'units of Sicilian migrants, closely associated with their families of origin, operated investment activities and formed echelons of criminal labor-force employed in criminal actions in Sicily'.[28]

This is not to deny that the Sicilian Mafia has suffered some setbacks. It has not been able to establish a monopoly in the drug market, although it tried to obtain the exclusive rights for imports to Italy and possibly Europe as a whole. In addition, the Mafia assault on the Italian judiciary and police forces between 1983 and 1993 ultimately proved counterproductive. The interlinking with political power and the establishment of a collusive relationship with some sectors of the state has also come under increasing attack. While it has been hurt in recent years by the commitment and effectiveness of a young generation of judges and prosecutors, the upsurge of popular sentiment and the related changes in the political situation in Italy, the Sicilian Mafia still remains an important criminal force. Although it is not the global octopus that it is sometimes portrayed as, the Sicilian Mafia, with increasing links to other criminal organizations, remains a major challenge to law enforcement.[29]

*Russian organized crime*[30]

Although there has been a major increase in organized crime in the Russian Federation and the other parts of the former Soviet Union, Russian criminal organizations are not an entirely new phenomenon. The 'centrally planned economies created scarcities that amounted to nationwide shortages of virtually any item consumers wanted. Organized crime groups ... exploited these shortages in the past and continue to do so'.[31] The underground economy in the Soviet Union and the pervasive corruption provided the potential for organized crime, but were kept under control by the dominance of the Communist Party. The reforms initiated by Mr. Gorbachev, however, destroyed the mechanisms of social, political and economic control. The collapse of the Communist Party, and with it the Soviet state, also removed the system of criminal justice. The new environment was a very permissive one for organized crime, with few laws against criminal associations and continued inefficiencies in the economic system. The transition to the market economy was also made without a clear regulatory framework. As noted above, the Russian Federation started to develop a free market without the rules and regulations that are necessary to ensure its integrity, efficiency and effectiveness.[32] At the same time, the end of the cold war made it easier for the groups in the former Soviet Union to engage in transnational criminal activity. The result has been a consolidation of existing criminal groups, the rise of new organizations, and the diversification of criminal activity. In 1993, it was estimated that there were 4,352 organized crime groups in the Federation; by April 1994 the figure had risen to 5,700. Moreover, 200 of these groups were regarded as very sophisticated and were believed to be operating outside the Federation in 29 other countries.[33]

One analysis has identified several major kinds of criminal enterprise. As well as the old style party officials, there are also many ethnic-based groups. These include the Georgian Mafia, which controlled much of the black market under the Communist system and has subsequently extended the range of its activities, the Chechens and Azerbaijani groups, and others who help to account for a major upsurge in trafficking activities not only in drugs but also in metals, weapons, nuclear materials and even body parts. Moreover, these organizations clearly operate with little regard for national boundaries. In addition to the nuclear materials smuggled from the former Soviet Union, other metals such as magnesium have also been stolen and sold in Western Europe. The scale of this activity is perhaps best illustrated by the fact that in October 1993 an attempt was made to smuggle 300 tones of magnesium ingots from the Russian Federation to Western Europe. Although this attempt was foiled, it reveals the audacity of groups that have been able to operate with relative impunity. Moreover, these groups have infiltrated the Russian banking system and have been unscrupulous in their use of intimidation and violence against bankers and businessmen who were not cooperative. As a result, banking, in particular, has become a high-risk profession in the Russian Federation.

Although several commentators have identified a group of particularly adept, renowned and high-status criminals, known as 'thieves in law', the organizations seem to be very fluid. While 'there have been instances of a powerful leadership of isolated groups, there is no discernible overall controlling figure or body'.[34] Indeed, there has been a proliferation of crime bosses in the Commonwealth of Independent States, around 500 having been identified and over half of whom are of Russian, Georgian or Ukrainian descent. The typical structure is for each boss to control four criminal cells through a brigadier and two spies. The cells tend to be specialized units, which focus respectively on drugs, prostitution, political contacts and enforcement.

From criminal investigation it is clear that the Russian Mafia has also spread its activities to other countries, including the United States. Among the most important groups are the Odessa Mafia, based at Brighton Beach, New Jersey, but also active in California, the Chechens, who tend to specialize in contract murder and extortion, and the Malina Organizatsia, a multi-ethnic group at Brighton Beach, which maintains extensive international ties and is active in a variety of areas, for example, drug trafficking, credit card fraud, extortion and tax fraud. Although these groups clearly pose a new kind of threat for American law enforcement, the threat is far less in the United States than in the Russian Federation itself, where, as has been pointed out, 'domination by the Communist party may be replaced by the controls of organized crime. As in other societies, organized crime will limit free elections and freedom of the press and media. Labor markets, once controlled by state planning and submissive trade unions, will instead be subject to the intimidation of organized crime, which is already a major employer. State ownership of the economy will be exchanged for control of the economy by organized crime groups which have a monopoly on existing capital.'[35] To the extent that Russia remains a sanctuary from which these organizations can operate with relative impunity, it is likely that the transnational nature of their activities will become even more pronounced.

*Chinese Triads*

Although some Chinese Triads operate from the Chinese mainland, they are based predominantly in the territory of Hong Kong, which is the home base for the Sun Yee On, the 14K, and the Wo Group, and Taiwan Province of China, where the United Bamboo has its own base. One estimate suggests that there are as many as 160,000 Triad members in Hong Kong, belonging to around 50 different organizations.[36] There has been considerable debate among both practitioners and analysts about the extent to which Triads are formally organized. Perhaps the best way of putting it is that they are like an alumni association. Membership in the Triad permits a degree of trust and allows members of the Triad to work together and give assistance even when they are not personally known to each other. Although there is a formal structure, therefore, with a 'dragon head' and specialists such as enforcers and administrators, many of their criminal activities tend to take place among members who operate on an *ad hoc* basis and establish fluid network systems that may change from one criminal operation to the next.

Triads are involved in a whole range of criminal activities, including extortion, drug trafficking, prostitution and gambling. They also have extensive overseas networks, which allow them to engage in transnational criminal activity with great ease. Indeed, some observers have concluded that the Triad societies have very close links with both the tongs, or chambers of commerce, and the youth gangs that exist in many Chinese communities throughout North America. Not surprisingly, therefore, the Triads are the major importers of heroin from Southeast Asia into the United States.

The Triads have also been active in Western Europe, especially Amsterdam and London, and a report in the first half of 1994 suggested that the Chinese Triads have been engaged in a variety of activities in Spain, where the smuggling of illegal aliens had become evident from the appearance of large numbers of Chinese nationals in Galicia.[37] As elsewhere, these aliens are often exploited by the criminals as slave labour, are pressed into serving as drug couriers or prostitutes, or are forced to engage in other forms of crime. It has been suggested that this activity is controlled primarily by the Sun Yee On Triad. Heroin trafficking, where sales of 'China White' increased as law enforcement authorities cracked down on Turkish trafficking organizations, is largely controlled by the 14K, whereas prostitution and pornography and trafficking in children is controlled predominantly by the Wo On Lok. In addition, there is considerable evidence of loan-sharking and extortion, carried out largely by Dai Hoon, which is in effect an illegal bank that lends money at very high rates, makes loans for gambling purposes and provides money for illegal immigrants.

The comprehensive nature of these criminal activities, the difficulties faced by law enforcement agencies in attempting to infiltrate closely knit ethnic groups, and the imminent reversion of the territory of Hong Kong to Chinese rule in 1997, resulting in a possible exodus of Triad members, suggest that the Triad problem is likely to increase rather than decrease.

*The Japanese Yakuza*

The Japanese Yakuza or, as it has also become known, the *Boryokudan*, the violent ones, has been much more visible in its home base than most other criminal organizations. There are several major organizations within the Yakuza, of which the most important is the Yamaguchi-gumi, which has an estimated membership of over 26,000 individuals affiliated with 944 smaller gangs. The second largest gang is the Inagawa-kai, with over 8,600 members, while the third largest organization, the Sumiyoshi-kai, has over 7,000 members.[38] The Yakuza has been characterized by considerable internecine warfare among its various branches, but this has not prevented it from infiltrating legitimate business and extending corruption into the political system.

Perhaps less ambitious than the Chinese in the transnational scope of their activities, the Japanese Yakuza has nevertheless been involved in significant criminal activities across national borders, including the trafficking of methamphetamine into Hawaii and California, as well as the smuggling of guns from the United States into Japan. Moreover, the Yakuza also has a significant presence throughout much of Southeast Asia, where Japanese criminals have become a major force in organizing the 'sexual slavery' of women. The Philippines, for example, has been used by the Yakuza as a base for the production and smuggling of amphetamines and hand guns, as well as an additional market for hand guns.[39] In addition, the Yakuza has moved into gambling, fraud and money-laundering. In Hawaii, Yakuza members have been deeply involved in the sex and drug trades and have also invested heavily in real estate.

*Colombian cartels*

The Colombian cartels are in many ways unique. Unlike most other transnational criminal organizations, which tend to engage in a range of illegal activities, the cartels are, first and lastly, in the drug business. Indeed, the cartels - and this is particularly true of the Cali cartel that has now become the predominant group in the cocaine industry - have amalgamated corporate and criminal cultures more than any other group. They have developed an industry that is based on sound management principles, such as specialization and division of labour.

During the 1980s, Carlos Ledher and other members of the Medellín cartel led the way in applying industrial style transport to the drug trafficking business, increasing the amounts that were transported to the United States by air. The Cali cartel has taken this a stage further and has applied successful business management techniques and meticulous accounting procedures to its activities. Although the Medellín cartel is still active in drug trafficking - and there have been allegations that the Ochoas are still running their drug business from prison - the killing of Pablo Escobar by government forces both highlighted and accentuated the shift in power from the Medellín to the Cali cartel.

Rather than confronting the government and law enforcement, however, the Cali cartel has adopted a strategy of infiltration. The leading members of the cartel present themselves as legitimate businessmen and have increasingly invested in licit businesses. Moreover, their co-option of the local power structure, together with their local patronage, has provided them with a very protective environment in Cali. By eschewing a frontal assault on the state, Cali has also attempted in the past to establish a *modus vivendi* with a government that was prepared to tolerate narco-trafficking but that responded vigorously to narco-violence.[40]

In its activities in both Colombia and the United States, the cartel has a very specialized cell structure, based around functions such as logistics, marketing etc., and possessing information solely on a need to know basis. This modular approach has the effect of limiting the damage that can be done by law enforcement; even if one group is infiltrated and dismantled, the ability of law enforcement agencies to exploit this and further penetrate the cartel is limited. Although these protective measures set it apart from legitimate business, in other respects the Colombian cartels act like any other transnational corporation. In recent years, for example, they have sought to diversify their markets, with particular emphasis on Western Europe and the newly emerging markets in Eastern Europe and the former Soviet Union, as well as their products, through the production of Colombian heroin that is more compact and cheaper to transport and has higher profit margins than cocaine. In addition, although the cartels continue to use aircraft to traffic drugs into the United States, they have also made increasing use of commercial cargo. At the same time there has been growing sophistication in concealment methods. The incorporation of cocaine base or cocaine into cardboard, glass, plastic and fiberglass reveals a degree of innovation and sophistication that is intended to circumvent law enforcement and interdiction activities.

*Nigerian criminal organizations*[41]

The rise of Nigerian organized crime is relatively recent and is often traced to the collapse of oil prices in the early 1980s and the dislocation that this caused to an economy that relied on oil for 95 per cent of its export earnings by the late 1970s. The result was that a lot of bright, articulate Nigerians - many of them college-educated and many of them living in other countries - were effectively deprived of their source of income. In some cases they turned to crime, with spectacularly successful results.

Indeed, Nigerians have developed large-scale trafficking activities and have been identified as second only to the Chinese in the import of heroin into the United States. Once again, this was facilitated by the fact that they were able to operate from a relatively safe home base, characterized by lack of legislation and law enforcement capacity, as well as a certain political instability, indications of corruption and few resources to devote to the fight against organized crime. They have proved to be very adaptable in terms of finding alternative trafficking routes, concealment techniques, courier profiles and choice of product, and have progressed from simply being couriers for other transnational criminal organizations to becoming major players in their own right. Although there is little evidence of a Nigerian cartel, a loose network of drug barons has been identified and it is clear that even the activities of couriers are carefully orchestrated, the couriers themselves being trained in methods of avoiding detection.

Nigerian criminal activities have not, however, been limited to drug trafficking. Nigerian organizations have also engaged in large-scale fraud and extortions, including credit card fraud and fraud *vis-à-vis* commercial banks and government assistance programmes. They have proved adept at obtaining the documentation for false identities that have facilitated cheque kiting, student loan fraud, social services fraud, insurance fraud, and electronic fund transfer fraud. They have not been involved in major schemes, generally exhibiting a preference for a large number of smaller-scale activities, and adopting a low profile. The members tend to live modestly and ship money back to Nigeria, where there is an absence of legislation directed against money-laundering. Their success has nevertheless bred imitation, and individuals and groups from Ghana, Benin and Sierra Leone have also become involved in various transnational crime operations including drug trafficking.

Although the law enforcement authorities have had some success in dealing with their activities, the Nigerian organizations have several natural defense mechanisms. The use of a variety of different dialects, for example, reduces the usefulness of wire-tapping and other electronic surveillance devices. In essence, they have a non-technological way of circumventing high-technology law enforcement. The fact that the organizations tend to be based on family or tribal ties also makes them very difficult to infiltrate. Although they may pose less of a threat in terms of corruption and violence than some of the other groups, that threat is certainly not insignificant. Moreover, the long-term ramifications and implications for development of the existence and expansion of transnationally operating organized criminal groups in the region deserve particular attention.

PROBLEMS AND DANGERS 21

*Other criminal organizations*

This survey is not, of course, comprehensive. Turkish drug trafficking organizations that supply heroin to Western Europe from Southwest Asia using the famous Balkan Route, and the variations on it that have been made necessary by the conflict in the former Yugoslavia, are not discussed in detail. Nor are Jamaican Posses, the indigenous American Mafia, Dominican criminal organizations or a variety of other groups. Their activities nevertheless highlight some of the strengths of transnational criminal organizations, showing that they are highly adaptable, very fluid, able to take advantage of weaknesses in particular nations or regions, and difficult to penetrate. As such, they pose a real challenge to the rule of law.

## Activities of Transnational Criminal Organizations

Transnational criminal organizations engage in a variety of illicit activities, and it would be impossible to draw up a comprehensive list of all their activities. Some of them are nonetheless particularly relevant and deserve major attention.

*The drug trafficking industry*

In addition to being a major source of income for most transnational criminal organizations, illicit drug activities can best be understood as an industry, with distinct stages of production and distribution at the wholesale and retail levels. It is also a very lucrative industry, largely because there is limited competition among the entities concerned and little threat from substitute products, and because both the supplier of the raw materials and the consumers of the final product have very limited power.[42] The money from the drug trafficking industry goes largely to the trafficking organizations, while the peasants who actually grow coca and opium earn a very modest return, albeit one that is generally better than the profits from growing other commodities. The emergence of the drug trafficking industry as a multi-billion-dollar-a-year industry has given a great boost to the development of transnational criminal organizations and has also led to the emergence of money-laundering as a high-profile activity. There are also increasing signs of a growing linkage with other kinds of trafficking, especially in arms. Furthermore, drug money has been a major source of the government corruption that helps to provide secure home bases for transnational criminal organizations.

## Smuggling of illegal migrants

One of the most serious developments in transnational crime has been the increase in the trafficking in people. There are several dimensions to this, the first of which concerns the illegal migrants issue. According to one informed estimate, criminal organizations are now attempting to smuggle as many as one million people a year from poor to wealthier countries. Not only does this once again threaten a basic ingredient of national sovereignty, it also places the immigrants themselves in grave danger.

Moreover, the would-be immigrants are subjected to considerable hardship, deprivation and indignity. They are highly vulnerable and women in particular are often forced into sexual slavery. Even those who arrive at their destination often owe money to the smugglers and are forced to engage in criminal activities to pay off the debt. Although this problem has received a great deal of attention in Western countries, largely in relation to Chinese immigrants, it is not only a problem for the United States or Europe alone, and it is not limited to Chinese.

According to some estimates, immigrants from China form only 20 per cent of those in a pipeline that encompasses India, Iraq, the Islamic Republic of Iran, Pakistan, Romania, Sri Lanka and the Sudan. Those in transit include 60,000 Chinese in Moscow, 80,000 or more Asians, Africans and people from the Middle East in Romania, and significant numbers in staging areas such as Guatemala, the Netherlands and Spain. The scale of the problem is also revealed by the fact that in 1993 there were 1.2 million attempts to enter the United States illegally. Moreover, the smuggling organizations offer substantial bribes to officials and are ingenious in the development of new smuggling routes through Mexico and the Caribbean. One estimate has suggested that the trade yields an annual profit somewhere in the region of $3.5 billion.[43]

For the destinations and sometimes the transit states, however, the trade imposes significant and unexpected costs in terms of medical care, food, housing and transportation for the illegal migrants. The problem has reached such levels that it is in danger of provoking a major backlash against legal immigrants and legitimate refugees.

## Arms trafficking

The difference between the licit and the illicit supply of armaments is not always clear. As with chemical capabilities and the capabilities required to develop nuclear weapons, it often has more to do with who the end user is than with the product itself. In some cases, the end user may be a rogue state that the international community is trying to isolate; in others, it may be an ethnic group trying to circumvent an arms embargo. Whoever the end user may be, however, black market arms deals have three characteristics: they are a covert activity, a large part of the cost is related to the surreptitious nature of the transaction, and the return flow of money is laundered.[44]

In addition to their other ramifications and the sizeable profits they generate, these transactions can have a significant effect on local and regional conflicts and on the capacity of terrorist groups to pursue their goals and threaten peace and security. The drug trafficking and arms trafficking businesses also seem to be increasingly interwoven with cases of ethnic involvement in the drug trade for the purpose of purchasing weapons. As one report has noted:

> There is abundant evidence that organized crime is involved in the illegal arms trade and subversive activities that tamper with the rule of law in different parts of the world. The weight of the evidence indicates that it contributes to the political turmoil and upheaval occurring throughout the world. Drugs for weapons deals have become common in the world of organized crime, and many ethnic and political conflicts are aggravated by this unholy alliance.[45]

The importance of these activities lies also in the potential for major disruption and the consequent threat to security and stability at the national and international levels. There is no telling whether organized criminal groups will resort to stirring and abetting political turmoil as a defense against successful efforts of law enforcement agencies.

*Trafficking in nuclear material*

Trafficking in nuclear material is, above all, a major problem in relation to the former Soviet Union and one that, not surprisingly, has provoked considerable alarm. The possibility that nuclear weapons grade material might be passed to terrorist groups or pariah states attempting to acquire some kind of strategic nuclear capability is a matter of considerable concern to the global community. This issue has placed Germany in the front line; the fullest analysis of the problem has been made by the Bundeskriminalamt and part of it has been made public in a testimony by Hans-Ludwig Zachert, President of the German Federal Police. According to this testimony, there were in 1992, 59 fraudulent offers of radioactive material, 99 cases of illicit trade and 18 seizures of actual material. In 1993, there were 241 cases altogether, with 118 fraudulent offers, 123 cases of illicit trade and 21 seizures (3 of which actually involved material from Germany itself and not from the former Soviet Union). In 1993, 545 suspects were identified, 47 per cent of whom were non-German, predominantly Czech, Polish and

Russian nationals.[46]

The threat appears to be a serious one. This was underlined very starkly by recent developments. According to reports in July 1994 a few weeks earlier, German police searching for counterfeiters had actually found one fifth of an ounce of weapons-grade plutonium, the first case actually to involve fissile material.[47] This reported seizure, as well as that of the neutron emitter, californium 252 in 1993, suggests that there is an increasing diversity in the types of material being seized. On 10 August 1994, the German police seized 350 grams of weapons-grade nuclear material (mixed-oxide fuel for reactors, containing plutonium enriched to 87 per cent), and arrested one Colombian and two Spaniards. Another incident, involving a considerably smaller quantity of nuclear material, but of the same quality, occurred two days later.[48] The presence of individuals of different nationalities adds an alarming element to the issue, leading the authorities to speculate on the involvement of organized crime groups from various countries and the possibility of links and cooperation arrangements between them. On 29 August 1994, the Hungarian authorities seized a quantity of nuclear material in a hotel room at Budapest, an incident suggesting that the illicit trade in nuclear material is not confined to certain countries only. The German and Russian authorities have reacted to the incidence of smuggling of nuclear material, concluding a bilateral cooperation agreement on 25 August 1994.

It is clear that this trade has considerable potential for extortion, as well as for significant environmental damage, if only as a result of improper handling of the materials. Although there are questions about whether there is actually an illicit end-user market, at least in Germany, there is a danger that the organization responsible may change tack if purchasers cannot be found and the material is in hand; extortion can then appear particularly attractive. The fact that nuclear materials are often procured from government-controlled installations in the Russian Federation suggests the involvement of criminal organizations seeking profit. If they cannot obtain these profits in one way, then it is only a small step to attempting to obtain them through some kind of nuclear blackmail. As nuclear disarmament continues, the availability of material is likely to increase rather than decrease.

*Transnational criminal organizations and terrorism*

In considering the activities of transnational criminal organizations, both the use of terror tactics and the links with terrorist and guerrilla organizations are recurring themes. If criminal organizations often resort to terror and develop alliances of convenience with terrorists, however, it is clear that the two kinds of organization have very different objectives. Transnational criminal organizations engage in terror simply to provide a more congenial environment for their criminal enterprises. They are generally willing to work within the existing system as long as this is malleable. In so far as they have political objectives, these are aimed against specific law enforcement policies rather than representing part of an effort to overthrow the existing power structure (much of which they may have already corrupted). Terrorist groups, in contrast, pursue political objectives often aimed at the overthrow of the status quo at either the state level or the international level. In so far as terrorist groups engage in criminal activity such as drug or arms trafficking, this is usually designed to provide resources to enable them to pursue more effectively their political agendas. If the means and ends of criminal and terrorist organizations are very different, however, there may be a growing, and perhaps irreversible, trend towards convergence.

One element in this trend is the direct use of terror tactics by transnational criminal organizations. Some transnational criminal organizations, such as the Italian Mafia and the Colombian cartels, have used terrorist attacks against the state and its representatives in an attempt to disrupt investigations, deter the introduction or continuation of vigorous government policies, eliminate effective law enforcement officials, coerce judges into more lenient sentencing policies, and create an environment more conducive to criminal activity. A second element is the willingness of transnational criminal organizations to develop direct links with groups that engage in the widespread use of violence for political purposes. In some cases this may be unavoidable. The narco-traffickers in Peru, for example, have had little choice than to deal with the Sendero Luminoso (Shining Path). Indeed, the Shining Path guerrillas operating in the upper Huallaga Valley have provided protection for the coca growers and narco-traffickers in return for a levy on the drugs. For the traffickers, Shining Path involvement has made decisive government action much more difficult. For Shining Path, the levy has provided funding for its campaign to overthrow the government. In effect, the linkage is 'a business relationship in which each side uses the other to achieve its respective goals'.[49] Similar synergies exist elsewhere. In Colombia, for example, the cartels and revolutionary movements such as the FARC and M-19 have developed complex cooperative linkages in spite of a basic ideological antipathy.

Another factor leading towards convergence between international terrorism and transnational criminal activity is the changed political context. With the end of the cold war, international terrorism has lost much of the sponsorship it enjoyed in the past. State-sponsored terrorism still exists, of course, but has become far less important. As a report by the Federal Bureau of Investigation noted, 'state sponsors of terrorism are less anxious to be connected to terrorist acts, and more countries are attempting to avoid fitting the criteria for inclusion on the state sponsors of terrorism list.'[50] Yet this should not lead to complacency. As terrorist organizations find that government financial support is drying up, they seem likely to turn to criminal organizations and activities as an alternative source of funds. In these circumstances, deals involving weapons for illicit products or services are likely to become more prevalent. Indeed, terrorist groups will almost certainly be increasingly willing to engage in criminal activities to fund political terrorism.

Another source of convergence is technological opportunity. The theft of nuclear material and its potential use for large-scale extortion and blackmail suggests that the distinction between crimes of extortion and political terrorism will become increasingly blurred. The theft of nuclear material by transnational criminal organizations and its purchase by terrorist organizations is one possibility. Another is that the groups that steal plutonium will themselves use it to blackmail governments. In short, the motives of terrorist groups and criminal organizations may differ, but the strategies they adopt to achieve their objectives could become indistinguishable if not inseparable. Moreover, the linkages between them will make both traditional law enforcement efforts and counter-terrorist strategies more difficult. The prospect is a formidable one, to which governments need to address their attention.

*Trafficking in women and children*

Prostitution has long been a major element in the activities of criminal organizations at the national level, and it is no surprise that it also has major international dimensions. Both the Triads and the Yakuza are particularly active in this arena and have held women as slaves in the tourist sex industry in the Philippines, South Korea and Thailand. This kind of trafficking treats women as 'commodities that have a market value ... sex work is not there by accident, sex work plays a great part in the world economy where women and children are seen as sources of pleasure and spare parts for the developed world'.[51]

A variant on this, but one that tends to be more tangential to criminal organizations, involves parents selling their children as brides, often to wealthy men from other countries. Adoption, too, is something that needs more careful scrutiny and regulation, as, according to several reports, international adoption has become a million dollar business, in which babies from South and Central America fetch up to $20,000. Not surprisingly, there have been about 30 cases a year in Guatemala of false mothers offering children for adoption. Concern about trafficking in babies has created a climate of suspicion and hysteria in some countries and has led to attacks on foreigners wrongly suspected of kidnapping.

*Trafficking in body parts*

One reason for the climate of suspicion about kidnapping has been concern that the abducted children would be killed for their body parts. Although there is little evidence that kidnapping for this purpose has taken place, it is clear that there are lucrative black markets in body parts, especially in Argentina and the Russian Federation. In Argentina, for example, there have been examples of serious transplant abuses, often involving the removal of corneas of patients who were declared brain dead after fabricated brain scans.[52]

The problem is perhaps even greater in the Russian Federation, especially as there are as many as 4,000 unclaimed bodies in Moscow morgues. One investigative report found one company that had extracted 700 major organs, kidneys, hearts and lungs, over 1,400 liver sections, 18,000 thymus organs, 2,000 eyes and over 3,000 pairs of testicles. Moreover, one Moscow forensic detective saw these activities as being firmly under the control of organized crime, which he suggested had 'elaborate criminal structures for kidnapping children and adults, using their organs for transplants and for medical experiments'. He even suggested that 'organ transplantation is the most profitable business in Russia and it will grow'.[53]

There have also been cases of organs being exported using false documents and of confirmed trafficking in Argentina, Brazil, Honduras, Mexico and Peru, largely with German, Italian and Swiss buyers. It is clear that this is an era where the potential for corruption in medical communities is enormous and will remain so until rules governing the purchase or sale of organs are systematically developed and implemented.

*Theft and smuggling of vehicles*

Another significant problem is the theft and smuggling of vehicles. The prevailing pattern here is the opposite of that in the drug trade, the cars being stolen from the advanced industrialized states and supplied to the élites of developing countries or countries in transition. This has proved to be a big problem in the territory of Hong Kong, where luxury cars are stolen and rapidly transported to China on extremely fast power boats. It has also become an extensive problem in Europe, where the number of motor vehicle thefts almost tripled between 1989 and 1993. The proportion of stolen vehicles that are permanently missing - at present more than 40 per cent - is an indicator of the amount moved to other countries. It is also a serious problem in many African countries.

Since the political opening, Eastern Europe has become a main area for the movement of stolen vehicles, with Poland as the central point of the illegal transport route. From there, the vehicles are taken to the Baltic republics, or the Ukraine, to the Russian Federation, the Caucasus region or Kazakhstan.[54] Bulgarian and Russian criminal groups have become a major force in this particular area of transnational crime. The same problem also exists in the United States, where 'the low apprehension, prosecution and conviction rate of auto thieves make this crime a booming industry, with high profits and low risks'.[54] The results are evident in the receiving countries: for example, 'in one Caribbean country, a survey conducted by various law enforcement agencies determined that approximately one out of every five vehicles on the docks awaiting clearance showed clear signs that it had been stolen and shipped from the United States. For vehicles worth over $15,000, the rate increased to nearly four out of five'.[55] While less serious than some of the other activities of organized crime, car theft is an additional source of revenue and can help these groups to consolidate their position in certain countries.

*Money-laundering*

One of the major activities of transnational criminal organizations is profit taking. Although a considerable portion of this comes from drug trafficking, other forms of transnational crime may account for a significantly high percentage of all the illegal proceeds that enter the global financial system. The problem for these groups, however, is that the money derived from illicit proceeds has somehow to be made legitimate.

The laundering process designed to achieve this involves three major stages. The first stage is the placement of cash proceeds into the financial system through banks or other financial institutions. In countries where there are reporting requirements for large cash transactions, this tends to be done through a larger number of small transactions, the so-called 'smurfing'. An alternative approach is physically to smuggle large amounts of cash out of the country and deposit it where the reporting requirements are less stringent. The second stage in money-laundering involves what is generally termed 'layering', which separates the funds from their source and is designed to disguise the origin of the funds and obscure the audit trail. The third stage is integration, which involves 'the introduction of criminally derived wealth into the legitimate economy without arousing suspicion and with some apparent legitimacy for its source'.[56] This third stage can consist, for example, in the purchase of real estate or can simply involve the complicity of banks in countries that lack money-laundering legislation.

*Other activities*

Inevitably, in an overview such as this, not all the activities undertaken by transnational criminal organizations can be included. For example, the illegal animal trade, the theft and trafficking of cultural objects or art pieces, and smuggling in precious metals have all been omitted, as have activities such as protection racketeering, the kidnapping of businessmen or the theft of intellectual property through large-scale software piracy. Other areas of criminal activity are old-fashioned piracy on the high seas, for instance in the Malacca Straits, counterfeiting, and activities such as cattle rustling across national borders in Africa. This is not to denigrate the importance of these activities, all of which deserve much more attention. The intent, however, has been to provide a flavor of the range of major operations that fall under the rubric of transnational crime and that are undertaken by transnational criminal organizations.

## Characteristics and Major Trends

An analysis of the major criminal organizations and their activities makes it possible to define the characteristic patterns and trends of transnational organized crime and thus to identify the key features of these groups that make them such a formidable problem for law enforcement authorities. The present analysis is also intended to point the way to effective preventive and control policies by national governments and to emphasize the importance of enhanced international cooperation in law enforcement and criminal justice activities.

*The resilience of transnational criminal organizations*

Transnational criminal organizations are diverse in structure, outlook and membership, but all of them operate across national borders with great ease and provide formidable challenges for law enforcement at both the national and international levels. One reason for this is their emphasis on loose network structures rather than excessively formal and structured hierarchies. In this respect, they have been ahead of transnational corporations: illegality has compelled them to operate in covert fashion with fluid networks and functional cooperation rather than fixed structures. Indeed, transnational criminal organizations have developed several mechanisms that help them to defend themselves against law enforcement efforts.

The flexibility of network organizations is the first and most important characteristic. Because such organizations are highly fluid and have a loose structure, they are able to respond rapidly to law enforcement challenges. The pyramid organizational structure is another relevant feature. The pyramid characterizes most transnational criminal organizations because it insulates their leaders, who are not easily connected with specific criminal activities and are unlikely to be caught engaging in criminal operations. In addition to this, the capacity for replacement of the top leadership and the strict rules for the recruitment of new members are essential to the maintenance of an efficient structure. The capacity for relocation plays an important role as well. Success in combating the operations of transnational criminal organizations can be countered relatively easily by moving operations to countries where the criminal justice and law enforcement systems are much weaker.

Other essential mechanisms exploited by criminal organizations are the infiltration of legitimate business, which often provides a veneer of respectability to the criminal organizations, and the use of patronage to provide excellent counter-intelligence capabilities that make it enormously difficult to mount surprise operations. Last but not least, in view of the dangers it poses to society, is the use of corruption to provide a congenial environment, in which the groups can conduct their business with relatively low risk of interference from law enforcement agencies.

The upshot of all this is that transnational criminal organizations are extremely difficult to dismantle or destroy. This difficulty was graphically described by a British customs officer, who compared a smuggling syndicate to spaghetti: 'Every piece seems to touch every other, but you are never sure where it all leads. Once in a while we arrest someone we are sure is important ... but once we get him, he becomes no more than a tiny cog. Someone else important pops up in his place.'[57]

*Growing sophistication*

Transnational criminal organizations clearly have a significant capacity for learning and adaptation. Some of them also appear to have a sense of strategic vision and engage in sound business practices, such as diversification of activities and the exploitation of new markets. They are increasingly characterized by sophistication and flexibility, resilient and efficient organizational structures, effective management techniques and the use of specialist advisers, and in some cases they have even initiated research and development programmes. This has been particularly evident in the area of money-laundering, but also in the way in which ever more ingenious methods of smuggling are being introduced. Indeed, the way in which the organizations use high technology, adopting what appears to be an intensive research and development programme, is illustrative of the innovative approach they are taking to their business and adds to the difficulties faced by law enforcement.

*Emphasis on strategic alliances*

Like transnational corporations, transnational criminal organizations are entering more and more frequently into strategic alliances. In the case of licit corporations, such alliances secure local knowledge and experience for marketing and distribution. Transnational criminal organizations pursue alliances for similar reasons. Strategic alliances permit them to cooperate with, rather than compete against, indigenous entrenched criminal organizations, enhance their capacity to circumvent law enforcement, facilitate risk sharing, make it possible to use existing distribution channels, and enable criminal organizations to exploit differential profit margins in different markets.

Operation Green Ice, which culminated in 1992 in around 200 arrests in several countries, revealed the links between the Cali cartel and the Sicilian Mafia. The Mafia was helping the Colombians to break into the New York heroin market in return for franchise arrangements for cocaine in Europe. Similar linkages seem to have developed between the Italian groups and some of the criminal organizations in the Russian Federation, between Pakistani and relatively small Danish drug trafficking organizations, in the Netherlands and Turkey, and even Italian and Japanese criminal organizations. The growth of strategic alliances is likely to continue in the future as the various groups see both formal and informal linkages as providing not only economic advantages but also additional means of circumventing law enforcement.

In concluding, the characteristics of transnational criminal organizations, as well as current trends and developments, reveal the extent of the threat they pose to national governments, to the legitimate economy, to licit businesses and to legal and normative framework at both the national and international levels.

## The Transnational Crime Threat

The threat from transnational crime and transnational criminal organizations is insidious, pervasive and multifaceted. As has recently been noted:

> Organized crime poses a direct threat to national and international security and stability, and constitutes a frontal attack on political and legislative authority, and challenging the very authority of the state. It disrupts and compromises social and economic institutions, causing a loss of faith in democratic processes. It undermines development and diverts its gains. It victimizes entire populations, targeting and capitalizing on human vulnerability. It co-opts, entraps and even enslaves segments of society, especially women and children, in its diverse and interrelated illegal undertakings, particularly in prostitution.[58]

Although that was an excellent summary of the threat posed by transnational criminal organizations, it may be useful to identify more carefully the various levels at which this threat manifests itself.

### *The threat to sovereignty*

Transnational crime, by its very nature, involves the violation of national borders. While it is clear that, in an age of high technology, global trade and financial systems, national borders have become more porous than ever, states still try to regulate what goes through their borders. This is a fundamental attribute of sovereignty. It is also something that is negated by transnational criminal organizations. Indeed, these organizations directly challenge the characteristics of state sovereignty and security that have long been taken for granted. They highlight the permeability of national borders and, in effect, penetrate territories that are nominally under the control of states. States retain sovereignty in a formal sense, but if they are unable to control the trafficking of arms, people and drugs into their territory, then sovereignty loses much of its real - as opposed to its symbolic - significance.

The concept of sovereignty retains usefulness as a basis for the international society of states, but no longer reflects real control over the territorial dimension of the state. Although the main purpose of transnational crime is profit, the inevitable by-product, therefore, is a generally implicit - but sometimes explicit - challenge to state authority and sovereignty. The threat is insidious rather than direct. It is not a threat to the military strength of the state, but it is a challenge to the prerogatives that are an integral part of statehood.

*The threat to societies*

Many transnational criminal organizations engage in activities that pose a threat to the fabric of societies. Drug abuse is an often cited example. Although it has to be dealt with in terms of the reduction of both supply and demand, the product, by its very nature, creates its own demand, as has become evident in the process whereby producer and transit countries have developed substantial user populations of their own. Not only does this result in lost productivity, with significant implications for economic competitiveness, but it also entails substantial costs for health care and law enforcement. Moreover, organized crime has developed sophisticated marketing techniques that target new users. The establishment and expansion of organized crime groups, however, irrespective of the activities they engage in, poses the most serious threat to society. Organized crime targets basic values, both legal and political, that constitute the cohesive element of societies. It does so by challenging the foundation of these values and by developing opposite 'values' of its own. The projection of organized crime as the provider of employment and prosperity and its replacement of the central authority as the ruler, legislator and law enforcer can have deleterious effects on any society, regardless of its degree of advancement or its cultural foundation. By corrupting or intimidating legitimate authority, organized crime undermines fundamental institutions, rendering them inoperative not only because of their lack of effectiveness, but in the long term by discrediting the values that form their basis.

Organized crime generally involves two kinds of violence: violence used by the organizations involved to protect their territory and profits; and violence against people and property resorted to by individuals in order to pay for illicit products or services. There is, in addition and with reference to drug trafficking, the violence perpetrated by individuals under the influence of psychotropic substances. It has been estimated, for example, that the average heroin user commits 200 crimes a year to feed his habit.[59] The overall result, therefore, is that transnational crime feeds into violence in local communities, providing a vivid example of the global-local nexus in relation to transnational crime.

## The threat to individuals

At the individual level, security can be understood as the provision of a relatively safe environment, in which individuals and entities can go about their daily business without fear of violence or intimidation. They are able to pursue their right to life and property without being put at risk by the violent actions of others. In this context, transnational criminal organizations have had what might be called a profound geosocial impact. If individual security is inversely related to the level of violence within society - the greater the violence, whether through civil strife, factionalism or criminal activity, the less security is enjoyed by citizens - then transnational crime poses a serious security threat. As well as the violence that is a consequence of drug trafficking, violence is often perpetrated on individuals by criminal organizations. Some organizations, for example, traffic in people, especially women and children, treating them essentially as products and fundamentally depriving them of their human rights.

## The threat to national stability and state control

Transnational criminal organizations affect not only the host or recipient state but also their home state. In some cases, they provide a rival authority structure, or what sometimes appears as 'a state within the state' based on a parallel or black market economy of very significant proportions. Their readiness to use force against the state and its agents challenges the state monopoly on the legitimate use of violence and imposes a level of harm that probably exceeds the damage resulting from the activities of most terrorist groups.

This has certainly been the case in Colombia and Italy. In both nations, home-based transnational criminal organizations have resisted efforts at state control and have resorted to extensive violence and terrorism. In Colombia, the Medellín cartel posed a fundamental challenge to the Colombian state and although, with the death of Pablo Escobar, the Colombian state has clearly emerged intact, the toll has been enormous. The Colombian judiciary has been decimated, the level of violence, at times, has reached proportions that are characteristic of civil wars, and Colombian political and economic life has been dominated by the threats posed by the narco-traffickers. The cartels have also been a threat to democratic values, killing journalists who were critical of their activities and corrupting the institutions of the state. Much the same kind of threat has been evident in Italy, where the Mafia has not only challenged efforts at control by launching similar attacks on members of the judiciary, but has proved to be a far more formidable enemy than such terrorist organizations as the Red

Brigades. One of the reasons for this is that the Mafia has created an illicit but effective authority structure over its own territory and population.

Having gained enormously in power and wealth through its involvement in the heroin trade from Southeast Asia and the cocaine trade from Latin America, the Sicilian Mafia, in particular, has used both corruption and violence. It has historically had very close links with ruling political parties and has infiltrated government not only at the local and regional levels but also at the national level. Moreover, throughout the 1980s the Mafia regularly killed magistrates, policemen, politicians, civil servants and trade unionists.[60] The assassinations of Paolo Borsellino and Giovanni Falcone represented a challenge to the Italian judicial system similar to the Medellín cartel's challenge to the Colombian judicial system. Although the challenge backfired, the events in Italy revealed the vulnerability of even advanced industrialized states to the threat posed by powerful transnational criminal organizations.

The challenge to state authority may be inescapable, as 'each crime network attempts to build a coercive monopoly and to implement that system of control through at least two other criminal activities, corruption of public and private officials, and violent terrorism in order to enforce its discipline'.[61] In other words, transnational criminal organizations, by their very nature, undermine civil society, add a degree of turbulence to domestic politics, and challenge the normal functioning of government and law. While they are particularly effective where government is already weak or unstable, criminal organizations add further layers of instability. Furthermore, as criminal organizations 'realize the extent of their influence and power in the face of weak government or half-hearted efforts to control them, it is not too fantastic a leap to see these groups going beyond efforts merely to neutralize government enforcement but to become the government'.[62]

*The threat to democratic values and public institutions*

Criminal organizations do not always confront the state directly. An alternative approach is to infiltrate and corrupt state authorities in an effort to neutralize efforts at law enforcement. The aim is generally to achieve a position in which the government is acquiescent and takes no serious initiative to deal with the organization or to suppress its activities.

One way of achieving this is to enter into a tacit agreement to limit violence so long as the government does not interfere with the group's economic enterprises. Another is to engage in corruption so that those who have the power or authority to initiate action against the criminal organization do not do so because of the benefits they obtain from the organization. The worst situation is one in which government officials and the criminal organization have a symbiotic or collusive relationship. In these circumstances, the government is little more than a protective front for criminal activity, and, at the same time, a hostage of the criminal organization. This is an extreme case, but, as suggested above, can occur under certain conditions. It is consequently not a contingency that can be ignored.

*The threat to national economies*

Unlike terrorist groups, the objectives of transnational criminal organizations are predominantly economic and not political. Moreover, it has been argued that even illicit enterprises add to wealth in national economies, enhance levels of employment and provide a safety net against recession. According to the same argument, transnational criminal organizations also offer opportunities for entrepreneurial and management skills that would otherwise be wasted. The profits from these activities are enormous and at least some of them are ploughed back into the local or national economy, usually with some multiplier effects. These positive results are only one part of the picture, however. The profits from transnational crime may also make economic management a much more difficult task, as they can encourage inflationary pressures, a distorted sectoral development, and spending on luxury products by a few when the greatest need is for a wider distribution of resources within the society.

Furthermore, in so far as they reduce the tax base, 'black' economies tend to have a harmful effect on the legitimate economy and can undermine development efforts and efforts to ensure economic equilibrium.

*The threat to financial institutions*

Transnational criminal organizations also pose a serious threat to the integrity of financial and commercial institutions at both the national and international levels. Infiltration of licit institutions, intimidation of their owners, distortion of their purposes, so that they no longer serve either the public interest or that of their shareholders, and reduction of management can lead to the misuse of funds.

Such a process is also central to the efforts of transnational criminal organizations to develop symbiotic relationships with both licit business and political élites. To the extent that this process succeeds, it is much more difficult for governments and law enforcement authorities to deal with these organizations. The analogy of a virus gradually breaking down the immune system of the body politic is a striking and appropriate one.

The pollution of financial institutions is a serious activity that could undermine public confidence and have a serious long-term effect on global confidence in the economy. At the international level, the amount of money that is being laundered further erodes the capacity of governments to manage, control and regulate the global financial system. At the same time there is also a danger of a backlash. In fact, the response to the challenge by transnational criminal organizations may be to take measures that could inhibit normal and legitimate financial activity. On the contrary, effective policies should resist the temptation of overregulation, thus avoiding measures that undermine growth and development.

## *The threat to democratization and privatization*

With the end of the cold war, many states have embarked on a difficult transition to the creation of democratic institutions and market economies. This dual transition has provided new opportunities for criminal activity, especially in areas where criminal justice systems are weak. Although there was initially some scepticism as to whether states in transition would be targeted by organized crime, partly because of the primitive stage of their economies, this assessment overlooked the fact that organized criminal groups operate in many ways like transnational enterprises and invest in the potential of economies in transition. This potential is measured by such factors as natural resources and other criteria affecting likely economic growth. Furthermore, the risks involved in these investments are significantly lower, as successful efforts on the part of law enforcement and judicial authorities are less likely'.[63]

Indeed, one of the problems is that, in cases where totalitarian systems were formerly in place, there is a considerable reluctance to do anything that appears to involve the reimposition of controls over the society. Moreover, efforts by friendly governments to bolster up criminal justice systems and enhance law enforcement capabilities may be seen as an unwarranted intrusion into the country's domestic affairs and a violation of sovereignty.

Such tendencies could obstruct efforts at international cooperation. At the other extreme, however, is the possibility that there will be a significant backlash against the crime and corruption that have accompanied democratization and that the populace will opt for a hard-line government that promises to restore order. In these circumstances, the potential for a reversal of the trend towards democratization is very considerable. The backlash effect of transnational crime, therefore, is not something that can be ignored. Indeed, there is an inherent danger that some governments may use the threat from transnational criminal organizations to establish restrictions on personal freedom and other fundamental elements of democracy.

*The threat to development*

The threat posed by transnational criminal organizations to developing states has both a systemic and a personal impact. At the systemic level, organized crime undermines development efforts, in that scarce resources have to be diverted from other projects in response to criminal activities. In addition, the corruption that often accompanies transnational crime tends to weaken 'the commitment of the citizenry to the sacrifices demanded by development policies', and to impair 'the rational decision-making process required by public administration'.[64] Corruption can occur at several levels, from the policeman on patrol to the highest level of government. Whatever the level, however, the result is invariably that it provides benefits to the few at the expense of the many. At the individual level, it is often the weakest and poorest members of society who are most at risk from criminal organizations. Indeed, for peoples who barely manage to subsist, transnational crime can have a devastating impact. Cattle theft and the transport of cattle across borders in parts of Africa, for example, have profound implications for those who depend on them for their very subsistence.

*The threat to global regimes and codes of conduct*

Attempts to regulate the global political system and establish codes of conduct, principles of restraint and responsibility and norms of behavior are increasingly being challenged by transnational crime and the criminal organizations that engage in it. Regimes to inhibit the proliferation of nuclear, chemical and biological weapons, as well as the technologies used for ballistic missiles, are highly dependent upon cooperation among suppliers and the ability to isolate rogue states that seek to obtain such capabilities.

Alliances of convenience, particularly between rogue states or pariah states on the one hand and transnational criminal organizations on the other, could do much to undermine the control regime. Once a trafficking network is in place and is functioning effectively, product diversification is easy. Organizations that traffic in drugs can just as easily traffic in technology and components for weapons of mass destruction. Whether the recipients are terrorist organizations or pariah states, the threat is obvious. If non-proliferation and other regulatory regimes are to function effectively in the future, therefore, it will be necessary to curb the activities of transnational criminal organizations.

**Conclusion**

Transnational crime and transnational criminal organizations pose serious and still not fully acknowledged threats to the dignity and safety of individuals to the sovereignty, security and stability of states, to the proper functioning of financial and commercial institutions at the national and global levels and to the order and stability of the international system. While these threats are very real ones in their home states and in the host countries in which they operate, failure to deal with the transnational criminal organizations from a global perspective only offers further opportunities for their growth and development. As was underlined by the Commission on Crime Prevention and Criminal Justice at its third session, in paragraph 5 of the annex to its draft resolution I,[65] adopted by the Economic and Social Council as resolution 1994/12, '... organized crime is, due to its nature, a pervasive phenomenon. Therefore, the international community should find ways to cooperate, not only in controlling current illicit behavior but also in preventing the expansion of the phenomenon in new areas where defense mechanisms against the spread of such criminal activities are weak'.

Organized criminal groups have already achieved enormous successes. As has been emphasized: 'The resources at its disposal, the generation and maintenance of enormous wealth and power, the continuity and resilience of its structures and activities, and its continuing recruitment and replenishment of operatives, as well as the unscrupulous ways in which "business" is conducted, enable organized crime to defeat criminal justice systems personnel.'[66]

In these circumstances, it is essential that governments initiate more stringent measures against transnational criminal organizations and engage in more comprehensive and effective cooperation. In particular, on the basis of the analysis made in the previous chapters, and drawing on the elements highlighted in the discussion document on the World Ministerial Conference on Organized Transnational Crime (see Economic and Social Council resolution 1994/12, annex), the following issues appear to deserve special attention for appropriate action:

    (a) Identification and regular monitoring, through a global assessment, of the various and ever-changing problems posed by transnational organized crime;

(b) A focus on specific types of criminality that are considered particularly dangerous or alarming;
(c) A better understanding of the problems arising from differences that exist or emerge among various countries in the perception and evaluation of transnational organized crime;
(d) A study of the problems related to the different degrees of development of laws and regulations in individual countries;
(e) An examination of the problems arising from the expansion or reallocation of transnational criminal organizations to other countries where the defense mechanism is weak;
(f) A study of conditions that are conducive to the rise and growth of transnational criminal organizations, namely: social, economic and political factors; structural characteristics of organized crime; and organizational shortcomings and lack of resources in the control agencies;
(g) The gradual development of a common perception of the phenomenon;
(h) A global strategy for more effective inter-state cooperation.

While it is hoped that the Conference will take action on the above proposals, it should be pointed out that there may be no guarantee of success: the dialectic between law enforcement and organized crime is a continuing one of measures and countermeasures. Unless governments pursue the issue much more vigorously than has hitherto been the case, with enough priority, determination and vision, as well as making the corresponding allocation of adequate resources, the danger persists that transnational criminal organizations will become ever more powerful.

NOTES

1. Gary W. Potter, *Criminal Organizations: Vice, Racketeering and Politics in an American City* (Prospect Heights, Illinois, Waveland Press, 1994), pp.2-7.
2. Ibid., p.19.
3. Some cases of organized crime, however, also involve extensive corruption; see, in this respect, Ethan Nadelmann, *Cops Across Borders* (University Park, Pennsylvania, Pennsylvania State University Press, 1993), especially pp.251-312.
4. Ibid., p.117.
5. Ibid., p.117
6. Robert Keohane and Joseph Nye, *Transnational Relations and World Politics* (Cambridge, Massachusetts, Harvard University Press, 971), p.xii.
7. Edward Morse, 'Transnational economic processes', in Keohane and Nye, op.cit., p.25.
8. John A. Mack and Hans-Jurgen Kerner, *The Crime Industry* (Lexington, Massachusetts, Heath, 1975), p.6.
9. Timothy Green, *The Smugglers* (New York, Walker, 1969), p.3.
10. Phil Williams, 'Transnational criminal organizations and international security', *Survival*,

Vol. 36, No. 1 (Spring 1973), pp.96-113.
11. *Discussion guide for the Ninth United Nations Congress on the Prevention of Crime and the Treatment of Offenders* (A/CONF.169/PM.1 and Corr.1), para.38.
12. Samuel Huntington, 'Transnational organizations in world politics', *World Politics*, Vol. 25, No. 3 (April 1973), pp.333-368.
13. This theme is developed in John M. Martin and Anne T. Romano, *Multinational Crime* (London, Sage Publications, 1992).
14. R. Vernon, *Storm over the Multinationals* (Cambridge, Massachusetts, Harvard University Press, 1977), p.2.
15. See *World Air Transport Statistics*, No. 37 (June 1993), pp.8-11.
16. *1990 International Trade Statistics Yearbook* (United Nations publication, Sales No. E.92.XVII.2), Vol. 1, pp.52-53.
17. L. Krause, 'Private international finance', in Keohane and Nye, op. cit., p.175.
18. Peter Lupsha, 'Organized crime: rational choice not ethnic group behavior: a macro perspective', *Law Enforcement Intelligence Analysis Digest*, Winter 1986, pp.1-7.
19. Kenichi Ohmae, *The Borderless World* (New York, Harper Business, 1990), p.xiii and pp.18-26.
20. Louis Kraar, 'The drug trade', *Fortune*, 20 June 1988, pp.27-38.
21. Joel Kurtzman, *The Death of Money* (New York, Simon and Schuster, 1993), p.19.
22. In the present context, the term refers to an area that is not the target of significant law enforcement attention, in some cases because of the absence of law enforcement capabilities.
23. Francisco E. Thoumi, 'Why the illegal psychoactive drugs industry grew in Colombia', *Journal of InterAmerican Studies and World Affairs*, Vol. 34, No. 3 (Fall 1992), pp. 37-64, especially pp.47 and 55.
24. See E/CN.15/1993/4, para. 14.
25. The term 'sovereign free' is used by James Rosenau, in *Turbulence in World Politics* (Princeton, New Jersey, Princeton University Press, 1989) to discuss a wide variety of non-state actors.
26. Giovanni Fiandaca, 'Mafia problems', in *Mafia Issues*, Ernesto U. Savona, ed. (Milan, International Scientific and Professional Advisory Council of the United Nations, Crime Prevention and Criminal Justice Programme, 1993), p.37.
27. Adolfo Beria di Argentine, 'The Mafias in Italy', in *Mafia Issues*, p.20.
28. Guido M. Rey and Ernesto U. Savona, 'The Mafia: an international enterprise?', in *Mafia Issues*, p.74.
29. The 'global octopus' argument is developed in Claire Sterling, *The Mafia* (London, Hamish Hamilton, 1990) and more recently in the same author's *Thieves' World* (New York, Simon and Schuster, 1994).
30. See Carl Johnson, *Russian Organized Crime: A Baseline Perspective* (Johnstown, Pennsylvania, National Drug Intelligence Center, November 1993).
31. Joseph Serio, 'Organized crime in the former Soviet Union: only the name is new', *Criminal Justice International* (July-August, 1993), pp.11-17.
32. Stephen Handelman, quoted in Seymour M. Hersh, 'The wild East', *The Atlantic Monthly*, Vol. 273, No. 6 (June 1994), p.79.
33. Carl Johnson, *Russian Organized Crime*, op.cit.
34. Ibid.
35. Louise Shelley, quoted in Seymour M. Hersh, op. cit., p.82
36. Ko-lin Chin, 'Triad societies in Hong Kong', *Rassegna Italiana di Sociologia*.
37. See *El Mundo*, 27 March 1994, p.71.
38. *Asian Organized Crime: The New International Criminal*, Hearings before the Permanent Subcommittee on Investigations of the Committee on Governmental Affairs, United States Senate, One Hundred Second Congress, Second Session, 18 June and 4 August 1992, p. 125.
39. David E. Kaplan and Alec Dubro, *Yakuza* (New York, Macmillan, 1986), p.208.
40. Such activities succeeded up until 1995 when the leaders of the Cartel were either arrested or surrendered voluntarily. The extent to which this has injured the Cartel, however, remains

uncertain.
41. *Nigeria - A Country Overview* (Johnstown, Pennsylvania, National Drug Intelligence Center, 17 March 1994).
42. For a fuller analysis of the industry, see Phil Williams, 'International drug trafficking: an industry analysis', in *Low Intensity Conflict and Law Enforcement.*
43. Josh Friedman, 'Smugglers move 1 million yearly to industrial world', *Houston Chronicle,* 12 June 1994, p. A 31.
44. R. T. Naylor, 'Covert commerce and underground financing in the modern arms black market', paper presented to the Committee on International Security Studies of the American Academy of Arts and Sciences, 24 Feb. 1994, p.6.
45. *Discussion guide for the Ninth United Nations Congress on the Prevention of Crime and the Treatment of Offenders* (A/CONF.169/PM.1 and Corr.1), para. 40.
46. Testimony by Hans-Ludwig Zachert to the *Permanent Subcommittee on Investigations of the Committee on Governmental Affairs, United States Senate,* 25 May 1994.
47. Ferdinand Protzman, 'Germany reaffirms origin of seized plutonium in Russia', *New York Times,* 21 July 1994, p.A 6.
48. See *Time,* No. 35, 29 August 1994, and *Newsweek,* 29 August 1994.
49. Gabriela Tarazona-Sevillano, *Sendero Luminoso and the Threat of Narcoterrorism* (New York, Praeger, 1990), p.100.
50. See *Terrorism in the United States 1982-1992,* Terrorist Research and Analytical Center, Counterterrorism Section, Intelligence Division (Washington, D.C., United States Department of Justice, 1993), p.13.
51. John Krenuske, quoted in Marilyn Goldstein, 'Human rights, if you're the right sex', *Newsday,* 13 Dec. 1993, p.8.
52. 'Organ trafficking a reality, says Argentine diplomat', *Reuters,* 22 Nov. 1993.
53. Quoted in 'The organ theft scandal', *The Times,* 18 November 1993. See also, 'Film exposes black market in human body parts', *Reuters,* 12 Nov. 1993.
54. M. E. Beekman and M. R. Daly, 'Motor vehicle theft investigations: emerging international trends', *FBI Law Enforcement Bulletin,* Vol. 69, No. 9 (Sept. 1990), pp.14-19.
55. Ibid.
56. Michael DeFeo and Ernesto V. Savona, 'Money trails: international money-laundering trends and prevention/control policies', background paper presented at the International Conference on Preventing and Controlling Money-Laundering and the Use of the Proceeds of Crime: A Global Approach, Courmayeur, Italy, 18-20 June 1994, p. 21.
57. Green, op. cit., p. 9.
58. *Discussion guide for the Ninth United Nations Congress on the Prevention of Crime and the Treatment of Offenders* (A/CONF.169/PM.1 and Corr.1), para. 39.
59. The Majority Staffs of the Senate Judiciary Committee and the International Narcotics Control Caucus, *The President's Drug Strategy: Has it Worked?* (September 1992), p.vi.
60. 'The Sicilian Mafia', *The Economist,* 24 April 1993, pp.21-24.
61. R. J. Kelly, 'Criminal underworlds: looking down on society from below', in R. J. Kelly, ed. *Organized Crime: A Global Perspective* (Totowa, New Jersey, Rowman and Littlefield, 1986), p.17.
62. Roy Godson and William J. Olson, *International Organized Crime: Emerging Threat to US Security* (Washington, D.C., National Strategy Information Center, 1993), p.14.
63. Report of the Secretary-General on the control of proceeds of crime, submitted to the Commission on Crime Prevention and Criminal Justice at its second session (E/CN.15/1993/4), para. 15.
64. See *Eighth United Nations Congress on the Prevention of Crime and the Treatment of Offenders, Havana, 27 August-7 September 1990: Report Prepared by the Secretariat* (United Nations publication, Sales No. E.91.IV.2), chap. IV, sect. C, para. 255.
65. See *Official Records of the Economic and Social Council, 1994, Supplement No. 11* (E/1994/31), chap. I, sect. A.
66. *Discussion guide for the Ninth United Nations Congress on the Prevention of Crime and Treatment of Offenders* (A/CONF.169/PM.1 and Corr.1), para. 38.

# National Legislation and its Adequacy to Deal with the Various Forms of Organized Transnational Crime
## Appropriate Guidelines for Legislative and Other Measures to be Taken at the National Level[1]

**Introduction**

In the present report, different strategies and policies adopted at the national level to combat organized crime are analysed and existing legislation against organized crime, both criminal and regulatory, substantive and procedural, is examined, together with law enforcement mechanisms and special programmes. Considering these strategies and policies in a systemic approach as goal-oriented,[2] the key elements that have proved successful are outlined and two types of goals analysed: prevention and control.[3] 'Preventive goals' are the goals pursued in order to reduce the opportunities for accumulating profits through illicit activities, and to reduce the vulnerability of societies and governments to infiltration by organized crime. 'Control goals' are the goals designed to weaken, disrupt and dismantle criminal organizations by prosecuting and convicting their members and tracing and confiscating the assets accumulated through, or used in, illicit activities. Drawing on existing United Nations documents, reports and resolutions,[4] as well as on the experience of some selected countries, this analysis offers elements for understanding the conditions and limitations of the policies adopted so far, and also suggests ways to enhance national capabilities for responding more effectively to old and new threats posed by transnational organized crime. The legislation reviewed was selected on the basis of availability, regional representation and the existence of a variety of measures designed to deal with organized crime.

**A Systematic Approach to the Problem of Organized Crime**

The goal of combating crime and the organizations that pursue wealth and power through criminal activities is often mentioned in official national and international documents, denoting an awareness of the problem and a will to take action. Shifting from the symbolic dimension to the reality of the situation in each country, many variables may influence the perception of the problem, the will to act and, hence, the effectiveness of the action that is taken. These variables include a number of objective elements, such as the level of resources available, the qualifications and professional skills of decision makers and of those who implement the action, in particular the criminal justice system personnel, including law enforcement agencies, as well as a number of subjective features or weaknesses, such as the level of corruption, or susceptibility to it, and other collusive relations between organized crime groups and some parts of the political, economic and bureaucratic system.

Owing to the inherent characteristics of organized crime, which is simultaneously engaged in providing illegal services and goods and in infiltrating the legitimate economy, the criminal justice system alone cannot successfully fight it. For these reasons, in the past few years, a range of 'preventive' policies have been conceived and adopted, aimed, for example, at reducing the demand for illicit goods and deregulating or regulating some markets in order to reduce their vulnerability to infiltration by organized crime groups. These preventive policies, as opposed to crime control policies, relate to various sectors of the social and economic systems. The increased use of such policies (for example, the regulation of non-bank financial institutions as an anti-money-laundering policy), in response to the organized crime emergency, calls for their close integration with crime control policies and, consequently, with the criminal justice systems.

A systemic approach designed to identify the most effective strategies against organized crime focuses on two elements: goals and policies. The more these are rationally linked, the more likely it is that the prevention and control system will be effective. The word 'rationally' is used judicially to mean that a given society or country should select its priorities from among the desired goals, with a readiness to accept trade-off effects, and that it should base its choice on the policies that are least costly and present the fewest political and legal constraints, bearing in mind the fact that organized crime is simultaneously a domestic and an international problem.

In terms of strategy, the main question is to identify the most effective policies for preventing and controlling organized crime. The distinction between prevention and control is based on whether the policies pursued are defensive or offensive. Although they may appear to be closely interlinked in terms of the effects they produce, the difference lies in the intended goals. On the one hand, with respect to prevention, there may be a policy to reduce the demand for illicit goods and services, thereby limiting the opportunities for organized crime and preventing it from expanding. Conversely, the deregulation of, for example, the construction industry, or the introduction of a different type of regulation, has tended to make it much less vulnerable, preventing criminal organizations from securing a dominant, often monopolistic, hold on the market and making it much more difficult for them to infiltrate the legitimate economy. On the other hand, crime control policies are intended to disrupt the structure of criminal organizations. The two policies, to be effective, should be integrated into a systemic approach. In fact, when crime control policies are adopted without considering the advantages of preventive measures, and when general deterrence receives overwhelming attention and is viewed as the only form of prevention, the criminal justice system becomes overburdened and, therefore, less effective.

*Preventive Strategies*

When considering how to prevent or reduce the incidence and expansion of organized crime, the main assumptions are that:

(a) Organized crime is a derivative of a complex society - the more complex the organizational structure of a society becomes, the more the crime problem reflects this complexity, taking on varying and more sophisticated organizational patterns;

(b) The criminal justice system is overloaded; some experts are questioning whether the economic costs of control policies have reached the point of diminishing utility - criminal law alone, and law enforcement in isolation, cannot succeed in dealing with the increasing complexity, flexibility and sophistication of large-scale organized crime operations;

(c) As organized crime is oriented to providing illicit goods and services and to infiltrating legitimate activities through a variety of methods, including corruption and violence, preventive strategies need to be identified, which, while reducing the opportunities for crime, will also increase the threshold of vulnerability of the economic systems to infiltration. These strategies need to be integrated into - and not opposed to - crime control measures.[5]

*Reducing the opportunities for criminal activities*

Strategies for limiting the opportunities for criminal activities involve different policies; for example the demand for illicit goods and services may be reduced, or an attempt may be made to make the goods and services monopolized by criminals legally available. These policies should be integrated, as their goal tends to be the same. On the one hand, there is the aggregated demand, while on the other, there is the demand for illegal goods and services only.[6] Since the problem is highly complex, it should be treated as such, taking into account the trade-offs and side effects that might occur. This aspect of preventive strategy calls for a deeper knowledge and a thorough evaluation of its various implications and of their effects in different regions of the world.

The strengthening of the values of morality and legality must occupy a prominent place in preventive measures against crime. These values are prerequisites for building a social and cultural consensus against organized crime. The operations of organized crime groups, and their continued existence in territories where they are established and traditionally located, require a social consensus that helps to lower the risk attached to law enforcement activities and, in the process, facilitates the recruitment of new members. Organized crime groups achieve a consensus by redistributing resources and, consequently, creating incentives to employment in economically and socially depressed areas, and also creating disincentives through corruption and fear of violence. Building and maintaining high moral standards in political and administrative structures through respect for the law is the first commitment for effective action against organized crime. A culture of morality and legality has strong messages to convey to those who violate the law and to those who allow them to do so. The values need to be implanted, nurtured with extreme care, and passed on to new generations. As organized crime represents the organized violation of these values, it is essential to devise and implement comprehensive strategies to restore legality wherever it has been eroded, and to create 'incentives for morality' for those who are exposed or susceptible to corruption. Measures for the protection of the criminal justice system against violence and the fear of violence are geared towards restoring legality[7] and codes of conduct in different areas of government and administration are geared towards restoring morality.

Policies that place emphasis on civic education can go a long way towards countering organized crime by building a social consensus against it, disseminating information and increasing awareness of the cost of organized crime to society. Here, the mass media play an important central role. The educational impact of messages transmitted by the media may, however, prove contradictory, since the emphasis is often on the spectacular or the sensational. Fictional crime stories and non-fictional accounts of crime are attracting increasingly wider audiences. Crime, violence, and corruption capture public attention in all parts of the world: the issue of reconciling the rights of information and freedom of artistic expression with the civic and social responsibility of promoting values of morality and legality is a very difficult one. The interrelationship between the media and crime, and their role in crime prevention, are truly challenging questions, which take on even more importance as time goes by.[8] Research and documentation on the experience gained thus far and increasing attention on the part of educational institutions are essential conditions for gaining the support of the media in this area.

## Reducing the vulnerability of legitimate industry

A second goal within the framework of preventive strategies is related to the need to reduce the level of vulnerability of legitimate industry to infiltration by organized crime groups. The assumption is that organized crime tends to infiltrate the legitimate economy for different purposes, such as:

(a) laundering and investing the proceeds of crime;
(b) acquiring respectability and social consensus for its members; and
(c) controlling the territory where it operates in order to maximize economic and political advantages and minimize the risk of apprehension, arrest, and conviction (what is termed the 'law enforcement risk').

Activities in the illegal markets and infiltration of legitimate business are not separate in the life and operations of an organized crime group. Opportunistic criminal organizations go where the money is, and 'mono-task' organizations, such as those specializing in drug trafficking, become opportunistic when they have to invest the money produced by their criminal activities. For both, the infiltration of legitimate business is part and parcel of their activities. In order to reduce the vulnerability of industry, there must be more transparency in the economic system.

Successful policies involve a good chemistry of regulation and deregulation. For example, a number of countries have recently been strictly regulating the licensing of all economic activities, including banking and financial services, that could be infiltrated by organized crime. In particular, a request for banks to monitor transactions in an attempt to frustrate the money-launderers may help to identify money-laundering operations and trace criminal organizations. Furthermore, new regulations and codes of conduct for businesses and professionals can also help in the fight against money-laundering by keeping standards of transparency high and avoiding infiltration by organized crime.

Conversely, however, regulation through licensing may reduce competition and lead to some inefficiency in the system. Reduction of the vulnerability of legitimate industries has therefore to be balanced by forms of deregulation that increase competition among different enterprises. Some industries (for example building and construction) are particularly attractive to organized crime groups.[9] It has been a long-standing practice in many countries for organized crime groups to use violence and corruption to obtain some form of monopolistic control over the bidding procedure for public contracts, especially in the construction industry. In these cases, deregulation, which increases the level of competition, may be beneficial.[10] When promoting and facilitating competition among enterprises for public contracts, special attention should be paid to structuring the general framework of competition in such a way as to reduce the opportunities for and the risk of infiltration by organized crime groups. Such a policy also has the advantage of reducing the risk of corruption because of competitive prices. Corruption requires some form of monopolistic control in order to keep prices high and thus cover its costs.

As regulation and deregulation policies may have their trade-offs in terms of efficiency, they should be regularly monitored and adjusted. For example, regulation is effective when transparency is required in order to identify the actors in the market, while deregulation is effective in order to decrease the opportunities for criminal groups to establish monopolies. The optimal amount of regulation and deregulation must be based upon variables determined by the structure and the power of organized groups acting in given areas, as well as basic characteristics of the economy, including its size, strength, level of development and ability to be flexible and functional.

Preventive strategies and policies, although not sufficiently used in the past, have increasingly been explored in recent times as a means of action against organized crime. They are promising and cost- effective if carefully planned and implemented. As such, they represent the natural complement to traditional crime control policies.

## Crime Control Strategies

### Substantive legislation

Substantive criminal law has adapted itself in different ways to the changes imposed by organized crime. The countries that have been exposed to the greatest threats from organized crime have been the first to react, by refining their legislation. The main changes relate to the criminalization of participation in the activities of criminal organizations and to the confiscation of assets acquired through, or used in, such criminal activities. In some countries, legislation allows the confiscation of crime proceeds through civil action against the proceeds themselves (*in rem*). This can be seen as a further expansion of the capability of the law in dealing with the changing trends of organized crime.

In many countries, the fact that an offence was committed as part of organized crime is frequently considered by criminal law to be an aggravating factor. In these cases, criminal codes define the commission of a crime by an organized group as a qualifying feature. A distinction is made between criminal activities engaged in by organized criminal groups and participation in an organized criminal activity. The former relates to activities traditionally conducted by organized crime groups. In the latter, membership in an organized crime group is penalized. In general, however, many countries punish differently the criminal activity engaged in by organized crime, according to their particular perception of this problem. For example, in some countries, in addition to the traditional offences, other less typical offences are considered by legislation as organized crime activities, including crimes such as participation in 'anti-revolutionary syndicates,' or 'loitering syndicates,' and offences against 'public order'.

Although there are exceptions, there is an emerging consensus on organized crime activities in different countries' legislation. The following list drawn from the legislation of some countries with considerable cultural diversities can give an idea of the most recurrent offences considered by legislation as organized crime activities: in Germany, illicit narcotics trafficking, gang robbery, the receiving of stolen goods, trading in illicit firearms, extortion, management and procuring of prostitution, and illicit gambling; in Italy the distribution of illegal drugs, kidnapping for profit, extortion, fraud, loan-sharking and counterfeiting of public money or securities; Jamaica has a Dangerous Drugs Act, an Offences against the Person Act, a Larceny Act, a Forgery Act, a Firearms Act and a Corruption Prevention Act. Statutory law in England and Wales considers the following as criminal activities: various forms of fraud, false accounting, handling of stolen property, drug trafficking, forgery, living off the earnings of prostitution, and various forms of assault. Criminal activities according to the common law in England and Wales are: murder, manslaughter, kidnapping and false imprisonment. In the United States of America there is no general national law against murder, robbery, burglary or rape; instead there are 51 different sets of laws, in the 50 states and the District of Columbia that provide for such crimes. Federal law acts in cases of criminal activity affecting the country as a whole, proscribing a number of criminal activities commonly engaged in by organized crime, such as trafficking in illicit drugs, extortion by private or public persons, illegal gambling, and the interstate transportation or receipt of stolen property or property obtained by fraud.

Countries of the new Commonwealth of Independent States are now updating their criminal legislation against organized crime. A process of convergence through known and well established offences is developing in the republics of the former Soviet Union. The perception of organized crime as a serious problem is bringing the legislation of many of these countries into a process of modernization in which the old ideological offences traditionally associated with organized anti-revolutionary activities have been deleted. Banditry, possession of contraband, embezzlement of government property, extortion, fraud, black marketeering, robbery, armed assault, premeditated murder, causing serious bodily harm, and drug-related crimes are the most frequent offences recognized by these countries. Their legislation, and also their criminal justice systems as a whole, are going through a deep process of change and modernization.[11]

A recent trend, which has substantially modified criminal legislation, is to consider 'participation in an organized criminal association' as a crime. In many countries, this coincides with the crime of 'conspiracy'. Conspiracy is defined as the formation of a combination of two or more persons on a continuing basis for the purpose of committing an indefinite number of unlawful or criminal acts through the common use of all necessary means to carry out the concerted criminal plan. In order to be found guilty of criminal conspiracy, a defendant must be permanently aware of his membership in the conspiracy, and must always be ready to operate with the aim of implementing the pre-established plans of the conspiracy. Italian law has separate provisions prohibiting conspiracies to distribute illegal drugs. Because of certain characteristics peculiar to the Mafia culture, especially the duty of silence, known as *omertà*, conspiracy has always been difficult to prove in a trial. In view of these difficulties, Italy enacted a law in 1982 introducing a new offence. This law makes it illegal to be a member of a Mafia-type association composed of three or more members. An association is defined as 'Mafia-type' when its members strive to secure the management or at least the control of economic activities, grants, permits, public works, contracts, and public services to make illicit profits or to acquire other illegal benefits for themselves or others. This crime is separate and distinct from the crime of general criminal conspiracy or the crime of drug conspiracy.

Born out of emergency, this law has turned out to be a powerful tool against organized crime. The crime of 'membership of an organized crime association' is based on the assumption that members of criminal organizations commit crimes. This assumption has made it possible to prosecute the top bosses of organized crime for this crime alone, on the basis of evidence provided by members of criminal organizations who have turned State's evidence. This crime has shown its potential in a long series of trials in which top Mafia leaders have been convicted and sentenced.

The Italian example of 1982 follows, albeit with many differences, the example set by the United States of America in the legislation of the 1970s. Although judicial interpretations of the United States Constitution did not allow the national legislature to prohibit mere membership in an organized crime group, the Racketeer Influenced and Corrupt Organizations statute, commonly known as RICO, makes it an offence for a person to participate in the affairs of an enterprise through a pattern of racketeering activity. The term 'racketeering activity' is defined in the RICO statute with great detail, and encompasses virtually all serious criminal activity prohibited by either state or federal law, such as murder, robbery, drug dealing, fraud and other serious crimes listed in the statute. The Continuing Criminal Enterprise statute (CCE) is directed only against persons who are engaged in large-scale drug dealing, and requires, *inter alia*, that the defendant commit at least three violations of the drug laws while acting as a manager or organizer of five or more people. In addition to these statutes, the United States has a statute prohibiting general criminal conspiracies and a separate statute prohibiting drug-related conspiracies.

Other countries, which do not have the extensive organized crime groups with which Italy and the United States, for example, have long been familiar, have hesitated to follow the Italian and American examples, considering the category of 'conspiracy crime' sufficient to deal with the emerging organizational typologies of organized crime. Law enforcement agencies, prosecutors and judges believe that including participation in a criminal organization as a specific crime has been a powerful tool in their hands for disrupting criminal organizations. The numerous indictments in the United States on the basis of the RICO legislation and the positive results of the implementation of article 416 *bis* of the Italian criminal legislation suggest that an extension of those categories to other national legislation may have definite advantages.

The success of efforts to combat the laundering of 'black money' directly depends on the level of accessibility of law enforcement agencies to the activities of financial bodies. A problem here is that opening up the activities of financial bodies to outside scrutiny can affect their competitive position. The activities of organized crime may, however, undermine the entire financial market, thus affecting society as a whole. Furthermore, the money derived from organized crime often circulates through the same channels as legitimate funds. In view of this, it is vital for the banks to maintain records of the identity of their clients, and to cooperate with law enforcement agencies whenever there are suspicious deposits or other transactions. It may be necessary to strengthen mechanisms of control over banking operations and even to centralize information of this kind.

In recent years, many countries have introduced into their criminal laws the crime of drug-money-laundering, in accordance with the United Nations Convention against Illicit Traffic in Narcotic Drugs and Psychotropic Substances of 1988. Because, however, drug trafficking is only one source of the proceeds of crime, there is a tendency in many Western European and North American countries, and in Australia, to expand the predicate offences from those related to drugs to virtually all serious crimes. In Central and South America and Asia, when money-laundering is criminalized as a separate offence its application is often limited to drug instrumentalities and proceeds. Eastern European countries are beginning to tackle these issues in the context of an overall re-examination of the law of property, banking regulations and criminal procedure. Few African countries have ratified the 1988 Convention and criminalized money-laundering.[12]

According to the conclusions of the International Conference on Preventing and Controlling Money-Laundering and the Use of Proceeds of Crime: a Global Approach, seven areas have been identified as implementation priorities for an effective anti-money-laundering global strategy. These areas are predicated on a number of assumptions about the presence of certain international and national enforcement mechanisms. Key among them is the concept that a net or web operates at three complementary levels - international, regional and national (which may be further divided into penal, cultural and administrative mechanisms at the national level). Political support, adequate resources, and high professionalism are essential conditions for effective action at all three levels. Governmental, multilateral, regional and international institutions must allocate adequate means and facilities to regulate or exercise successfully other types of control over highly sophisticated activities that may involve a large number of legitimate transactions, as, for example, in the case of wire-transfer technology.[13]

Corruption greatly facilitates the activities of organized criminal groups. In view of this, many countries have enacted special anti-corruption legislation. The fight against organized crime would be greatly assisted if all countries were to follow the anti-corruption recommendations adopted by the Eighth United Nations Congress on the Prevention of Crime and the Treatment of Offenders in its resolution 7.[14]

Specific domestic criminal legislation dealing with the problem of corruption can be found in many countries. Some examples can help to highlight the categories used for criminalizing corruption. For example, in Germany, under the penal code, active or passive bribery of public officials, civil servants or employees, is a criminal offence. In addition, with respect to commercial transactions, German law makes it a criminal offence to bribe any employee in connection with that employee's official functions. Italian law has a wide variety of penal offences calculated to reduce the opportunities for, and the impact of, corruption. Italian law was recently modified to strengthen the provisions against corruption. It is a criminal offence for public officials to embezzle money or illegally enrich themselves. It is also a crimina offence for a public servant to abuse a position of power by soliciting or receiving a bribe in order to perform an act related to the duty of the office held by such official. The penal law also punishes a public servant who performs an act contrary to his official duties.

In Jamaica, the Corruption Prevention Act deals with corruption of public officials and covers the soliciting or receiving of bribes, the offering of such bribes, or acting as an intermediary to facilitate a bribe. There is no legislation covering bribery and corruption in private enterprises. Federal Mexican law establishes the following penal offences: wrongful exercise of public office, abuse of public authority, wrongful use of the powers of public office, extortion by a public official, intimidation by a public official, abusive exercise of a public official's functions, selling the influence of a public official, bribery of a public official, embezzlement of public funds, and unlawful enrichment.

The United Kingdom of Great Britain and Northern Ireland has a variety of criminal offences related to official corruption. Some of these are crimes created by common law, while others are governed by statutory law. In the United Kingdom, there are common law offences for misconduct in public office, bribery or attempted bribery of a public officer, or accepting bribes when in public office either to act in a manner contrary to public duty or to show favour in the discharge of public functions. One of the earliest statutory offences in English law is the Sale of Offices Act of 1551, which prohibits the buying or selling of any public office concerned with the administration of justice. In 1809, these prohibitions were extended to all offices held under the Crown throughout the United Kingdom. Similarly, the Public Bodies Corrupt Practices Act of 1889 makes it an offence for any member, officer, or servant of a local governmental authority corruptly to solicit or receive any gift as an inducement or reward for performing any act associated with the office held by the official. In the private sphere, the Prevention of Corruption Act of 1916 prohibits a person who acts on behalf of another, for example, an employee, from accepting money to act to the detriment of the person for whom he is acting, for example, an employer.

United States law prohibits a public official of the federal or national government from demanding, seeking or receiving a bribe. The same law prohibits anyone from giving, offering or promising a bribe to such public official. In addition, various laws limit the type of private business and legal relationships a former government official may have with current government officials after leaving office. Federal law also requires certain public officials to relinquish control of their financial investments to another person so that their actions in public office will not be influenced by even an unconscious desire to increase their own personal wealth. In addition certain individuals are required to file financial disclosure forms indicating all their financial interests. The federal government also has at its disposal many laws to battle corruption by local officials of the 50 states. For example, the RICO statute discussed in paragraph 21 above has been used to prosecute public officials who have used their office corruptly. Finally, all 50 states have statutes designed to fight corruption.

Preventive strategies against corruption have been adopted in a number of countries and specific mechanisms have been set up, such as the Independent Commission against Corruption in Hong Kong and in New South Wales, Australia. In the context of preventive strategies, codes of conduct have been elaborated and an increasing number of countries are implementing them.

Prosecution of corruption is difficult and the adjudication of the alleged offender even more so, especially when organized crime is involved, owing to the problems in obtaining evidence. Laws often create incentives for solidarity between corrupted and corruptor, both being punished equally. For these reasons, it is necessary to develop new sets of policies against corruption, from regulatory to criminal ones. Many regulations in areas sensitive to corruption need to be reshaped (preventive policies) by incorporating incentives for reporting corruption cases into the same legislation that punishes the corrupted officials and by creating (at a legislative or judicial level) a conflict of interest between the corruptor and the corrupted, in order to obtain evidence.

Corruption is part of the transnational dimension of organized crime and international corruption is growing as a related phenomenon. Many countries do not punish business executives who bribe foreign officials and, in some ways, they have legalized corruption practised outside the borders through a system of financial and tax advantages. The contradiction between domestic and international morality is thus a stark one. A special commission of the Organisation for Economic Cooperation and Development has drawn up recommendations dealing with international corruption, with a view to harmonizing the laws of different countries.[15] This is in line with the efforts of other institutions, such as the Council of Europe and the International Chamber of Commerce, which have recommended the adoption of international measures (treaties, conventions) as crucial instruments in the fight against corruption.[16] It is essential that all countries respond positively to these recommendations.

In addition to the traditional sanctions of imprisonment or fines that may be imposed upon conviction, consideration should be given to other sanctions designed to deter organized criminality. Some countries use judicially imposed limitations on the property, residence, association and daily activitie of persons formally judged to be criminally dangerous, often taking past convictions into account. The granting of licences and public contracts may be conditional on the absence of criminal connections and proof of good reputation. Individuals and legal entities engaged in economic or financial activities involving great risk to the public, for example deposit-taking institutions or those dealing with toxic wastes, should be subject to adequately strict and enforced regulation to prevent wrongdoing, in particular since penal sanctions rarely provide proper compensation for victims.

Particular attention should be paid to the deterrence and punishment of misconduct by legal entities, such as multinational and other corporations. Individual executives may frequently be beyond national jurisdiction and personal responsibility may be difficult to establish. Criminal punishment of the entity itself, by fine or by forfeiture of property or legal rights, is used in some jurisdictions against corporate misconduct, and an increasing number of countries are including corporate crimes in their legislation. The establishment of criminal responsibility of a legal entity for corporate crimes is a powerful deterrent, intervening in the invisible or intangible good of the 'reputation'. The growth of economic crimes strictly connected with organized crime, such as frauds, calls for more attention to the activities of legitimate enterprises. These are the places where the infiltration of organized crime begins the process of polluting the legitimate economy and corporate sanctions can help to reduce the vulnerability of economic systems.

Crime committed for economic gain can be successfully countered by the forfeiture of such gains and of any other assets of the individuals and organizations involved. In some legal systems, great significance is attributed to the freezing, seizure, and confiscation of assets related to illegal activity. The need for more effective organized crime control makes it necessary to regard forfeiture as a strategic weapon, an economic method of discouraging organized crime activities and a means of eliminating the financial advantages of such antisocial activities.

The procedures for freezing, seizure, and confiscation need to be of broad scope and to permit the confiscation from the offender of a wide range of assets in order to eliminate all gain from the criminal activity. As a secondary benefit of such action, law enforcement agencies would be able to use confiscated assets or funds to further the activities of the agency. This can act as a powerful incentive. International agreements may also provide for the sharing of such assets.[17]

When dealing with organized crime, and on the basis of existing legislative provisions and practice, it may be appropriate to make any property constituting the proceeds of organized crime actions and any assets obtained with the help of these proceeds and any property used or intended to be used, in any manner or part, to commit or facilitate the commission of a crime by an organized group, including land, buildings and other private property subject to confiscation.

Consideration may also be given to allowing certain flexible evidentiary rules to be used in the procedures for confiscation of the assets of criminals involved in organized crime. For example, if it is proved that defendants had acquired assets during the time they were committing offences for which they had been convicted, and there is no other likely method by which they could have acquired the assets, then it may be reasonably inferred that the assets are the proceeds of crime. In the legislation related to confiscation, the liberty and property rights of individuals should be protected, in accordance with national constitutional principles and existing international instruments.

As may be seen from a recent analysis,[18] there is a marked convergence of country policies on asset forfeiture and confiscation of the proceeds of crime, which appear to be more widely accepted than the criminalization of a money-laundering offence *per se*. In the numerous countries where there are no specific money-laundering provisions, it is possible to find confiscation provisions deriving from more generic laws dealing with stolen property or the proceeds of a criminal act. Some examples drawn from the legislation of countries which have recently considered this issue can help in understanding recent trends. German law allows for both forfeiture and seizure of property under certain circumstances. A defendant may forfeit any financial advantage which he gained through the offence or as a result of his unlawful act. Forfeiture applies not only to tangible assets but also to accrued financial advantage. German law establishes various mechanisms to provide for the rights of third-party claimants to the property who are not involved in the activity. The concept of forfeiture allows property accrued in violation of law to be forfeited even if the defendant did not show the required intent to commit a criminal offence. If the defendant has violated a law for which forfeiture is a penalty, then the property acquired through the violation of that law is subject to forfeiture. In addition to the legal concept of forfeiture, German law provides for seizure of tangible assets which are acquired through the defendant's intentional commission of a criminal offence, or used by the defendant for the purpose of committing that offence, or in preparation for the commission of the offence, or intended by the defendant for use in intentionally committing a criminal offence. The principle of proportionality applies to both seizure and forfeiture, requiring that the seizure or forfeiture of the asset be in proportion to the extent of the harm caused as a result of the illegal act.

Italian law provides for two types of forfeiture. The first type is of a preventive nature; it allows a court to order the seizure of assets belonging to a person if that person's lifestyle is inconsistent with the person's apparent or declared income. In that event, the person is required to explain the nature and source of the asset. If the person can articulate and prove a lawful basis for his possession of the asset, then he is allowed to retain it. If, however, the person is unable to provide the authorities with an explanation as to the lawful acquisition of the asset, the court may order the asset forfeited. The second type of forfeiture or confiscation involves assets which have been used to commit a crime or are the products or profits of such crime. Confiscation is mandatory upon a defendant's conviction of a criminal offence related to his use or acquisition of the property in question.

In Jamaica, in addition to the forfeiture under the Exchange Control Act, the Dangerous Drugs Act provides for the confiscation of conveyances, for example boats, aeroplanes and motor vehicles, used in the commission of the offence. Particular attention is given to the forfeiture of assets acquired from the illicit trafficking of drugs and psychotropic substances. Mexican law permits the forfeiture of the instruments used to commit a criminal offence. The Mexican Constitution, however, prohibits confiscation, which is understood to be a non-judicial seizure of property. In the United Kingdom, confiscation of drug proceeds is allowed for the entire value of the drug proceeds, including property transferred to third parties as a gift or sold for significantly less than its full value. In addition, instrumentalities of drug trafficking crimes may be forfeited.

In the United States, the following laws allow the confiscation of assets: the RICO statute, the CCE statute, the anti-drug laws, and a wide variety of other federal criminal statutes. The drug law permits the forfeiture of the proceeds and instrumentalities of drug trafficking. If the government proves that a defendant violated the drug laws and acquired property during the time he was committing the drug offence for which there is no other likely source of funds, then it is presumed that such property was acquired with drug-related money even though that fact cannot be specifically established. The defendant, however, is free to offer evidence showing that the property was obtained in a legal manner. In the former Soviet Union, confiscation of property was permitted only if specifically provided for by statute. In general, confiscation of property is allowed for all types of specified profit oriented crime. The confiscation law exempts property needed by the defendant or his dependants, for example, a residence, foodstuffs, and money totalling the monthly salary of the criminal.

The main sanctions applied to cases of organized crime are imprisonment and confiscation of assets derived from crime. The latter has acquired growing importance as a necessary complement to anti-money-laundering policies, drawing on the experience of countries that have imposed it. Drawing on that same experience, other countries could be encouraged to introduce such sanctions into their legislation. Modifications in property laws may, however, be necessary, just as it is necessary to ensure the efficient functioning of legal enterprises that are objects of confiscation.

*Procedural legislation*

On the basis of a review conducted by the International Seminar on Organized Crime, held at Suzdal, Russian Federation, from 21 to 25 October 1991 (see Economic and Social Council resolution 1992/23, annex II), it would seem that most countries have procedural provisions empowering the courts, prosecutors, investigators and the police, as appropriate and in accordance with their respective competencies, to carry out investigations whenever there are indications of a crime. There may, however, be discretionary powers that allow the law enforcement authorities to decide whether or not to investigate or to initiate prosecution. Where this discretion exists, it is often used by investigators when working with informants from criminal circles. Its use requires a high degree of professional responsibility on the part of the investigators. Legal systems do recognize the possibility, in some cases, of granting minor offenders immunity from prosecution, in return for disclosing identities of leaders of organized criminal groups.

The criminal laws of many countries specify the elements that must be established to prove an offence. These may include: the commission of an offence; the defendant's guilt and motives for the crime; any aggravating or extenuating circumstances, including the defendant's record; and the nature and amount of damage inflicted by crime. The evidence is evaluated by the official performing the investigation, by the prosecutor, and finally by the court. In practice, there is no difference in the standard of evidence required in respect of crimes committed by organized crime groups compared with other crimes. Deciding on the verdict remains a task for the appropriate authority exercising judicial powers over serious offences committed by organized crime. In doing so, the principle of the presumption of innocence must be followed.

The experience of many countries suggests that there are advantages to be gained by using information obtained with the help of electronic surveillance, undercover agents, controlled delivery, the testimony of accomplices and similar methods of preliminary investigation for the collection of evidence. The acceptability of such methods is limited by the strict observance of legal requirements and criminal procedural principles. The use of the testimony of accomplices can be extremely helpful in prosecutions involving organized crime. Careful assessment and use of such testimony can enable law enforcement authorities to penetrate the layers of secrecy that are characteristic of criminal organizations and that would otherwise protect them from prosecution. Some countries have also found it advantageous to enact legislation obliging witnesses to testify truthfully and providing for sanctions if they refuse to do so.

The restriction of the liberty of the defendant prior to conviction is frequently allowed by the law when there are specified grounds. The main form of such restriction is pre-trial incarceration. This can be ordered if it is appropriate, in view of the seriousness of the case and the possible sentence upon conviction and for other reasons, for example because the defendant has tried to escape or because he or she may seek to evade justice or conceal evidence, or that he or she may commit further offences or pose a threat to witnesses, or otherwise be a danger to the community. If there is a bail system, the defendant who has been accused of an offence could be released upon the payment of a certain sum of money, unless the judicial authorities believe that pre-trial incarceration is necessary. The question whether a criminal may be released on bail should normally be a matter for a judicial or other appropriate body but the financial resources of those engaged in organized crime are often such as to make release inappropriate, since forfeiting bail may be considered as an acceptable cost of their business. The appropriateness of granting conditional release and other benefits of law in cases of organized criminality must be evaluated, taking into account the criminal record of the accused and the severity of the accusation.

Two questions appear to be of particular relevance in procedural legislation: mandatory or discretionary principles of prosecution; and issues of proof.

Some examples drawn from existing legislation can lead to a better understanding of the way in which these questions are considered by domestic laws. In Brazil, police and investigative authorities are allowed some discretion with regard to whether to arrest or proceed with an investigation of an offence known to them. No discretion is granted to prosecuting authorities if there is sufficient evidence to bring charges against a defendant.

Under German law, both the police and the Department of Public Prosecutions have the duty to institute criminal proceedings if there is sufficient evidence to show that a person is guilty of a criminal offence. Thus, Germany follows the principle of mandatory prosecution. Italy also follows the same principle. The police must report to the prosecutor, within 48 hours, any crime that has come to their attention. Similarly, the prosecutor is required to initiate criminal proceedings if the evidence so warrants. However, under certain circumstances, the prosecution may request from the appropriate judicial authority a reduction in the charge or reduced punishment, in exchange for the defendant's cooperation in a criminal investigation.

In Jamaica, some discretion is allowed to enable the police to overlook minor offenders in order to further their investigations of major offenders in organized crime. The final authority for prosecution is the Director of Public Prosecution, who is a constitutionally independent officer, not subject to the directions of anyone. The Director may determine at any time to commence a prosecution, take it over or discontinue it. In the United Kingdom, the decision whether to investigate a report of criminal activity rests entirely within the discretion of the chief officer of the force responsible for conducting the investigation. Crown Prosecutors have discretion at all the various stages of prosecution, including the power to terminate proceedings or offer no evidence. This discretion is exercised in light of the Code for Crown Prosecutors, which details the manner in which crown prosecutors perform their duties. In the United States, the investigative agencies have discretion whether to investigate or report a criminal offence to a prosecutor or judge. This discretion is frequently used by investigators to develop sources of information regarding criminal activity. A prosecutor has discretion not to bring charges against a potential criminal defendant, and to enter into plea agreements asking the court to impose a reduced sentence based on the defendant's cooperation. This discretionary authority is frequently used, and is an important tool for obtaining evidence concerning other criminal activity; it is, however, to be exercised in accordance with appropriate guidelines.

Related to the issue of proof, the first problem is the burden of proof. There is a general convergence, and it is part of legal tradition, that the burden of proof lies upon the State. The prosecutor should be able to prove guilt backed by strong evidence (beyond reasonable doubt in the United Kingdom and the United States). The presumption of innocence until conviction is universally recognized as an essential condition of legality.

With regard to evidence-gathering, electronic surveillance has been one of the most powerful technologies for collecting evidence. The difficult balance between the right to privacy and the need for law enforcement to trace alleged criminals characterizes the definition and the implementation of this powerful technology. Domestic laws authorizing or denying such use are influenced by this debate. Systems of balance have been found in many countries, which have used this technology successfully against organized crime groups. For example, Brazilian law allows electronic surveillance after the requesting officials receive judicial authorization. In Germany, electronic surveillance, along with the other forms of investigation, are within the competence of the investigatory authorities and are still considered permissible. Legislation specifically addressed to electronic surveillance and other forms of sophisticated criminal investigations provides that evidence produced through such methods is admissible with some limitations. Under current legislation, the admissibility of these methods is limited by a strict interpretation of the constitutional law relating to proportionality with respect to criminal investigations, and also by other principles of constitutional law, together with basic principles of law and justice. Investigative methods that affect the domain of individual personality to any considerable extent, or methods that are employed in secrecy, are only admissible in connection with serious offences. In addition, the government must establish that other investigative procedures less injurious to the persons concerned are considered.

In Italy, in cases concerning serious offences, telephone wire-tapping and interception of telephone communications are allowed. The order for such surveillance is issued by a preliminary investigations judge at the request of the prosecutor. In urgent cases, the prosecutor can order the interception by issuing a decree stating all the reasons for such a measure. The prosecutor must, however, submit within 24 hours a written application to the preliminary investigations judge for such wire-tap authorization. The judge must confirm or deny the request within 48 hours. In addition, the anti-Mafia law provides for preventive telephone tapping. Wire-tapping must be authorized by the public prosecutor and carried out in compliance with the relevant statutory provisions governing such surveillance. Information obtained under this law may be used to develop evidence, but may not itself be offered as proof at trial. In Jamaica, the law does not allow the use of electronic surveillance for collecting evidence but the possibility of enacting such legislation is being considered. The United Kingdom allows electronic surveillance evidence to be admitted under the Police and Criminal Evidence Act of 1984. The decision to use electronic means in an investigation is contained in non-statutory guidelines, which require investigators to obtain approval from appropriate authorities before beginning the surveillance.

In the United States, electronic surveillance is allowed if an order is obtained from a judge. The requirements for obtaining such an order are governed by statute. If authorized by a judge, a suspect's conversations with other individuals may be monitored without the consent or knowledge of any of the parties to the conversation. It is a serious crime to conduct electronic surveillance without a court order. In addition, electronic surveillance conducted in an improper manner will not be admitted in evidence under the exclusionary rule of evidence, to deter misconduct by law enforcement officials. No court authorization is needed, however, for an undercover agent or consenting witness voluntarily to record a meeting with the subject of an investigation.

The effectiveness of such technology is limited by rapid changes in communication technology. Criminals are adapting their methods to this technology, frequently using encrypted phones and faxes, thus making any kind of interception by law enforcement agencies impossible. The development of crypto-technology is placing serious strains on electronic surveillance. It is a moot point whether only one standardized type of crypto-technology should be available, giving law enforcement agencies the capacity to intercept it, or whether, owing to market pressures, different crypto-technologies can be used, making interception more difficult.

Differences are also evident in the use of undercover agents and controlled delivery, new powerful instruments that are being used successfully against organized crime. Some countries do not allow the use of undercover agents, others place some restrictions on their use in terms of the crime involved (for example only for drug trafficking), while others prohibit incitement to commit a crime. In many countries the court wants to see clearly that no entrapment was initiated by the police. Some countries allow the controlled delivery and sale of drugs to an undercover officer, and in some limited cases allow an undercover officer to deliver drugs to another person.

Positions differ with regard to testimony by accomplices. Some countries permit the testimony of such witnesses. Others specify that testimony of co-defendants charged with the same crime, or the testimony of defendants in a related case, cannot be admitted unless they have been irrevocably cleared of charges. In other countries, the court weighs the testimony of an accomplice witness with greater caution and care than that of an ordinary witness, because the accomplice could be motivated to falsify his or her testimony.

With reference to evidence gained as a result of confidential informants, some countries prohibit the use of anonymous testimony in judicial proceedings. Confidential informants can, however, be used by the police in conducting investigations into criminal activity. Other countries provide that anonymous reports cannot be used at trial. Documents containing unsigned statements can neither be admitted as evidence nor otherwise used. Information supplied by confidential sources can nevertheless be used by the police for investigative purposes and may provide the probable cause needed to justify a physical search or electronic surveillance, the results of which may be admitted in court.

Within certain limits, countries are veering towards admitting enforced testimony. In Germany, if a witness declines without lawful reason to make a statement, the court will declare him to be in contempt of court and impose a disciplinary fine. In Italy, the witness is required to appear before the judge and comply with the judge's orders relating to proceedings, as well as to answer all questions by telling the truth. If the witness has been regularly summoned but fails to appear without reasonable excuse or justification, the judge can order the witness to be forcibly escorted into court. In the United Kingdom, witnesses can be compelled to attend court, but they generally cannot be obliged to make a statement in advance. There is a requirement for persons with knowledge of terrorism offences to disclose that information to the police. In the United States, the Fifth Amendment to the Constitution provides that no person shall be compelled to be a witness against himself. However, a federal prosecutor, with the written finding of a senior official in the Justice Department that it is in the interest of justice to secure the testimony of a reluctant witness, can obtain a compulsion order from a federal judge, who orders the witness to testify. This order must also provide that nothing the person says while testifying can be used against him or her as evidence or to develop evidence against the witness. If a person still refuses to testify, he can be incarcerated for refusal to comply with the court's order until he testifies, for up to a maximum of 36 months, or prosecuted for any false declaration.

The presence of organized crime has led to important changes in the criminal law procedure of many countries, particularly those, such as the United Kingdom, that are sensitive to the political version of such crime, namely terrorist activities. There are factors for and against two models of mandatory and discretionary criminal action and it is difficult to make a comparative evaluation without considering the political and social framework in which the criminal justice system operates. Discretionary systems are more efficient but can produce more inequalities. Mandatory systems theoretically provide a better guarantee of equal rights and reduce the possibility of discrepancies, but they may be less efficient. This inefficiency can, in the end, lead to a practical discretionality, which may be worse than discretion established as a principle by law and properly regulated.

*Special programmes*

Provisions that ensure the protection of witnesses are of great importance in the fight against organized crime.[19] Some national systems of criminal justice have paid close attention to this question, and have enacted legislation providing for the security of witnesses. In particular, attention has been focused on measures to protect witnesses by allowing for them to move to a new place and change their identities and providing physical protection if a threat has been posed by a defendant or the defendant's associates. This can necessitate making arrangements to provide the witnesses with documents enabling them (and members of their family) to establish a new identity, providing temporary housing, arranging for the transportation of household furniture and other personal belongings to a new location, making subsistence payments, helping the witnesses to obtain employment, and providing other necessary services to help the witnesses to lead a full and normal life. In considering the type of protection to be provided, the financial circumstances of a country must be taken into account. In addition, provision needs to be made for the safe custody of incarcerated witnesses, including separate accommodation. Legislation may also be necessary to deal with the practical problems that may arise in connection with relocated witnesses, such as child custody disputes and crimes committed under their new identity.

These programs are usually included in appropriate legislation, which also deals with the protection of confidential sources and the protection of accomplices. For example, in China, the identity of an individual who makes a report concerning a criminal violation is protected throughout the investigation, unless that individual consents to have his or her identity disclosed. Informants who cooperate with the police are also protected. In Germany, there is no specific legislation permitting the relocation of witnesses and a change in identity. German law does, however, provide various other means of protecting witnesses; for example, the police authorities may take security measures for the protection of a witness within the framework of their normal duties. There are no similar provisions for protecting criminal informants who do not agree to testify in court. Italy has recently enacted legislation specifically providing for the protection of witnesses. This legislation includes provisions for their relocation. The program is administered through a special central protection service within the Department of Public Security of the Ministry of the Interior and through an office under the National Anti-Mafia Prosecutor (Procuratore Nazionale Antimafia). Informal measures also exist for the protection of informants by the police.

Although the United Kingdom does not have any legislation regarding the protection of witnesses, the police can provide for the protection, relocation and change of identity of witnesses who have given evidence in criminal trials and are known to be in danger. These measures are available to accomplices who testify against the defendant, but there are no provisions for the protection of informants. The United States operates a witness protection program, established by legislation, whereby the relocation of witnesses and the creation of new identities are authorized. This programme, which is governed by detailed rules and procedures, authorizes the following services, in addition to simple guarding of the witness and family:

(a) issuing documents to enable the witness to establish a new identity;
(b) providing temporary housing for the witness;
(c) providing for the transportation of the household furniture and other personal goods to a new location;
(d) providing subsistence payments to the witness;
(e) helping the witness to obtain employment;
(f) providing other necessary services to enable the witness to become self-supporting.

In addition to the formal witness protection programme, investigative agencies can also provide some assistance in relocation, for example in the form of cash payments. Finally, some informal procedures exist for the protection of informants who do not give evidence in court.

Witness assistance programmes have been key issues in the fight against organized crime in countries where the problem is widespread and the number of cooperative accomplices is consequently very large. The quality of their contribution and of the evidence they make it possible for the authorities to collect depends also on the quality of protection (physical, psychological and economical) that is provided. Questions arise about the most suitable agency for administering these programmes. The dangers entailed in a close relationship between the police or the prosecutor and cooperative accomplices are being discussed in countries where these authorities are in charge of protecting cooperative accomplices and witnesses. An independent authority may be the best way to manage the matter.

Another programme in the fight against organized crime is that which compensates the victims of acts of organized crime (for example, extortion). Such programmes are designed to increase resistance to the infiltration of organized crime into the legitimate economy, which sometimes starts as extortion, and to increase the cooperation of citizens who have been subjected to this kind of pressure.

*Law enforcement methods and organization*

If effective action is to be taken against organized crime, the law enforcement authorities must be able to collect and analyse systematically all relevant information from all appropriate sources in order to produce and use intelligence for both strategic and tactical purposes. The methods employed for the collection and use of such information should be authorized and controlled by legislation. Even so, it is important that the technical facilities and techniques that law enforcement authorities are allowed to use should always be sophisticated enough to enable them to match those employed by organized crime.

The production of intelligence requires the collection, processing and analysis of a wide range of information on the persons and organizations suspected of being involved in organized criminal activity, even including information that at first sight is not directly related to organized crime. There may be no rigid borderline between strategic and tactical intelligence, but the main aim of tactical intelligence is to help in the planning of particular law enforcement operations and to identify the sources for obtaining the evidence that will make it possible to arrest a suspect and to prove guilt. Analysis by trained personnel greatly increases the effective application of law enforcement intelligence. It is important to note that there is often a need to continue the collection of information throughout all the relevant stages of the legal process. Intelligence should always be collected in such a manner that even years later it can be retrieved and used as evidence.

Where resources permit, computerized information systems can be of particular benefit in combating organized crime.[20] Computers are used to store information on the various persons and organizations suspected of being involved in organized crime, as well as information about crimes already committed or being planned. Where there are different law enforcement agencies collecting information, appropriate arrangements need to be made to permit a regular exchange of information between local and national (or federal) authorities, and between local police forces in different areas. Careful attention must be paid to the compatibility of computerized systems, and the convertibility of manual systems to computerized ones. The creation of a centralized data bank may be appropriate in some countries, the information being shared internationally on the basis of mutual agreements. Furthermore, technical assistance in setting up and organizing criminal intelligence systems is advantageous to both developing and developed countries.

Particular attention has to be paid to information from confidential police sources, including prisoners. Important intelligence comes from other sources as well, however, and in particular from financial and taxation bodies. When permitted to do so, they can be of great assistance, as they frequently find themselves directly in contact with organized groups seeking to make use of the proceeds of crime. Legislative inquiries and official and public records may also be of value. An essential resource in the effective investigation of organized crime is the capability to collect, and present in an intelligible manner as evidence, complicated financial and commercial information. The collection of information concerning forfeitable assets permits the forfeiture of such property and makes it available for state use.

The infiltration of organized crime into legal enterprises and any contacts it may make in political circles can create a superficial respectability, facilitate corruption and be used by criminals to hinder investigations of their activities. Therefore, law enforcement agencies, when collecting data on the criminal activity of a particular person or organization, need to obtain the most comprehensive intelligence picture possible. A range of measures have been adopted. These include measures:

(a) to develop intelligence, through informants, searches and other techniques, in order to uncover large-scale organized criminal enterprises;

(b) to determine the factors and conditions facilitating the development of organized criminal activity;

(c) to provide for the centralized collection, storage and analysis of information (including the use of criminal organization charts) and for the tactical application of such information;

(d) to ensure cooperation with law enforcement authorities and other bodies involved, using a multi-agency approach;

(e) to study other countries' experience of organized crime control; and

(f) to develop on the basis of the above factors a systemic approach to criminal policy, based on appropriate legislation, proper allocation of resources and mobilization of public support.

To lift the veil of secrecy, conspiracy and fear-induced silence of possible witnesses, as well as to understand how the criminal groups function, who directs their activities and where their illegal income is channelled, police bodies generally collect intelligence and evidence by using undercover methods. With appropriate safeguards, secret operations directed against organized crime can be conducted effectively through the use of undercover agents and informants, often in conjunction with the use of technical facilities to intercept and to record conversations, the contents of which may facilitate the disclosure of crimes. These techniques may include wire-taps, surveillance by means of closed circuit systems, night vision equipment, and video and audio recording of ongoing events. In some jurisdictions, such technical surveillance may be used only in cases when other mechanisms of investigation have failed, or there is no reason to think that they will lead to the desired results, or where other mechanisms are too dangerous.

If extreme care is exercised with regard to the reliability of accomplices or their testimony, and due account is taken of the severity of their offence, the cooperating witnesses for the prosecution may be a valuable means of infiltrating organized crime groups. Mitigation of sentence or even dismissal of charges, where possible, can motivate lesser criminals to assist in investigations of organized crime. The incorporation of such procedures into national legislation or recognized practice, together with the protective services previously discussed, has served to attract such cooperating witnesses.

The ways in which law enforcement agencies operate are related to three basic issues:

(a) the management of intelligence;
(b) the strategies for targeting the objectives; and
(c) the techniques for gathering intelligence and evidence.

With reference to the management of intelligence, countries have different forms of organization, depending also on their political structure. In Germany, for example, each individual state in the Federation has a structurally similar command post, which collects and coordinates intelligence information related to organized crime. These individual offices are linked together with the Federal Criminal Investigation Department headquarters. In Italy, intelligence is collected by the three major police forces in Italy, which are the State Police, the Carabinieri and the Customs Police and by the new Anti-Mafia Investigative Board (Direzione Investigativa Antimafia) expressly created for intelligence gathering and operations against organized crime. Each of these police forces has a local office to investigate criminal acts. The intelligence gathered by these organizations is stored in a data-processing centre within the Office of Police Coordination and Planning of the Ministry of the Interior. The data-processing centre runs the collection, classification, storage, and dissemination of the intelligence that has been collected and submitted by the investigative agencies.

The Jamaican police force has an organized crime unit whose function is to collect and analyse intelligence information related to organized crime activities. This information is gathered from a variety of sources, including contacts the police force has with investigative agencies in other countries. The information is analysed to identify the subjects who are engaged in criminal activities. In the United Kingdom, criminal intelligence gathering is conducted, processed and analysed by the National Drug Intelligence Unit, nine regional criminal intelligence offices, and the Metropolitan Police. A recent development is the creation of a National Criminal Intelligence Service.

In the United States, the Federal Bureau of Investigation (FBI) is the primary investigative agency responsible for investigating organized crime activities. In addition, other investigative agencies, such as the Drug Enforcement Administration, the Internal Revenue Service, the United States Customs Service, the Immigration and Naturalization Service, and other federal, state and local investigative agencies, play an important part in attacking the problem of organized crime. The intelligence information gathered by these organizations is used in formulating a national organized crime strategy, which is developed from a variety of sources.

With reference to targeting strategies, in Brazil, for example, individuals are targeted for investigation mainly as a reaction to information received by the police. In China, in order to prevent the spread of organized crime, industrial companies, schools and street organizations closely monitor possible criminal elements and educate them to prevent them from falling into criminal ways. In Germany, the coordination of investigations is undertaken by the Federal Criminal Intelligence Division (BKA) headquarters, which informs the Public Prosecutors's Investigative office of its findings if that investigation reveals concrete suspicion of criminal activity. The BKA is charged with acquiring information relating to the fundamental structures of organized crime for use in determining proper investigative strategies with respect to those organizations. In Italy, the data base in the Ministry of the Interior is used to develop investigative strategies. The directors of the investigative agencies at the local and central level are responsible for the implementation of the investigative strategies developed through the analysis of the information contained in the data base. In Jamaica, decisions to target individuals or groups are usually based both on reaction to information received and on intelligence reports arising out of proactive plans.

In the United Kingdom, targeting strategies are determined at the senior level by using the intelligence collected through the process described. Targeting may be a reaction to information received, but more probably entails a detailed evaluation of intelligence gathered and the preparation of a proactive investigative plan by the police force and intelligence officers for the relevant force or agency to implement. Prior to any targeting, the operational plan ensures that all information is researched, as far as is practically possible. The United States uses long-term sustained investigations and resulting prosecutions to attack the prominent organized crime groups which pose a significant threat to the country. This is a proactive as opposed to a reactive approach and is based on intelligence-gathering efforts identifying major criminal conspiracies.

With reference to intelligence and evidence gathering, many countries use a wide range of techniques, such as searches, informants, financial investigations and physical surveillance; electronic surveillance of telephone conversations and other types of telecommunication; undercover operations; debriefing of convicted persons; open sources, for example, public records, the media and articles in the press; liaison officers; embassies and missions abroad; foreign law enforcement intelligence agents; and fortuitous discoveries made during routine investigations. Patterns for collecting and analysing strategic intelligence have been developed in many countries. An important example is the FBI 'enterprise theory', whereby the organized crime enterprise itself becomes the focus of the investigation. While individual criminal acts are investigated, the investigation seeks to link the acts to an overall portrait of the organization's criminal activity and in this manner attack the entire criminal organization as opposed to isolated criminal acts committed by members of that organization. The RICO statute is a critical tool in the successful investigation and prosecution of criminal organizations.

*Problems of coordination*

Organized crime may be investigated by a variety of law enforcement agencies with different jurisdictions. It is essential to ensure that close coordination is maintained between central and peripheral structures as well as effective liaison between intelligence and operations. In countries with federal structures, it is also essential that effective mechanisms be established to ensure coordination of jurisdiction, intelligence and operations among federal policing agencies and those of other governmental units. While coordination within and between agencies and units is a condition for successful action against organized crime, a clear delineation of jurisdiction contributes to a harmonious and effective working relationship.

When resources permit, the formation of one or more specialized units dedicated to the investigation of organized crime could be very useful, particularly in the areas of corruption and money-laundering. The danger must be recognized, however, that exclusive jurisdiction over an area of investigation may create susceptibility to corruption, and appropriate safeguards should be developed.

Within any individual law enforcement agency, a strictly centralized senior management system, which can scrutinize all aspects of investigations and monitor their course, is necessary to ensure that all investigations are conducted in accordance with national laws and with a proper respect for individual freedoms. It is important for senior management officials to take into account the necessity of ensuring financial, logistical and moral support.

Investigators, and in particular those leading the investigation, should be selected on the basis of their ability, experience, moral qualities and dedication. The importance of basic and in-service training, not only for the police but also for prosecutors and judges, should not be underestimated. Two keys to success are specialization and a high degree of professionalism.

The relationships between investigative functions and prosecutorial and judicial organs vary markedly from one legal system to another and in any system, smooth coordination among them is an essential condition for effectively combating organized crime. Obviously, due respect must be paid to maintaining the proper relationships between the functions, keeping in mind the importance of preserving the independence and impartiality of the judiciary, as well as the proper role of defence lawyers.[21]

Regarding specific patterns of coordination, in Germany, for example, there are special offices within the BKA and in the criminal investigation divisions in the various states. These organizations are responsible for conducting investigations that have a regional impact. When coordination is required at a level above that of the region, this task is undertaken by the Organized Crime Commission, which is composed of the heads of the BKA and the criminal investigation divisions for the individual states. In Italy, in addition to the three police forces, there is a new one devoted to the fight against organized crime and another devoted to the fight against drug trafficking: The State Police, the Carabinieri, the Customs Police, the Anti-Mafia Investigative Board and the Central Anti-Drug Board (Direzione Centrale Antidroga). Each of these police forces has its own local offices to investigate criminal acts, and also dispose of special units to investigate organized crime and drug trafficking. These investigative agencies have numerous regional and interprovincial offices to address crime problems that cross local and provincial boundaries. At the national level, these police forces operate through their own appropriate offices and regularly coordinate their activities. For example, intelligence information is coordinated by use of the data base which is jointly operated and is located at the Data-Processing Centre of the Interior Ministry. Special anti-Mafia district attorneys (Procure Distrettuali Antimafia) and a national anti-Mafia prosecutor have recently been established. Their role is to coordinate the investigation and prosecution of organized crime cases.

In Jamaica, the police department has an organized crime unit, headed by a superintendent of police, who is accountable to the Deputy Commissioner of Police. This unit conducts undercover operations and is specifically charged with the responsibility of investigating various posses and gangs. In addition to the Organized Crime Unit, the following specialized agencies in the police department gather evidence with regard to organized crime prosecutions: Narcotics Division, Special Operations Division, Criminal Intelligence Division, Flying Squad, and the Monitoring and Analysis Division. The Organized Crime Unit, by use of regular conferences and meetings among the heads of the various agencies, coordinates the various activities under the Deputy Minister of Police. In the United Kingdom, there are no specialized units devoted to the prosecution of organized crime, in that traditional criminal organizations such as the Mafia do not at present have a large operational base in the United Kingdom. There are, however, nine regional crime squads located in England and Wales, which are composed of officers detailed from the 43 metropolitan police forces for three-year tours of duty. The responsibilities of these units are:

(a) to identify and arrest those responsible for serious criminal offences which transcend the jurisdiction of individual police forces;

(b) to cooperate with the regional criminal intelligence offices in gathering intelligence;

(c) at the request of the chief of one of the 43 police forces, to assist in the investigation of serious crime.

All operations conducted in relation to organized crime are recorded within the intelligence system and are cross-referenced to the individuals that are under investigation. Close liaison is maintained between the 43 municipal police forces and the regional crime squads. These organizations frequently conduct joint operations.

In the United States, the principal investigative agency responsible for organized crime investigations is the FBI, although many other investigative agencies make crucial contributions to this effort. In areas where the Cosa Nostra has a major presence, there are special units termed 'strike force units', composed of experienced federal prosecutors dedicated to the investigation of organized crime cases. There is also a strategic reserve of prosecutors in Washington, D.C., who are available to develop organized crime cases in any particular area. In areas where there are large-scale drug activities, there are 'drug task force' units devoted to prosecuting drug offences. In any event, the investigation and prosecution of organized crime at the policy level is coordinated by the Attorney General's Organized Crime Council, which is composed of the directors of the various investigative agencies and high ranking officials within the Justice Department.

With reference to the relationship between prosecutors and investigators, the situation varies according to the different structures of the criminal justice systems and law enforcement agencies. For example, in Brazil, the police are responsible for gathering evidence, which is later presented to the court for its decision. The prosecutor assists the court in developing the evidence during the trial of the case. Unlike some South American countries, there are no investigating magistrates in Brazil. In Italy, the new code of criminal procedure provides that the prosecutor bears the ultimate responsibility for investigating criminal activity. Owing to their high degree of complexity, organized crime cases may involve more than one public prosecutor. In that event, prosecutors are to share and exchange documents and other relevant information, as well as to coordinate with each other all instructions given to the judicial police. The district anti-Mafia attorney's offices and the National Anti-Mafia Prosecutor are responsible for implementing this cooperation procedure.

In Jamaica, the Director of Public Prosecutions is in charge of all criminal proceedings on the island and works closely with the police in the investigation of organized crime. The magistrate's role is to adjudicate on matters presented to the court for trial and to issue, for example, warrants to ensure the satisfactory conclusion of the trial process. In Mexico, as previously noted, the Public Prosecutor is the official who bears the ultimate responsibility for both the investigation and prosecution of criminal offences. In performing such functions, assistance is provided by the Federal Police.

In the United Kingdom, the Crown Prosecuting Agency is an independent prosecuting agency, and is generally viewed as standing apart from the investigation of the crime and the operation of the police. The majority of the investigations are conducted without reference to the Crown Prosecution Service until such time as there is sufficient evidence available to institute criminal proceedings. An exception to this general principle is in cases involving serious fraud falling under the responsibility of the Serious Fraud Office. In the United States, the prosecutive and investigative agencies have forged a close working relationship when it comes to organized crime. For example, the law requires that all electronic surveillance must be applied for and supervised by a prosecutor, who then has the responsibility of reporting the status and progress of the surveillance to the court that authorized it. Coordination between the prosecutor and the investigative agency is maintained at all steps in an organized crime investigation, taking into account the distinct areas of responsibility, that is to say, the function of the investigator is primarily related to the pre-trial preparation of a case, while the primary responsibilities of the prosecutor are the charging decision and the trial of a case before a jury.

In any case, whether or not a separate unit is created to deal with organized crime, there should be accountability for responsibility and resources. If, for example, one police agency is assigned the primary responsibility for organized crime investigations, or if one or more agencies receive budgetary allocations to fight organized crime, the assignment of responsibility should be clear. In this way, at the end of the year or when controversies arise, the public and legislative oversight body could demand accountability from the responsible agency or body, regarding, for example, what accomplishments were achieved, how many persons were convicted and what assets were seized as a result of the budgetary resources or legal authority given to any particular agency.

### Conclusions: Towards an Integrated Approach

From the preceding analysis some brief conclusions may be drawn, which are also in line with the issues highlighted by the Commission on Crime Prevention and Criminal Justice at its third session.[22]

It will be recalled that the General Assembly, in its resolution 45/123, invited member states to make available to the Secretary-General the provisions of their legislation relating to money-laundering and other measures to counter organized crime. Member states were requested, accordingly, by three *notes verbales* of 6 March 1991, 7 November 1991 and 9 July 1992, to provide to the Secretariat information on their legislative and other measures to combat organized crime and money-laundering. To date, 46 Member States have responded to this request. A survey of their replies demonstrates that, while certain countries have made considerable progress in establishing and implementing substantive and procedural legislation, law enforcement methods and other measures suitable to combat organized criminal activities, there are still a number of countries that lack any adequate legal provisions, and the judicial and investigative means and structures required to fight organized crime. In fact, most of the national legislative provisions reported to the Secretary-General pertain to drug related crimes, as a result of the efforts of Member states to implement the United Nations Convention against Illicit Traffic in Narcotic Drugs and Psychotropic Substances of 1988 (E/CONF.82/15 and Corr.2). The rapid expansion of organized crime across borders, particularly at a time when efforts to liberalize trade and secure economic integration are being accentuated, makes the adoption and implementation of effective prevention and control measures essential. A lack of such measures at the national level, in addition to the threat that it poses to national economic development and security, will adversely affect international cooperation, to the detriment of efforts already under way and to the benefit of criminal organizations. The absence of legal and regulatory measures against organized transnational crime reflects the difficulties faced by a number of countries, particularly developing countries and those in transition, in coping with the problem.[23] It also demonstrates the urgent need for strengthened international cooperation and assistance to those countries, which, because of their particular situation or economic potential for the future, have become a primary target for transnational criminal organizations.

For action against organized crime to be effective, priority objectives must be determined and resources need to be efficiently managed. As it may realistically be impossible to fight all forms of crime with the same intensity in any particular society, a decision has to be taken on which of the most dangerous or serious ones should be pursued, taking into account the limited resources available. The difficulty lies in determining the criteria for such a selection. For example, is organized crime more dangerous than other forms of street crime or the so-called 'victimless' crimes? The answers can be totally different, depending on the level of awareness and perception of the problem, which have a bearing on people's fear of crime; this, in turn, increases in proportion to the probability of experiencing that crime.[24] It is possible that in countries where organized crime does not strike the public as being as violent or as damaging as it does in other countries, it may not be regarded to as a top priority. Also, street crimes are closer than transnational organized crime to the day-to-day experience of the general public. Decision-makers, who are necessarily sensitive to public opinion and are also aware of the costs and the impact of these forms of crime on society at large, may be forced to take decisions that favour an immediate response to violent street crimes. The reality, however, is that there clearly exists a global-local nexus in relation to organized transnational crime.

In the area of substantial legislation, efforts against organized transnational crime would be considerably strengthened through the introduction of legislative reforms focused on:

(a) Criminalization of participation in a criminal organization;
(b) Criminalization of conspiracy or similar forms of inchoate offences;
(c) Prohibition of the laundering of criminal profits;
(d) Sanctions and other measures, such as the confiscation of goods and measures to prevent the preservation of illicit profits, aimed at defeating the economic power of criminal organizations.

As far as police action and criminal proceedings are concerned, strategic measures are required in the following areas:

(a) The improvement of intelligence in order to identify the organizational structure of criminal groups, types of activity of these groups, interrelations between the various groups and the means they use for self-perpetuation;
(b) The development of investigative methods that make it possible to 'penetrate' criminal organizations, such as the creation of specialized investigative units, the interception of communications, the use of undercover operations and controlled deliveries, the protection of witnesses and victims, and the reward and protection of cooperative witnesses and accomplices;
(c) The development of investigative methods and other mechanisms aimed at seizing and freezing illicit profits and thus facilitating confiscation, for example the establishment of appropriate structures at the national level (integrated proceeds of crime units and seized property management directorates).

Strategic measures also include those addressed to the law enforcement agencies, in terms of enhanced capability, professionalism and coordination. Strategic intelligence should not be sacrificed to tactical intelligence. Investment in this area is essential, as is cooperation between different agencies. The concentration of energies and resources against organized crime in a specialized agency could be an innovative organizational measure only if this concentration truly happens. When this is not possible because of the notorious difficulties inherent in such a measure and the resistance to it, substantial and effective coordination among existing agencies and between the agencies and the prosecutors should be consistently pursued. Different patterns of cooperation and coordination can be found in the most experienced law enforcement agencies of many countries.

The growing threat to the economy posed by organized crime requires the progressive development of preventive strategies, mostly designed to preserve the stability of financial institutions and focused on:

(a) The provision of technical and forensic training for police, prosecutors and judges, enabling them to understand financial operations and collect evidence;
(b) The limitation of bank secrecy and other relevant regulations;
(c) A more active role for financial institutions in appropriate situations, for example in reporting suspicious transactions.

The criminal justice system on its own, overburdened and overloaded as it usually is, suffers from structural limitations in its ability to control organized crime. This situation calls for heavy investment in preventive strategies, which have probably been neglected in the past. The different systems to which these strategies are addressed therefore need to be increasingly integrated. The process, which began with the call for more cooperation between the banking system and the criminal justice system, should be extended to the educational system and to all areas of media communication. Commissions of inquiry and overviewing legislative committees could encourage such a process, which is a progressive one, involving a wide set of new policies and institutions traditionally outside the area of criminal justice. Administrative law and other forms of regulation of public contracts could reduce the probability of corruption and defend legitimate businesses from the infiltration attempts of organized crime groups. Together with the existing 'hard laws', a new set of 'soft laws' is necessary both domestically and internationally for achieving new standards of morality. The progressive elaboration of codes of conduct is a positive signal, as are other soft laws, such as the recommendations made by the Financial Action Task Force on Money-Laundering, set up by the Group of Seven major industrialized countries, which are influencing domestic policies.

The integration of strategies, policies and mechanisms, with effective and transparent management, is a challenging answer to the growing danger posed by transnational organized crime.

## NOTES

1. For a fuller analysis of the industry, see Phil Williams, 'International drug trafficking: an industry analysis', in *Low Intensity Conflict and Law Enforcement*.
2. The main components of this approach can be found in E. U. Savona, 'Strafrechtssystem und organisiertes Verbrechen', in *Soziologisches Jahrbuch*, Vol.3, 1987.
3. For the theoretical framework of preventive and crime control policies see, E. U. Savona, 'The organized crime/drug connection: national and international perspectives', in H. Traver and M. Gaylord, eds., *Drugs, Laws and the State* (Hong Kong: Hong Kong University Press), pp.126-127.
4. Working paper on effective national and international action against: (a) organized crime; and (b) terrorist criminal activities, prepared by the secretariat of the Eighth United Nations Congress on the Prevention of Crime and the Treatment of Offenders (A/CONF.144/15); resolution No. 24 on the prevention and control of organized crime of the Eighth United Naitons Congress on the Prevention of Crime and the Treatment of Offenders (see *Eighth United Nations Congress on the Prevention of Crime and the Treatment of Offenders, Havana, 27 August - 7 September 1990: report prepared by the Secretariat* (United Nations publication, Sales No. E.91IV.2), chap. I, sect. C); report of the Secretary-General on the strengthening of international cooperation in combating organized crime, submitted to the General Assembly at its forty-seventh session (A/47/381); account of the discussion on national and transnational crime, economic crime, including money-laundering, and the role of criminal law in the protecion of the environment in the Commisssion on Crime Prevention and Criminal Justice at its second session, chap. II, sect. A; General Assembly resolutions 44/71, 45/123 and 47/87 on international cooperation in combating organized crime; Economic and Social Council resolution 1992/23 on organized crime and Economic and Social Council resolution 1994/12 on organized transnational crime.
5. See E. U. Savona, 'La réglementation du marché de la criminalité', *Revue internationale de criminologie et de police technique*, Vol. XLV, No. 4 (1992).
6. See R. J. MacCoun, J. P. Kahan, J. Gillespie and J. Rhee, 'A content analysis of the drug legalization debate', *Journal of Drug Issues*, Vol. 23, No. 4 (Fall 1993).
7. See 'Conclusions and recommendations of the meeting of the Ad Hoc Expert Group on Managing the Risk of Violence in a Criminal Justice System: a Framework of Analysis, held at Chicago, United States of America, from 18 to 20 August 1993' (E/CN.15/1994/4/Add.3, annex).
8. See 'Discussion guide on demonstration and research workshops to be held at the Ninth United Nations Congress on the Prevention of Crime and the Treatment of Offenders', prepared for the Commission on Crime Prevention and Criminal Justice at its third session (A/CONF.169/PM.1/Add.1), chap. III, sect. B, paras. 40-51.
9. New York State Organized Crime Task Force, Corruption and Racketeering in the N.Y. City Construction Industry (final report to Governor M. Cuomo, December 1989).
10. E. U. Savona, op. cit., para. 6.2.
11. See Joseph Serio, 'Organized crime in the former Soviet Union: only the name is new', *CJ International*, Vol. 9, No. 4 (July-August 1993), p.11.
12. See E. U. Savona and M. DeFeo, 'Money trails: international money laundering trends and prevention/control policies', report prepared for the International Conference on Preventing and Controlling Money-Laundering and the Use of the Proceeds of Crime: a Global Approach, held at Courmayeur, Italy, from 18 to 20 June 1994, p.97.
13. Report and recommendations of the International Conference on Preventing and Controlling Money-Laundering and the Use of the Proceeds of Crime: a Global Approach, held at Courmayeur, Italy, from 18 to 20 June 1994 (E/CONF.88/7, annex).
14. See Eighth United Nations Congress on the Prevention of Crime and the Treatment of Offenders, Havana, 27 August-7 September 1990: report prepared by the Secretariat (United Nations publication, Sales No. E.91.IV.2), chap. I, sect. C.
15. See Recommendations on Bribery in International Business Transactions, adopted by the

Organization for Economic Co-operation and Development on 27 May 1994.
16. See Resolution No. 1 on civil, administrative and criminal aspects of corruption, adopted by the Council of Europe 19th Conference of European Ministers of Justice, held at Valletta in 1994; see also 'Extortion and bribery in international business transactions' in the report adopted by the Council of the International Chamber of Commerce at its 131st session on 27 November 1977.
17. United Nations Convention against Illicit Traffic in Narcotic Drugs and Psychotropic Substances 1988 (E/CONF.82/15 and Corr.2), art. 5, para. 4.
18. See E. U. Savona and M. DeFeo, op. cit., p. 97.
19. See 'Conclusions and recommendations of the meeting of the Ad Hoc Expert Group on Managing the Risk of Violence in a Criminal Justice System: a Framework of Analysis, held at Chicago, United States of America, from 18 to 20 August 1993' (E/CN.15/1994/4/Add.3, annex, sect. III).
20. Guide to Computerization of Information Systems in Criminal Justice, Studies in Methods, Series F, No. 58 (United Nations publication, Sales No. E.92.XVII.6).
21. Compendium of United Nations Standards and Norms in Crime Prevention and Criminal Justice (United Nations publication, Sales No. E.92.IV.1), Part One, sect. D.
22. See Official Records of the Economic and Social Council, 1994, Supplement No.11 (E/1994/31), chap. II, paras. 19-29 and Economic and Social Council resolution 1994/12 on 'Organized Transnational Crime', annex.
23. See the reports of the Asian and Pacific, European, Latin American and Caribbean, African, and Western Asia Preparatory Meetings for the Ninth United Nations Congress on the Prevention of Crime and the Treatment of Offenders A/CONF.169/RPM.1/Rev.1,A/CONF. 169/RPM. 2 ,A/ CONF. 169/RPM. 3, A/CONF. 169/RPM. 4 and A/CONF. 169/RPM.5).
24. A. Alvazzi del Frate, U. Zvekic and J.J.M. van Dijk, eds., *Understanding Crime. Experiences of Crime and Crime Control,* No. 49 (Rome: United Nations Interregional Crime and Justice Research Institute, 1993).

# Most Effective Forms of International Cooperation for the Prevention and Control of Organized Transnational Crime at the Investigative, Prosecutorial and Judicial Levels

**Introduction**

As organized crime has long since crossed national borders to come a highly transnational phenomenon, the response to it should also be transnational if it is to be at all effective. Although the degree of international cooperation in response to transnational crime has increased significantly in the last 20 years, there are still many gaps in patterns of cooperation that can be exploited by the criminals - especially those who belong to highly sophisticated and adaptable transnational criminal organizations. These organizations pose a formidable threat to States, which can be contained only if those States cooperate even more closely.

Against this background, the present report identifies the major forms of international cooperation that have already been developed and suggests ways of further enhancing cooperative strategies and mechanisms. The report focuses on arrangements at the operational level, more than at the policy level. First, though, the rationale for cooperation is defined. This is shown to be both compelling and multifaceted; yet there are still powerful obstacles and inhibitions that stand in the way of cooperation. If these are to be overcome, it is important that certain principles of cooperation be observed. Having identified these principles, the discussion focuses on various kinds of cooperation. Informal modalities of cooperation, such as personnel and information exchanges, as well as various types of assistance in both the investigation and prosecution of transnational organized crime, are examined. Consideration is also given to more formal modalities of cooperation, and particular attention is paid to efforts to bring criminals to justice via the process of extradition and the provision of evidence through mutual assistance. While all these methods of cooperation are important, major initiatives need to be taken at the political level to generate awareness of the threat and of the sustained cooperation necessary to counter it.

## The Rationale for Cooperation

The rationale for international cooperation to deal with transnational criminal organizations is very powerful. These organizations are not only becoming stronger and more diverse but they are engaging more and more frequently in systematic forms of cooperation designed to further their criminal activities, extend the reach of illicit markets and expand their capacity to infiltrate legitimate business. Their enhanced mobility and their capacity to exploit licit commerce for concealment, and to use the global banking system for accumulating, moving and laundering the proceeds of their crimes, make it extremely difficult for any single government, no matter what means and resources it has at its disposal, to develop an adequate response without some form of international cooperation. Indeed, the inability of any government acting alone to make major inroads on criminal organizations that operate transnationally is the single most important factor underlying the need for international cooperation. In fact, global conglomerates dealing in illicit activities survive and flourish because unilateral enforcement efforts by a single country generally disable only small segments of such operations.[1] In other words, host nations may be able to do something about the branch office or local franchise but find it much more difficult to reach the corporate headquarters, especially as most transnational criminal organizations operate from a safe haven in home bases in which criminal justice systems are weaker. Moreover, these organizations profit from the lack of homogeneity of national countermeasures and have proved capable of adapting themselves to the different national settings and law enforcement obstacles by choosing the activities they can carry out more easily in different countries and by always being quick to transfer their activities to other countries when national countermeasures become more efficient.

Even when efforts are made to compensate for the weaknesses of the domestic system, through extradition and subsequent prosecution in other countries, criminals use nationalism and sovereignty as defensive symbols against extradition efforts. Consequently, extensive cooperation with, and assistance to, countries that are having the most difficult problems and, consequently, may be used as sanctuaries or safe havens, remain essential.

International cooperation is not only an essential condition for controlling transnational crime and dismantling the organizations that engage in it but it is also important as a preventive measure. There must be universal awareness of the fact that no country is immune to the challenges posed by transnational criminal organizations. Even if they are not in the immediate line of fire, as trafficking needs change or new market opportunities arise, particular countries might find themselves involuntarily acting as transit nations or new host nations for criminal organizations. In fact, if transnational criminal organizations find one nation becoming less hospitable as a result of more vigorous and effective suppression activities, some of their members may simply move their base of operations elsewhere. It is essential, therefore, to strengthen the States with weaker criminal justice and law enforcement systems. Indeed, to maximize law enforcement risks for transnational criminal organizations, international cooperation should produce a more resilient and uniform law enforcement environment that makes it much more difficult for them to continue to operate with impunity in certain countries, to infiltrate others by relocating their operations and to move their profits through the global financial system.

The challenge posed by transnational organized crime can only be met if law enforcement authorities are able to display the same ingenuity and innovation, organizational flexibility and cooperation that characterize the criminal organizations themselves. They have to be not only as flexible as the organizations they are trying to combat, but as adaptable and sophisticated as well. In particular, to be successful, they will have to be more innovative in their use of existing and new bilateral and multilateral legal mechanisms, and action at the country level will have to be more uniform or homogeneous, so that law enforcement officials can display the same mobility and efficiency as the criminals themselves.[2] Moreover, in addition to the transnationality and adaptability of organized criminal groups, increasing cooperation between them, especially through a growing but still relatively small number of agreements, has highlighted the inadequacies in the fight against organized crime. New agreements and new judicial measures and instruments are therefore needed, which could involve the whole international community.[3]

Law enforcement cooperation should endeavour, *inter alia*, to achieve the following goals:

(a) To identify and immobilize the criminal; this will involve 'identifying individuals who engage in criminal activity, finding and arresting them, gathering the evidence necessary to indict and convict them, and finally imprisoning them';[4]

(b) To disrupt the activities of transnational criminal organizations, which entails making it more difficult for these organizations to operate with impunity and to use safe havens: one response to the safe haven problem might be to seek rendition and prosecution in countries where the criminal justice system is more effective;

(c) To deprive the criminal organizations of assets obtained through illicit activities, by means of seizure and forfeiture of assets: this is one of the most important strategies that can be used against transnational organized crime, as it limits their opportunities to reinvest in legitimate business and to engage in bribery and corruption;[5]

(d) To dismantle the criminal organizations themselves: as transnational criminal organizations have a ready source of manpower. Even if a few high-level individual members of the group are incarcerated, there are usually others who can replace them, so unless the organization itself is placed at risk, law enforcement action may simply create a more rapid turnover and greater promotion opportunities within the criminal group.

To achieve these strategic goals, cooperation is essential, as evidenced by the recent patterns of cooperation among law enforcement authorities, which have become stronger and more pronounced. Nevertheless, many countries still have a long way to go before they can achieve the kind of comprehensive cooperation necessary to deal with the formidable array of transnational criminal organizations and activities. Countries should base their countermeasures upon effective organizational and management techniques and, like organized crime itself, should take advantage of technological advances as a strategic defence against vulnerability. The development of frameworks are therefore essential for inter-state cooperation aimed at building a strong collaborative global infrastructure, more effective cooperative mechanisms.

## Factors Inhibiting Cooperation

The agenda for international cooperation itself may become more clear if existing obstacles to the establishment of an infrastructure are identified. In fact, in spite of the imperatives for cooperation, criminal law has long been not only a matter of national jurisdiction but also one of the main expressions of national sovereignty - the key assumptions of which are that the state recognizes no higher legal and constitutional authority than itself and has a monopoly on the legitimate use of force. Furthermore, the duty of the state to protect its citizens is generally taken to mean that citizens who transgress should be prosecuted under the state's own law and should not be subject to foreign jurisdiction. Consequently, a state is often reluctant to extradite its own nationals to another jurisdiction even if the other state has good reason to prosecute them. And even if the state is willing to extradite its own citizens for prosecution in another country, this may provoke violent opposition on the part of the transnational criminal organizations in their home base.[6]

The ability of States to cooperate in criminal justice and law enforcement matters depends in part upon the political relations between them. The more difficult the political relationship, the more sensitive such cooperation is likely to be - especially when different ideologies or value systems are in play, or when the levels of respect for human rights and freedoms differ. One of the problems here is that law enforcement cooperation has traditionally been treated as a matter of 'minor' policy to be subordinated to the 'major' policies associated with diplomatic relations, political and military alignments and security relations. The threat from transnational criminal organizations, however, makes law enforcement cooperation a priority.

The diversity of legal systems based on different principles, in which different activities are criminalized, sometimes makes it very difficult for States to cooperate. In fact, the difference between civil law and common law jurisdictions and between the different civil or common law systems can hamper the development of concerted approaches. A good example of this is that many civil law countries have a rule of compulsory prosecution that limits prosecutorial discretion and makes it more difficult to use criminal informants to obtain information on their organizations. Although the practice of using informants and initiating undercover operations has developed in many countries, these approaches - which are crucial to the fight against transnational criminal organizations - still encounter considerable resistance in others. Indeed, differences of attitude and approach and variations in criminal justice cultures remain evident even in regions where there is a high level of political and economic cooperation among States and where there is some progress towards the creation of 'common judicial spaces'. For example, in spite of the United Nations Convention against Illicit Traffic in Narcotic Drugs and Psychotropic Substances of 1988 (E/CONF.82/15 and Corr.2) and the steps taken towards political union, the patterns of legislation on drug abuse control differ widely in the States of Western Europe. When countries with different levels of economic development and very different cultural traditions are involved, the variations become even more pronounced, and the difficulties in the way of cooperation even greater. These different legal traditions have very important practical consequences on such issues as the admissibility of evidence.

Different countries also have different levels of sensitivity to particular problems. It is no accident, for example, that the United States of America and Italy have developed the most comprehensive legislation against organized crime, as this is something that Italy has had to deal with since the nineteenth century and that has been a problem in the United States since at least the prohibition era. For countries where the problem has not materialized to the same extent, readjusting the criminal justice system to respond to the threat from transnational criminal organizations is rarely a high priority.

Also, criminal justice systems have varying levels of effectiveness and efficiency. Even if there is a high level of sensitivity to the threat posed by transnational criminal organizations, it does not necessarily follow that the reaction to it will be sufficiently strong. For many of the countries making the transition to democratic governance and market economies - and certainly for most developing countries - the problem is a shortage of the human and material resources necessary for an effective criminal justice and law enforcement system. What makes this all the more disturbing is that 'differences in effectiveness of legal system are exploited by transnational criminals and pose problems and frictions for law enforcement'.[7]

Therefore, harmonization of national legislation is the premise on which the whole process of coordinating national efforts at least to check, if not to eliminate, the phenomenon of organized transnational crime is based.[8] For this, however, a strong political will is necessary, not only at the legislative level but also at the implementation stage. As a basis for the process of legislative harmonization there is a common perception of organized crime within the international community. A general agreement upon the essential concept and the use in all nations of similar, if not identical, types of criminalization for members of criminal organizations can help slow the spread of organized crime and will facilitate legal cooperation, especially when it is based on the principle of dual criminality.[9]

Another pervasive problem for cooperation is what has been termed 'institutionalized corruption'.[10] Law enforcement agencies can sometimes be reluctant to share information or engage in cooperative ventures with their counterparts in other countries because of the possibility that the information could be passed on to the criminals. As well as undermining the efficacy of law enforcement operations, leaks of this kind could place operatives in danger. When corruption also occurs at the government level, it can do much to undermine the will to respond to transnational criminal organizations - even if there is an acknowledgement of the threat and the capacity to do something about it.

A major, but rather sensitive, problem is posed by the fact that in certain circumstances it is not in everyone's interest to cooperate. This is the case when corruption has reached the highest levels of government, as cooperation can undermine government officials or even the government as a whole. It is also the case with off-shore banking centres that act as tax havens. Not surprisingly, the authorities of these areas, and the banks themselves, are reluctant to provide for disclosure of information. Indeed, in many of these cases there are laws against such disclosure. This is the very antithesis of the transparency that law enforcement authorities need to respond to transnational laundering. Since many of these havens are, however, highly dependent upon their banking systems as major sources of finance and employment, national self-interest works against major changes and the development of sustained cooperation.

These problems, the restrictions on cooperation that result, and the frustrations they create for law enforcement may be understandable. They do, however, pose 'a basic challenge to the state: how to control growing domains of transnational activities that either ignore or take advantage of national borders when the powers of the state remain powerfully circumscribed by the political, geographical, and legal limitations that attend notions of national sovereignty'.[11] This challenge can be met only if the continued preoccupation with the symbolism of maintaining national sovereignty in law enforcement efforts is mitigated by the acknowledgment that sovereignty can be systematically and consistently undermined by transnational criminal organizations. The concomitant is that some nominal sacrifices of sovereignty that may help to make transnational law enforcement more effective are essential to respond to the growing transgressions against it. To relinquish some of the formalities of sovereignty means to restore the rule of law, taking into account existing realities, in order to 'nullify the advantages that criminals derive from operating across borders and to reduce, circumvent or transcend the frictions that hamper international law enforcement'.[12] This point was made very graphically by the former Minister of Justice of the Netherlands in his comment that the Russian Mafia is too dangerous a foe to allow the rule of law to be hindered by national borders: 'The countries of Europe must be prepared to do away with customs and traditions that evolved over the centuries ... defending national sovereignty is a luxury we can no longer afford.'[13] The comment is an important one, with a much wider applicability than Europe.

**Factors Enhancing International Cooperation**

While increased cooperation is a matter of urgency, it must, wherever possible, be accompanied by an acute awareness of the political and structural constraints faced by many governments. Voluntary cooperation will generally work better than compulsory cooperation. At the same time, there may be cases, such as the offshore banking havens, where pressure from the international community has to be exerted in order to overcome the vested interest in maintaining the status quo.

Cooperation can take place in several different ways and at several levels. It can be informal and formal in nature, and both bilateral and multilateral in scope. Bilateral forms of cooperation undertaken by States with similar preoccupations and approaches tend to have a high payoff. Yet there are occasions, especially involving high-profile bilateral cooperation between unequal powers, when they can become unpopular in the weaker country. In these circumstances, it may be much more expedient politically to opt for a multilateral approach, rather than simply operating on a bilateral basis. Moreover, the various levels of cooperation should be regarded as complementary to one another rather than as alternatives. A 'variable geometry' approach to cooperation, based on a thickening web of bilateral linkages complemented by multilateral approaches that provide a framework of principles, has certain advantages, especially if it can be developed in ways that allow it to take on its own dynamism. Incremental forms of cooperation help to build up trust and make it possible to move to more comprehensive activities. To the extent that cooperative ventures are successful, then the inhibitions to further cooperation are likely to be eroded, encouraging new initiatives.

International cooperation, although it has various components, needs to be integrated into a holistic approach. The logic of this was recently brought out in the Commission on Crime Prevention and Criminal Justice at its third session, and subsequently in the Economic and Social Council, when the importance was noted of using:

> Normative and organizational measures that can be applied to every aspect of criminal activity. In other words, there is a need to devise strategies related to the structural characteristics of organized crime which, besides the essential element of having more individuals organized in a group, include the goal of profit-making; the use of violence, intimidation and corruption; the hierarchical links or personal relationships that make it possible to closely control the activities of the group; the economic control of whole territories; the laundering of illicit profits in order not only to organize other criminal activities but also to set up legal businesses (with the consequent effect of corrupting them); the great potential expansion beyond national boundaries; and the tendency to organize international operations together with other groups of different nationalities.[14]

In short, effective international cooperation needs to be as comprehensive as possible in order to attack the groups' structures, to disrupt their activities, to seize their assets and to incarcerate their members. In considering issues for international cooperation, the importance of preventive measures must not be overlooked. International cooperation can play a significant role in terms of defensive measures or target hardening. It can help States to reduce the vulnerability of administrative and law enforcement agencies to corruption and to protect financial and commercial institutions against infiltration and ultimate domination by criminal organizations. Assistance with administrative laws and banking regulations, for example, could help to ensure greater transparency in company ownership, better scrutiny of acquisitions and transfers, and higher standards of ethics and accountability in both governmental institutions and the private sector. Such assistance should be aimed at mobilizing the private sector to act voluntarily to make the objectives of transnational criminal organizations more difficult to achieve. Furthermore, the establishment of international databases on national financial legislation and their implementation (namely, control of financial transactions and assets) certainly constitutes an important tool for both the control and the prevention of organized transnational crime. A basic principle of all international cooperation to deal with transnational crime is that it should be compatible with respect for human rights and the protection of individual freedoms. Without this basic safeguard, the measures that are taken could attract criticism and fail to obtain legitimacy - something that transnational criminal organizations would be quick to exploit. If vigorous actions against transnational criminal organizations and the crimes they commit are to be accepted by domestic constituencies, these actions have to take place within a framework of high legal and ethical standards. Cooperation and especially forms of mutual assistance should be sensitive to cultural norms and political sensibilities. In other words, as was noted in the Commission on Crime Prevention and Criminal Justice at its first session, 'cooperation should not assume forms that placed the receiving countries in a passive and disadvantaged position. On the contrary, since it was the shared responsibility of all countries, international cooperation against escalating transnational crime should be structured on the basis of true partnership'.[15] At the same time, it must be recognized that partnership means that countries receiving mutual assistance also have a responsibility to make good use of it.

One of the major objectives of international cooperation must be to create greater harmonization in criminal justice systems, by improving the standards of countries with weaker criminal justice systems in general or by developing national legislation specifically directed against organized crime. It is crucial to eliminate 'sanctuary states' and ensure that national legislation against transnational organized crime is as compatible as possible. Complete harmonization is, of course, impossible, for some of the reasons identified above. Yet there is a level of harmonization, perhaps better described as inter-operability, that allows for continued national differences while still achieving the necessary degree of complementarity for effective concerted action against transnational crime. It has been emphasized that 'investigation of transnational crime, no less than its prosecution, will likewise involve multiple jurisdictions and cooperation among different governments. To be useful, the products of these investigations should be as nearly interchangeable as possible. Procedures need not necessarily be identical but they should incorporate rules to protect the accused, limit police power, ensure equitable tribunals and provide decent prisons'.[16] Growing interchangeability and the capacity to use information and evidence across national jurisdictions are of major importance in the fight against transnational crime.

Effective international cooperation requires speedy exchanges among nations and heightened responsiveness to requests for information or assistance. There are occasions, for example, when criminals are arrested but then allowed to go free because the paperwork from another country has not arrived. A more rapid response is crucial for dealing with urgent situations. Indeed, expediting responses to requests for assistance should be given high priority. Where necessary, technical assistance, especially in the form of computers and data-processing capabilities, could significantly improve the responsiveness to such requests.

It is important to build on the work of existing organizations, such as the International Criminal Police Organization (ICPO/Interpol) and others, and to consolidate the very extensive but still *ad hoc* arrangements that currently exist for cooperation so as to consolidate these activities and achieve more effective and efficient outputs. Cooperative institutions and arrangements already in place include ICPO/Interpol, the Financial Action Task Force on Money-Laundering, set up by the Group of Seven major industrialized countries, the Council of Europe, the European Union, the Schengen Group and the Commission on Crime Prevention and Criminal Justice. Contacts, coordination and cooperation among these bodies should be encouraged. In particular, it is of fundamental importance that all existing technical, bilateral and multilateral activities involving technical cooperation be well focused and that the means for coordinating such activities be studied in order to avoid overlapping.[17]

Cooperation should be commensurate with the threat - and the threat is more formidable than is usually realized. In a world in which a growing number of countries are affected by a crisis of governance, the opportunities for transnational crime are ever increasing.[18] Indeed, it is arguable that in the 'post-cold-war' era, mutual assistance will take on greater importance, at the same time as military assistance is declining in significance. In these circumstances, governments should be prepared to allocate significant appropriations for assistance in dealing with transnational crime.

Cooperation should not be pursued at the expense of all other goals - and in particular at the expense of the integrity and effectiveness of national investigations. The sharing of information, for example, is usually highly desirable, but when it could undermine national efforts to apprehend a particular criminal or group, withholding it or postponing it to a later stage is the preferable option. Such caveats are a recognition of the fact that cooperation is merely a means - albeit a very important one - rather than an end in itself. And at times, other objectives may override the impulse for cooperation.

Cooperation should be multifaceted - and should encompass such activities as extradition and mutual assistance, a willingness to enforce foreign judgements, and a readiness to transfer criminal proceedings and offenders from one jurisdiction to another. In addition, cooperation could be extremely useful in mobilizing both public opinion and the business sector against transnational crime. The media, for example, has enormous potential to expose corruption in government and could be a considerable asset in efforts to achieve greater transparency.

Cooperation is not simply a substantive matter but also a procedural one. In this connection, the process of cooperation itself needs to be enhanced. One way of doing this is to assign to a central authority the task of facilitating and coordinating international cooperation efforts, including such matters as extradition requests and the implementation of treaties.[19]

Cooperation against transnational organized crime requires the development of particular kinds of investigative and prosecutorial capabilities that are not readily available. One of the main themes of cooperation, therefore, should be to mobilize, pool and jointly use 'available resources, including expertise and facilities such as training centres, and through the transfer of knowledge, information and technology to foster operational compatibility on a global scale'.[20]

**Informal Methods of Cooperation**

The detection, investigation, prosecution and adjudication of organized transnational crime are laborious and complex activities because of the involvement of authorities of many countries and of different legal systems, and of the various difficulties of communication across borders. Therefore, the establishment of links at the operational level and direct communication in a more informal fashion can be invaluable in smoothing out difficulties and preventing delays or misunderstandings, provided such informal arrangements do not jeopardize the fundamental rights of those involved in investigations or criminal proceedings.

*Personnel exchanges*

One of the most effective ways to enhance the capacity to deal with transnational criminal organizations is to take relatively informal measures that are designed to reinforce the so-called 'law enforcement's transnational subculture' based on common functions and objectives: '... it is this transnational identity - based on the notion that a cop is a cop and a criminal is a criminal, no matter what their respective nationalities - that provides the oil and the glue of contemporary international law enforcement.'[21] One of the best ways of doing this is through personnel exchange programmes.

Although criminal justice attachés at embassies and consulates play an important role in enhancing understanding of their countries' laws and judicial procedures, their work needs to be supplemented by personnel exchange programmes at the level of criminal intelligence and law enforcement operations against transnational criminal organizations. Such programmes could be a very useful means of facilitating effective cooperation in response to transnational crimes.[22] To be really effective, however, international exchanges should be built into the patterns of career advancement in such a way that they become attractive to the most able law enforcement officers. Such schemes would have several advantages. For example:

(a) A systematic personnel exchange program would be of enormous help in generating trust and building up the necessary contacts to form a network of law enforcement officials able and willing to work together with those from other countries. It is crucial to establish extensive transnationalnetworks that can operate informally as well as formally. Indeed, building up relationships of trust between individuals from national police forces is essential if the kind of loose network structures that characterize the criminal organizations are to be countered by similar structures in law enforcement. It also means that there will be a greater willingness to work together even where there are political and bureaucratic obstacles;

(b) Personnel exchanges would assist in bringing in experts who can provide novel insights into the problem, based on national or ethnic backgrounds and past law enforcement experience. Law enforcement establishments in Western Europe and the United States, for example, could benefit considerably from the incorporation - on a temporary or permanent basis - of law enforcement officials from Hong Kong experienced in dealing with the challenges posed by Chinese Triads. More generally, exchanges would make it easier to infiltrate ethnically based criminal organizations by helping to surmount the barriers of language and ethnicity;

(c) Personnel exchanges would lead not only to a greater willingness to respond positively to requests for assistance, but also to a better understanding of the constraints that affect counterparts in different countries. This in turn could help contribute to a realization that lack of cooperation may be a result of external factors, rather than a lack of desire or will on the part of the national police forces themselves;

(d) It would be extremely useful not only for law enforcement and criminal justice personnel but also for staff of relevant administrative bodies, for example those in the financial sector that are responsible for analysing financial transactions, to take part in these exchanges.[23]

There are, of course, some dangers involved, not least of which is the risk of infiltration by foreign law enforcement officers who may have been corrupted by criminal organizations. Such exchanges, therefore, require very careful vetting to ensure the reliability of those involved. So long as these precautions are taken, however, this is a relatively modest step - and it is a case of systematically building on what has already been done in this area - that can have substantial benefits.

*Sharing and exchange of information*

One of the most important commodities in the efforts to deal with transnational criminal organization is information. Even at the national level, however, information is all too often jealously guarded, bureaucratically fragmented and treated as a resource in inter-agency power struggles rather than one of the keys to an effective response to transnational organized crime. In recent years, some efforts have been made to go beyond this by setting up national centres responsible for amassing intelligence on drug trafficking and other transnational criminal organizations. The creation of the National Drug Intelligence Center in the United States and the National Criminal Intelligence Service in the United Kingdom of Great Britain and Northern Ireland are good examples of the kind of centralized intelligence organizations that are likely to prove increasingly useful in the struggle against organized crime. Moreover, in certain countries, specialized investigative units dealing with organized crime,[24] such as the Anti-Mafia Investigative Board (Direzione Investigativa Antimafia) in Italy, gather information that is necessary for investigation and prosecution, thus functioning as an intelligence service.

Such agencies can provide both up-to-date and analytical assessments of transnational criminal organizations and their activities. By encouraging a better understanding of the 'complex combination of activities, people and means' that make up transnational organized crime, they facilitate the exchange of intelligence that is essential for both day-to-day policy-making and strategic planning.[25] To this end, important categories of information need to be further developed, analysed and shared. These include the profile of organizations and their power structures, evidence about the leadership, the extent to which the organization has infiltrated legitimate business, the nature of the interrelations between the street and intermediary levels on the one side and the main organization on the other, and the strategic alliances that are developing among organizations.[26] Upgrading the quality of organization analyses at the national level provides a much better basis for exchange of information at the international level.

Although any scheme for intelligence sharing has to combine the transmission of sensitive information with the need for security, both in transmission and with the recipient, the provision of real time information can be very helpful in apprehending those engaged in transnational crime.[27] This was reflected in March 1993, when Germany and the Russian Federation signed a protocol establishing rules for cooperation. In a different context, an encrypted communication system has been set up between the Federal Bureau of Investigation (FBI) in the United States and the Anti-Mafia Investigative Board in Italy, with routine exchanges which include:

(a) Information on those who have committed crimes and might be moving into one's jurisdiction. This is provided, as a rule, in the red notices supplied by ICPO/Interpol;

(b) Information on stolen art objects and antiquities that is passed on in an effort to prevent the illegal sale of movable cultural property;

(c) Information that can be used in passport and travel controls and that identifies vehicles and vessels used in transnational criminal activity;

(d) Information on new trafficking patterns and new trends in drug abuse (for example, the use of methcathinone);
(e) Information on money-laundering and financial transactions;
(f) Information on methods of concealment - as currently provided by the Customs Cooperation Council.

Such exchanges are designed to share information on who the criminals are, where they are, what they are doing, and how they are doing it, with continuous improvements at both the operational and the strategic levels, in order to identify the major transnational players and their impending operations. In considering ways of further improving the exchange of information, however, it is important to ensure that good use is made of existing data nets, such as that provided by ICPO/Interpol, which has created a database on enterprises and groups of persons engaged in illegal profit-making activities. Moreover, the range of countries that are provided with the information should be extended - although this also requires that the relevant authorities make good use of such information, protecting it from unauthorized leaks. There is an inescapable trade-off between the need for security and the need to share information. This difficulty is compounded by the fact that, with the end of the cold war, a number of national intelligence services have become increasingly involved in the struggle against transnational organized crime and drug-trafficking. This poses problems regarding the sharing of information even with law enforcement agencies at the national level, let alone with other nations. An additional complication is that a number of countries have adopted legislation that requires data to be protected in order to guarantee the privacy of their citizens.

Efforts should nevertheless be pursued to develop a more coordinated and extensive sharing of information based on the upgrading of national efforts, the development of interfaces with relevant organizations and the provision of information and computer technology and assistance to developing countries[28] and countries in transition. The increase of fax capabilities means that it is possible to have extensive 'hot line' type capabilities at a relatively modest cost. The other requirement is that national contact points should be designated, which would be computerized and would provide continuous liaison and rapid responses both to requests for and receipt of information.

As for the researching and passing on of information, at the international level, on organized crime and on legislative and organizational regulations set up in individual countries, an important role could be played by the United Nations,[29] provided that there is appropriate input and feedback, on a continuing basis, from all countries concerned, as well as a minimum of resources to process and disseminate relevant information.

*Bilateral and multilateral task forces*

Other types of initiatives that have yielded good results are the multinational task forces.[30] Increasing both the scope and the number of joint operations against transnational criminal organizations could help to disrupt their activities and result in major seizures of their assets. In certain cases it could be necessary for a specific country to take the lead, as the United States Drug Enforcement Administration did with Operation 'Green Ice', an undercover money-laundering operation that led to numerous arrests in 1992 in Canada, Italy, Spain, the United Kingdom and the United States. Such operations are able to attack the organizational structures underlying transnational crime and are generally extremely disruptive. They can also yield new information on the activities of the criminal organizations. In addition, they help to establish habits of cooperation that can be consolidated and extended in the future. Although such operations are generally easier to implement on a bilateral rather than a multilateral basis, as the linkages among transnational criminal organizations become more pronounced, multilateral operations will become even more important. National participants can provide complementary skills and expertise in ways that have a multiplier effect on law enforcement. This requires a certain minimum level of skill and expertise from all the participants. In some cases, however, this expertise is lacking. It is therefore crucial to enhance the capabilities of States with weaker criminal justice and law enforcement systems, by means of proper training and assistance programmes.

*Strengthening law enforcement capabilities*

The challenge posed by transnational organized crime is a formidable one, and one that most States are not equipped to meet. One of the crucial tasks for the international community, therefore, is to ensure that law enforcement is equal to the challenge it faces, especially in the developing and transition countries. In fact:

> A highly qualified, interdependent and coordinated response is an essential ingredient of more effective refine cross-sectoral professional training of high calibre, using the normative yardstick of international standards. The upgrading of specialized technical skills is necessary, together with development of an effective individual and collective operational capacity at the field level. It requires personnel conversant with organized crime techniques, as well as with substantive and procedural law of domestic and other relevant

jurisdictions. It also requires familiarity with the provisions of existing international conventions, standards and norms, agreements and other arrangements (including those related to seizure of the proceeds of crime, mutual legal assistance, extradition, prisoner transfer, transfer of criminal proceedings, and procedures such as controlled delivery). These are all designed to enable better collaborative transnational action.[31]

There are several schemes already in place that are designed to bring the level of criminal justice systems up to a point at which they can cope more effectively with all forms of crime, including transnational organized crime. These schemes include arrangements initiated or supported by individual countries, those that are carried out on a regional or subregional basis and action. This will involve a considerable human resource investment in order to provide or those under the rubric of international agencies and organizations.[32] Assistance should be regarded as a matter of self-interest and not altruism: the developed countries themselves will eventually benefit if they provide the means of empowering developing countries to respond to problems of organized and transnational crime in all its forms. Although the specific needs of the countries requiring assistance must be the final determinants of the shape of assistance packages, assistance is generally needed in four main areas: establishing the legal framework, training personnel to implement it, providing the technology that is necessary to manage it effectively, and providing support to protect the criminal justice system and its members against corruption, intimidation and violence.[33]

A viable legal framework can be established in countries that do not have a penal system suitable for fighting organized crime at either the national or the transnational level through assistance in the drafting of new laws. Technical assistance in drafting, revising and implementing relevant legislation is crucial, in particular in terms of the provision of available options and models, which could be adapted to the specific legal, political, cultural, economic and social contexts of each country.

In order to implement the framework it is necessary to have trained personnel. This need can be met through increased resources for training courses for law enforcement officials at the regional and interregional levels. In addition, the provision of special courses for personnel involved in detecting, investigating, prosecuting and adjudicating cases involving transnational organized crime (namely the police, investigating judges and magistrates, and technical and investigative support staff) is essential. One of the aims should be to produce law enforcement personnel able to form specialized investigative units that are able to develop information -gathering techniques such as the interception of communications, controlled deliveries, and cooperating witnesses. Another priority area should be training programmes designed to help law enforcement personnel to 'follow the money trail' and develop ways of confiscating the proceeds of crime, since the laundering and use of proceeds of crime are among the primary objectives of organized crime, and international cooperation to counter these activities is essential.[34] In addition, training programmes to deal with new threats, such as the smuggling of radioactive materials, would seem to be crucial. Finally, where necessary, the capability to prevent, detect, and prosecute instances of corruption by public officials and members of the criminal justice system itself should be developed. Anti-corruption training courses should emphasize prevention and education, as well as control measures.

It is also important that developing countries and countries in transition should receive assistance in developing or operating the technological capabilities that permit them to use and share information effectively. As transnational criminal organizations make full use of technology, it is essential that law enforcement agencies should also have access to computerized systems and, in some cases, other high-technology devices, including those necessary to detect radioactive material. Greater computer awareness is essential not only for the exploitation of data but also because of the growth of computer-related crimes and because money-laundering transactions and other economic crimes are carried out through sophisticated computer operations.

An efficient and effective criminal justice and law enforcement system should take special measures to protect itself against corruption, intimidation and violence. Ensuring the implementation of national codes of conduct for public officials is certainly helpful, as would be the designation of specific units at the national level charged with investigating corruption.[35] Transnational criminal organizations have large resources available for bribery and corruption and the temptations are particularly great for police officers, who often barely earn a subsistence wage.

Measures should also be initiated to protect the criminal justice system as a whole, that is, the persons, institutions and structures involved in the mission of investigating, charging and adjudicating. Indeed, the importance of protecting both prosecutors and cooperative witnesses from coercion and violence by transnational criminal organizations is difficult to overestimate. Consequently, it is essential to 'create disincentives to attempted interference ... by minimizing the results of any interference and by maximizing the costs to the criminal and the difficulty involved in any such attempt'.[36]

The results of interference can be minimized through arrangements that make individual officials less attractive targets for bribery or intimidation. For example, for police and prosecutors, task forces and collegial arrangements give the investigation greater resilience and mean that, even if one or more individuals are killed, action can still be taken against the criminal organization; for judges, a sentencing regime in which there are clear and fixed guidelines limits discretion and makes them less susceptible to bribery and intimidation; juries are less vulnerable to 'fixing' if they operate according to majority verdict rather than on the unanimity principle; witnesses are less likely to be targeted to the extent that a case can be made on alternative methods of proof, obtained, for example, by electronic surveillance, physical surveillance and seizures of documents and other incriminating matter.

In addition, steps can be taken to make it more difficult for criminals to use violence, intimidation or corruption against either witnesses or members of the criminal justice system. This can be done by moving the trial to another area where protection schemes are more effective, or through cooperation in the international relocation of witnesses and the establishment of new identities that would make it difficult for the criminal organizations to find them and seek retribution.

With regard to international relocation, it will be necessary to create the equivalent of the sanctuaries that the transnational criminal organizations themselves use so effectively. There might be a problem in terms of determining how the financial burden of such a scheme is to be shared; the possible reluctance of some witnesses to move to another country could also cause difficulty. The former problem could be overcome through the establishment of an international fund to provide for relocation of witnesses and in some cases for judges and jurors. Moreover, the principle could be established that relocation must involve a net improvement in the standard of living for the witness, which could help to overcome the latter difficulty and in some cases might even encourage witnesses to testify. This implies, however, that there must be a willingness on the part of the governments involved to facilitate immigration and to share the responsibility for relocation and for any attendant matters.

Together, these measures can contribute to the creation of effective and viable criminal justice systems, which will be better equipped to withstand the assault of transnational criminal organizations and to challenge their determination to maintain safe havens.

**Formal Cooperative Arrangements**

In addition to the relatively informal methods of cooperation outlined above, there are also more formal arrangements in relation to the apprehension of fugitives and the provision of information for prosecution. In particular, national and international efforts to achieve more effective strategies to deal with transnational crime focus, *inter alia*, on cooperation through extradition, mutual legal assistance, enforcement of foreign judgements and transfer of criminal proceedings and offenders.[37] The United Nations model treaties could be very useful to member states in their efforts to combat crime at the national, regional and international levels.[38]

*Facilitating extradition*

Extradition is one of the most important areas for international cooperation. It may, however, touch a sensitive chord in the matter of sovereignty, and in certain cases it could be politically controversial; there may also be some weaknesses in current practices and procedures. For example, the civil law tradition that underpins the legal systems of many countries forbids extradition of their citizens to other States (although they are able to prosecute citizens for crimes committed elsewhere). Furthermore, even if there is a treaty on extradition, this may not be implemented in particular instances because it does not cover a particular offence, as most treaties usually include the 'dual criminality' and the 'reciprocity' principles. Yet another problem is that countries may sometimes interpret the political offence exception clause in ways that allow them to refuse extradition without outright rejection of the request.[39]

In the face of such weaknesses, countries have opted for other alternatives, such as asserting extraterritorial jurisdiction, for example, in which a country authorizes its law enforcement officials to enter another state and seize wanted criminals. This option, however, is unpopular and usually leads to controversy instead of furthering cooperation. Two somewhat less unpalatable alternatives are: informal assistance, where the offender is expelled from the country rather than formally extradited; and informal circumvention where the target criminal in one country is lured into the territory of the country trying to bring him or her to justice. Ultimately, though, these are only palliatives that do not solve the fundamental problems, while they also raise a number of issues regarding their compatibility with international law.

Extradition is important in denying sanctuary to criminals and in compensating for the uneven development of criminal justice systems. Given its importance, therefore, serious consideration needs to be given to making the process much smoother and making countries more receptive to requests. One way of doing this is through the creation of greater inter-operability and harmonization among criminal justice systems. This would make it far easier to establish dual criminality. The introduction of conspiracy crimes in countries where the category does not exist would also be an important step in this direction.

In a sense, this would make it easier to meet the existing requirements. An alternative approach, however, is to ease these requirements. In particular, consideration should be given to reassessing the principle of reciprocity and the requirements on dual criminality and speciality. A more stringent approach could also be taken, before the political offence exception is brought into play, while a more permissive policy could be adopted towards the extradition of nationals. The political offence exception, in particular, should not be a bar to extradition for involvement in transnational organized crime.[40]

A further change that would help to make extradition more effective would be to improve upon existing procedures to ensure that, in cases where it is permissible, extradition is effected without undue delay. This could be done by establishing designated central authorities to process requests for mutual assistance in criminal matters and extradition. In this connection, the Council of Europe has established procedures that have gone a long ways towards reducing the difficulties associated with the technical requirements for extradition.[41]

Another improvement would be for countries to extend cooperation through new extradition treaties, as part of multilateral conventions, regional treaties or bilateral agreements. The Model Treaty on Extradition (General Assembly resolution 45/116, annex), which has received the necessary universal consensus of the international community, can serve as a basis for negotiations. The model is broad in scope and involves the agreement to extradite any person who is wanted in the requesting state for prosecution for an extraditable offence (namely an offence that is punishable under the laws of both parties by imprisonment for at least a year). Although the Model Treaty allows for optional refusal if the person is a national, the requested state has an obligation - if asked - to submit the case to its own authorities to consider prosecuting the person for the offence for which extradition was requested. The Model Treaty also has provisions related to procedures, which emphasize the need for specific channels of communication and clarify the documentation requirements. Application is allowed for provisional arrest where this is a matter of urgency and a formal request is pending. Significantly, the Model Treaty also contains provisions for the surrender of property acquired as a result of the offence.

The possibility of using transfer of proceedings, for which another model treaty (General Assembly resolution 45/118, annex) has been drawn up, as an alternative when extradition is not possible, is an attractive one. The Convention on the Transfer of Proceedings in Criminal Matters,[42] drawn up within the framework of the Council of Europe, may also be useful in cases in which extradition appears to be unsuitable.

Widespread reliance on extradition treaties would not, however, solve all the problems associated with the many issues related to extradition. There may, in fact, be an irreducible minimum of cases that would remain both difficult and extremely controversial.[43] Nevertheless, the steps outlined would certainly increase the capacity of governments to bring to justice members of transnational criminal organizations.

## Encouraging Mutual Assistance

Mutual assistance, like extradition, falls under the heading of international cooperation, which involves assistance in another country's penal processes, usually within a treaty framework. While extradition is concerned with rendition of offenders, mutual assistance deals especially with various forms of cooperation at the investigative stage, in order to collect evidence.

Obtaining evidence and witnesses from another country in ways that can be used in one's own courts is crucial at the prosecutorial level to deal with transnational organized crime. Yet it is also highly dependent upon legal formalities, offering little latitude for informal understandings and tacit cooperation, as 'differences between national law enforcement systems - in particular between the adversarial, common law system of the United States and the inquisitorial, civil law system found in much of Europe and Latin America - generate confusions, misunderstandings and tensions'.[44]

Mutual assistance treaties represent the primary response to this and are designed to facilitate the collection of evidence from foreign jurisdictions in a form admissible in one's own courts.[45] They are an attempt to reduce the frictions and obstacles to international evidence gathering, and contribute to the gradual homogenization of criminal procedures.[46] Moreover, although they still have limitations, such treaties are far superior to 'letters rogatory', which tend to be very slow, and 'have proven ill-suited to the increasingly complex and voluminous needs of modern international law enforcement methods'.[47] Mutual assistance has done much to fill the gap.

In fact, the inroads made into transnational criminal organizations through the use of mutual assistance treaties have been very considerable. For example, the United States treaty with Switzerland signed in 1977 has had significant results in providing information related to drug trafficking and money-laundering. Switzerland has provided evidence admissible in

United States courts and has even agreed to make the provision of assistance obligatory in organized crime cases, even where the alleged offences did not meet the requirement of dual criminality. Although there were initial problems, these were gradually overcome - especially after Switzerland in 1989 passed legislation making money-laundering a criminal activity. Thus, in April 1994, Swiss authorities seized 150 million dollars from bank accounts in Zurich that had accumulated since the 1970s and was believed to be the proceeds of drug trafficking. The accounts, belonging to two Colombian drug traffickers who had been indicted by a Miami grand jury, were seized as a result of a request by the United States under the treaty.[48]

Such treaties, as an instrument of international cooperation, have gradually become more innovative and extensive. For example, the treaty between the United States and Italy, which came into force in 1985, includes an 'international subpoena', whereby one state can request the other to compel a person to appear and testify in the requesting state, as well as a provision authorizing the immobilization of assets in the requested state and their forfeiture to the requesting state. The treaty between the United States, The United Kingdom and the Cayman Islands includes provision of documents, location of persons, transfer of persons in custody to give testimony, implementation of requests for search and seizure, and assistance in the freezing and forfeiture of assets. The treaty between Thailand and the United States is even more far-reaching. For instance, 'no requirement of dual criminality is imposed on requests for assistance, thereby permitting Thai assistance in drug conspiracy cases despite the lack of an exact counterpart in Thai law, and authorizing US assistance in violations of Thai currency control laws for which dual criminality might not be found in US law'.[49]

It is clear, even from these few examples, that such treaties have been one of the successes of international law enforcement cooperation. They could, indeed, be used even more extensively. The Model Treaty on Mutual Assistance in Criminal Matters (General Assembly resolution 45/117, annex) provides an important basis for further development of such treaties. The Model Treaty has a broad scope and suggests, in article 1, paragraph 1, that states 'afford to each other the widest possible measure of mutual assistance in investigations or court proceedings'. This includes the taking of evidence, assistance in making detained persons available to assist in investigations, the execution of searches and seizures, and the provision of information and evidentiary items. Although safeguards are also built in to allow refusal, the treaty makes it clear, in article 4, paragraph 2, that assistance 'shall not be refused solely on the ground of secrecy of banks and similar financial institutions'.

Once again there is a provision for the designation of authorities to receive requests, which are to be promptly executed and kept confidential. Attached to the Model Treaty is the Optional Protocol regarding assistance in forfeiture of the proceeds of crime, which could be particularly attractive if the states involved reach an agreement to dispose of the proceeds among themselves, as an incentive to cooperation.

To have maximum effectiveness, these model treaties - like other bilateral and regional treaties or conventions such as those drawn up by the Council of Europe[50] - have to be supported by legislation at the national level, which should be as streamlined as possible, both as to substantive law and as to procedural matters. They should also be implemented efficiently, using standard request forms and going through the designated authorities. In addition, they would need to be reviewed periodically, to encompass new forms of criminality, such as computer-related crimes.

In order to assist member states in such endeavours, the Crime Prevention and Criminal Justice Branch of the United Nations Secretariat is preparing two manuals providing guidelines on how to implement the Model Treaty on Extradition and the Model Treaty on Mutual Assistance in Criminal Matters, drawing on current experience and practice. Moreover, assistance has been provided by the Branch to the Executive Secretariat of the Economic Community of West African States (ECOWAS) in the elaboration of a new Convention on Mutual Assistance in Criminal Matters, based on the Model Treaty. The Convention was adopted by the Heads of states and government of ECOWAS at their annual summit, held at Dakar on 29 July 1992. The Branch also provided expertise to ECOWAS in the preparation of an additional draft convention on extradition, again based on the Model Treaty on Extradition.[51]

**Conclusions**

Although progress has been made towards achieving the level of cooperation that is necessary to respond to transnational criminal organizations, much remains to be done. Ultimately, however, this depends upon the will of governments to allocate both human and financial resources to the efforts to control and prevent transnational organized crime. This in turn requires that there be a recognition of the threat throughout national governments, and not just in ministries of justice or of the interior. It might be advisable to consider whether international conferences on the issue of transnational organized crime and its implications should be held periodically, in order to establish and update goals and benchmarks and systematically assess the extent to which they have been achieved. Annual international meetings, both at the regional and subregional levels, of heads of national law enforcement agencies responsible for preventing and controlling organized and transnational crime could be another suitable setting in which to identify proper countermeasures to be implemented at the national level.

These meetings would not only provide an added impetus for better cooperation, but they could also assist in making public opinion more sensitive to the threat of transnational organized crime and in mobilizing the private sector to take protective measures against it, especially through the adoption of measures to achieve greater transparency. Furthermore, they would offer opportunities to refine the agenda of cooperation, both from the substantial and the procedural points of view, for consistent review by the Commission on Crime Prevention and Criminal Justice. The fight against organized transnational crime, whose activities are becoming more and more internationally widespread, calls for the use of modern, flexible and effective countermeasures on an international scale. The main issue, however, is the urgent need to implement such measures, as no effective results can be obtained from attempts to curb organized transnational crime when they are neither timely nor comprehensive. There should therefore be a widespread awareness at the political level of the fact that this struggle is a matter of 'high priority' on the international agenda.

What emerges clearly, is the urgent need for strengthened international cooperation with the main focus on the following areas:

(a) Harmonization of legislative and other countermeasures;
(b) Training and exchange of law enforcement and criminal justice personnel;
(c) Information-sharing among relevant agencies;
(d) Joint force operations or task forces;
(e) Protection of witnesses, investigators and judges;
(f) Elaboration of new measures and updating of existing ones, on the basis of a periodic assessment of results achieved;
(g) Technical cooperation and assistance in drawing up such counter measures;
(h) Clear identification of coordinating authorities in the individual countries;
(i) Measures to encourage the adoption and improve the implementation of existing cooperation arrangements (for example, conventions and model treaties on extradition, mutual assistance and transfer of proceedings);
(j) Effective coordination of activities at the bilateral, regional and multilateral levels.

## NOTES

1. Malcolm Anderson, *Policing the World: Interpol and the Politics of International Police Cooperation* (Oxford: Clarendon Press, 1989), p.26.
2. Bruce Zagaris and Sheila Castilla, *Implementation of a Worldwide Anti-Money Laundering system: Constructing an International Financial Regime* (Washington, Police Executive Research Forum, July 1993), p.62.
3. See Economic and Social Council resolution 1994/12, annex, para. 38.
4. Ethan A. Nadelmann, *Cops Across Borders* (University Park, Pennsylvania: Pennsylvania State University Press, 1993), p.4.
5. Discussion document on the World Ministerial Conference on Organized Transnational Crime (Economic and Social Council resolution 1994/12, annex), paras. 17-18.
6. This actually happened in one country, where the campaign of violence against extradition mounted by one drug cartel group resulted in a new constitution in which the extradition of nationals was expressly forbidden.
7. Nadelmann, op. cit., p.5.
8. Recommendations of the Ad Hoc Expert Group Meeting on Strategies to Deal with Transnational Crime, held at Smolenice from 27 to 31 May 1991 (Economic and Social Council resolution 1992/23, annex I), subparas. 7 (a) and 7 (b).
9. Discussion document on the World Ministerial Conference on Organized Transnational Crime (Economic and Social Council resolution 1994/12, annex), paras. 8 and 13.
10. Nadelmann, op. cit., pp.251-312.
11. Ibid., p.xiv.
12. Ibid., p.6.
13. 'Dutch see Soviet Mafia casting shadow across Europe', *Reuters*, 20 April 1994.
14. Discussion document on the World Ministerial Conference on Organized Transnational Crime (Economic and Social Council resolution 1994/12, annex), para. 9
15. See *Official Records of the Economic and Social Council, 1992, Supplement No. 11* (E/1992/30), chap. III, para. 62.
16. *Testimony* of Philip B. Heymann, Deputy Attorney General to the Foreign Affairs Committee, United States House of Representatives, 14 September 1993, p.3.
17. Discussion document on the World Ministerial Conference on Organized Transnational Crime (Economic and Social Council resolution 1994/12, annex), para. 34.
18. Roy Godson and William J. Olson, *International Organized Crime: Emerging Threat to US Security* (Washington, National Strategy Information Center, 1993).
19. Recommendations of the Ad Hoc Expert Group Meeting on Strategies to Deal with Transnational Crime, (Economic and Social Council resolution 1992/23, annex I), subpara. 7 (c).
20. *Discussion guide for the Ninth United Nations Congress on the Prevention of Crime and the Treatment of Offenders* (A/CONF.169/PM.1 and Corr.1), para. 43.
21. Nadelmann, op. cit., p.468.
22. Recommendations of the Ad Hoc Expert Group Meeting on Strategies to Deal with Transnational Crime... (Economic and Social Council resolution 1992/23, annex I), subpara. 15 (d).
23. Discussion document on the World Ministerial Conference on Organized Transnational Crime (Economic and Social Council resolution 1994/12, annex), para. 29.
24. Ibid., para. 21.
25. Ibid., para. 20.
26. A useful assessment of information needs can be found in the *discussion guide for the Ninth United Nations Congress on the Prevention of Crime and the Treatment of Offenders*, under topic 2 (A/CONF.169/PM.1 and corr.1).
27. Recommendations of the Ad Hoc Expert Group Meeting on Strategies to Deal with Transnational Crime, (Economic and Social Council resolution 1992/23, annex I), subparas. 7 (g) and 7 (o).

28. Ibid., subparas. 7 (g), 7 (p) and 15 (f).
29. Discussion document on the World Ministerial Conference on Organized Transnational Crime (Economic and Social Council resolution 1994/12, annex), para. 30.
30. Recommendations of the Ad Hoc Expert Group Meeting on Strategies to Deal with Transnational Crime (Economic and Social Council resolution 1992/23, annex I), subpara. 7 (g).
31. Discussion guide for the Ninth United Nations Congress on the Prevention of Crime and the Treatment of Offenders (A/CONF.169/PM.1 and Corr.1), para. 44.
32. One example of training provided by a particular country is the International Criminal Investigative Training Program, established by the United States Congress in 1986 to enhance the capacity for investigations in democracies in Latin America and the Caribbean. This scheme is under the authority of the Deputy Attorney General but is funded by the State Department. The scheme has obtained considerable support from the Department of Justice, and the FBI which is not only providing assistance with training programs but is also sharing its resources, including facilities at the FBI Academy at Quantico. The program includes academic instruction for criminal justice personnel and is designed to improve the investigative, administrative and management abilities of law enforcement agencies. Although its main thrust is assistance for police agencies, it also works with judges and prosecutors. In addition, specialized training has been provided under the Colombian Judicial Protection Program (which began in 1989 under counter-narcotics legislation) and involves protection strategies for judges and others who are under threat. The scheme not only enhances the criminal justice and law enforcement capacity of states in the region but also contributes to the creation of law enforcement networks and the promotion of regional cooperation (Roger Yochelson, 'International police training', in *Law Enforcement Bulletin*, Vol. 62, No. 4 (April 1993), pp.6-11). Examples of assistance provided at the regional or subregional level include the Demosthenes Program carried out by the Council of Europe and the assistance provided to the Baltic States by the Nordic Council, which has established liaison offices in Estonia, Latvia and Lithuania, as well as at St. Petersburg, and provides assistance with border controls and crime prevention (Christopher J Ulrich, 'The growth of crime in Russia and the Baltic region', *RFE/RL Research Report*, Vol. 3, No. 23 (10 June 1994), pp.24-32). At the global level, both the United Nations International Drug Control Program and the Crime Prevention and Criminal Justice Branch of the United Nations Secretariat provide practical assistance through institution building. (See the note by the Secretariat on the coordination of drug-related activities and cooperation between the United Nations International Drug Control Program and the Crime Prevention and Criminal Justice Branch of the Secretariat (E/CN.7/1994/7).
33. Regarding the need to reform existing legislation, develop new legal frameworks and train law enforcement personnel in order to achieve effective international cooperation, see the report of the Secretary-General on the status of preparations for the World Ministerial Conference on Organized Transnational Crime (E/CN.15/1994/4), para. 25.
34. See the report of the Secretary-General on the status of preparation for the World Ministerial Conference on Organized Transnational Crime (E/CN.15/1994/4), para. 23.
35. The Code of Conduct for Law Enforcement Officials, adopted by the General Assembly in its resolution 34/169, provides in its article 7 that 'Law enforcement officials shall not commit any act of corruption. They shall also rigorously oppose and combat all such acts'. See also the special double issue of the International Review of Criminal Policy, Nos. 41 and 42, 1993 (United Nations publication, Sales No. E.93.IV.4), devoted to practical measures against corruption.
36. Conclusions and recommendations of the meeting of the Ad Hoc Expert Group on Managing the Risk of Violence in a Criminal Justice System: a Framework of Analysis, held at Chicago, United States of America, from 18 to 20 August 1993 (E/CN.15/1994/4/Add.3, annex), para. 7.
37. Recommendations of the Ad Hoc Expert Group Meeting on Strategies to Deal with Transnational Crime (Economic and Social Council resolution 1992/23, annex I), subpara. 7 (c).

38. Report on the meeting of the Ad Hoc Expert Group on Implementing Legislation to Foster Reliance on Model Treaties, held at Vienna from 18 to 21 October 1993 (see E/CN.15/ 1994/ 4/Add.1, annex), sect. II, paras. 9-26.
39. Richard A. Martin, 'Problems in international law enforcement', *Fordham International Law Journal*, Vol. 14, No. 3 (1990-1991), pp.519-539.
40. Recommendations of the Ad Hoc Expert Group Meeting on Strategies to Deal with Transnational Crime (Economic and Social Council resolution 1992/23, annex I), subpara. 7 (e).
41. See European Convention on Extradition (European Treaty Series, No. 24) and its First and Second Additional Protocols (European Treaty Series, Nos. 86 and 89).
42. 'European Convention on the Transfer of Proceedings in Criminal Matters' (European Treaty Series, No. 73).
43. See, for example, 'La batalla de Montevideo', *El País*, 26 August 1994. Two persons died and seventy-five were wounded as a result of a violent protest against the extradition from Uruguay to Spain of three fugitives.
44. Nadelmann, op. cit., p. 313.
45. Ibid., p.14.
46. Ibid., p.317.
47. Ibid. p.319.
48. 'US-Swiss MLAT yields $150 million seizure in Swiss bank', *Money Laundering Alert*, Vol. 5, No. 8 (May 1994), p.3.
49. Nadelmann, op. cit., p.377.
50. For example, the European Convention on Mutual Assistance in Criminal Matters and its additional protocol (European Treaty Series, Nos. 30 and 99); the European Convention on the Supervision of Conditionally Sentenced or Conditionally Released Offenders (European Treaty Series, No. 51); the European Convention on the International Validity of Criminal Judgments (European Treaty Series, No. 70); and the European Convention on the Transfer of Sentenced Persons, on 21 March 1983 (European Treaty Series, No. 112).
51. Report of the Secretary-General on Technical cooperation and advisory services of the United Nations crime prevention and criminal justice programme, including appropriate mechanisms for the mobilization of resources (E/CN.15/1994/6), paras. 21 and 22.

# Appropriate Modalities and Guidelines for the Prevention and Control of Organized Transnational Crime at the Regional and International Levels

**Introduction**

Pursuant to General Assembly resolution 45/108, the Ministerial Meeting on the Creation of an Effective United Nations Crime Prevention and Criminal Justice Programme was held at Versailles from 21 to 23 November 1991. The meeting spearheaded the integration and consolidation of efforts by the international community to prevent and combat transnational crime, as well as the strengthening of regional and international cooperation in combating all forms of crime. The meeting was also the culmination of an intergovernmental review that had begun in 1985, aimed at strengthening the United Nations crime prevention and criminal justice programme and rendering it more responsive to the priority needs of its global constituency.

The World Ministerial Conference on Organized Transnational Crime will be meeting exactly three years later, at Naples, setting a new landmark in the fight against transnational crime. Its agenda bears witness to the growing concern of the international community about the threat posed by the increasing dimensions of organized transnational crime and its determination to act jointly at the highest level in order to devise viable and effective defence mechanisms.

The two meetings are linked by more than the coincidence of dates. In fact, the World Ministerial Conference would not have been possible if the meeting at Versailles had not set precise goals and priorities for the United Nations crime prevention and criminal justice programme, particularly in terms of international cooperation and efforts to prevent and combat transnational crime. In the three intervening years, the message conveyed by the international community at Versailles has been further elaborated and amplified through the combined action of the Commission on Crime Prevention and Criminal Justice, the Economic and Social Council and the General Assembly.

The Ministers gathered at Versailles stressed the need for the growing internationalization of crime to generate new and commensurate responses. The incidence and scope of transnational crime was going to increase further in the coming years unless member states were put in a position to enact suitable preventive and control strategies. International cooperation represented the main strategy against transnational crime. Most problems arising in collecting evidence, extraditing offenders and solving conflicts of jurisdiction, which, in the past, had traditionally weakened the inter-state fight against crime, could be eased through mutual assistance and cooperation.

In the statement of principles and programme of action of the United Nations crime prevention and criminal justice programme (General Assembly resolution 46/152, annex), the participants declared their determination to translate their political will into concrete action, *inter alia*, by establishing a framework for inter-state cooperation and coordination to respond to the serious new forms and transnational aspects and dimensions of crime. It was emphasized that one of the big challenges confronting the international community was to match any increases in the capacity and capabilities of perpetrators of crime with similar increases in the capacity and capabilities of law enforcement and criminal justice authorities. Less stringent border controls, designed to facilitate legitimate trade and development, were being exploited by organized crime, and the increased free movement of people accompanying democracy was creating new opportunities for crime. In order to combat the new developments, additional resources needed to be made available to developing countries and countries in which democracy was beginning to emerge. The role of the United Nations as the focal point for coordinating international efforts, setting up projects and acting as a clearing-house to match needs and resources, was acknowledged at the Versailles Meeting.

This challenge continues to occupy the international community today. It has become more daunting because of the rapid expansion and increasing sophistication of organized transnational crime. Cooperation at every level is urgently needed if the challenge is to be met.

The present report contains an overview of existing modalities of international cooperation and an analysis of the goals that should be achieved. In this analysis some of the basic concepts and prospects of international cooperation are also considered, in an effort to lay down guidelines that will enable it to respond more effectively to the changing characteristics of organized transnational crime and the corresponding needs of states.

## International and Regional Initiatives

The first involvement of the United Nations in the issue of organized crime dates back to 1975, when the Fifth United Nations Congress on the Prevention of Crime and the Treatment of Offenders, held at Geneva from 1 to 12 September, examined the changes in forms and dimensions of criminality - transnational and national. At that time, the focus was on crime as business at the national and transnational levels: organized crime, white-collar crime and corruption. It was pointed out how, in addition to ordinary criminals who escaped detection, there were powerful perpetrators of harmful acts who wielded their power and influence with impunity to the detriment of the community as a whole. Crimes of corporations and 'organized' or syndicated crimes had many similarities and might involve the corruption of law enforcement and political authority. They also tended to be characterized by a high degree of secrecy and, as 'invisible' crimes, they were difficult to detect.

'Crime as business' was recognized as a more serious threat to society and national economies than traditional forms of crime. While 'crime as business' was a serious problem in many developed countries, in developing countries the national welfare and economic development of the entire society might be drastically affected by such criminal conduct as bribery, price-fixing, smuggling and currency offences. Definitions of terms relating to that type of crime were often vague and ambiguous, as the issue had been neglected by criminologists.

The Sixth United Nations Congress on the Prevention of Crime and the Treatment of Offenders, held at Caracas from 25 August to 5 September 1980, in its discussion of agenda item 5, 'Crime and the abuse of power: offenses and offenders beyond the reach of the law',[1] added new elements to the international perception of organized crime. Emphasis was placed on the concept of abuse of power in its various forms: political, economic and social. Abuses of economic, social and political power were often interlinked. For example, economic crime served as a causal and aggravating factor in the corruption of the governmental process and of public officials.

Among offenses beyond the reach of law discussed under agenda item 5 of the Sixth Congress, there were those legally defined as crimes but with respect to which the law enforcement agencies were relatively powerless because of the high economic and political status of their perpetrators, or because the circumstances under which the crimes had been committed were such as to decrease the likelihood of their being reported or prosecuted. Organized crime, bribery and corruption were among the first examples mentioned in the discussion.

It was noted that the lack of data on offences involving abuse of power was hampering a proper understanding of the problems involved and the development of more adequate means of combating them. Problems were posed by transnational corporations in the abuse of economic power, often because of the inability of the victimized country to deal with them effectively, especially if it was a developing country. International cooperation to combat corporate crime on a global basis was called for. It was also stressed how individual countries were not always in a position to fight corporate abuses that transcended national borders. An international strategy was needed to combat, deter and prevent corporate crime worldwide, beginning with an immediate compilation, study and analysis of all current national and international laws in this area. With the emergence of new and more dangerous types of criminal activity, further studies were required on this issue.

It was becoming more and more evident that the growing activities of organized crime were posing a serious threat worldwide. The issue was considered further by the Seventh United Nations Congress on the Prevention of Crime and the Treatment of Offenders, held at Milan from 26 August to 6 September 1985, under topic 1, entitled 'New dimensions of criminality and crime prevention in the context of development: challenges for the future.'[2] It was emphasized that multiple illicit operations carried out by international criminal networks represented a major challenge to national law enforcement and to international cooperation. National boundaries no longer constituted effective barriers against those criminal activities. By exploiting the discrepancies in the legislation of different countries, organized crime achieved a high degree of impunity.

In many parts of the world, great social alarm was caused by the deleterious impact of drug abuse on many young people. The illicit traffic in narcotic drugs was one of the main illegal operations conducted by organized crime. Corruption added to the difficulties of preventing and controlling such international crimes.

The Seventh Congress adopted the Milan Plan of Action,[3] in which it fully recognized the international dimensions of crime and the need for a concerted response from the community of nations to combat its various forms. It also emphasized how certain forms of crime could hamper the political, economic, social and cultural development of peoples and threatened human rights, fundamental freedoms, and peace, stability and security. The United Nations had a significant role to play in contributing to multilateral cooperation in this field. The Plan of Action was to be implemented as 'the collective endeavour of the international community to deal with a major problem whose disruptive and destabilizing impact on society is bound to increase unless concrete and constructive action is taken on an urgent and priority basis.'[4]

In 1990, within the framework of its topic III, 'Effective national and international action against: (a) organized crime; (b) terrorist criminal activities', the Eighth United Nations Congress on the Prevention of Crime and the Treatment of Offenders examined the problem of organized transnational crime in the light of the new historic developments.[5] In fact, the rapid increase in the number of independent countries, together with a true internationalization of criminal activities, had created the need for new international institutions that could introduce a measure of order and enhance the effectiveness of crime prevention efforts.

In the past, a few states had jointly enacted cooperation policies as necessary. These activities had been on an *ad hoc* basis and were never institutionalized. The changes in the world balance had created a need for institutionalization of the relations of sovereign and independent countries in all areas, including relations in the area of criminal law. A considerable body of international criminal law had been developed in recent decades; its systematization was the next logical step.

The pernicious effect of organized crime on economic, political and social institutions was once more underlined. Criminal undertakings discouraged domestic and foreign investments and adversely affected the daily flow of economic activities, undermining economic growth as well as political and social stability. As the financial aspects of organized crime were very frightening, there was an urgent need for new legislation that would effectively deal with the attempts to launder the proceeds of crime.

It was becoming increasingly obvious that the problem could not be solved at the domestic level. The degree of sophistication attained by organized crime and its international dimension called for joint efforts: domestic legislative action and administrative reform, together with coordinated international action.

More effective cooperation in crime prevention was possible, as had been demonstrated by some initiatives at the subregional level. Political will and the willingness to revise certain traditional approaches were necessary, together with substantial increases in technical cooperation at all levels. All countries had to be put in a situation in which they could participate effectively in the cooperative network. The United Nations crime prevention and criminal justice programme had to be strengthened to respond to the rising number of requests for assistance.

A substantive step towards international cooperation was made in 1990, when the General Assembly adopted the Model Treaty on Extradition, the Model Treaty on Mutual Assistance in Criminal Matters , the Model Treaty on Transfer of Proceedings in Criminal Matters, and the Model Treaty on the Transfer of Supervision of Offenders Conditionally Sentenced or

Conditionally Released. In the resolutions, member states were invited to take these model treaties into account when establishing treaty relations with other states, and to strengthen international cooperation in combating organized crime. The General Assembly also adopted resolution 45/123 on international cooperation in combating organized crime, in which member states were urged to implement the guidelines for the prevention and control of organized crime, contained in the annex to resolution 24 of the Eighth Congress,[6] and invited them to make available to the Secretary-General national legislation pursuant to that resolution.

On the basis of the above-mentioned appeals for cooperation in combating organized transnational crime, the Ad Hoc Expert Group Meeting on Strategies to Deal with Transnational Crime was held in May 1991, at Smolenice. The meeting, attended by experts representing the five geographical regions and by representatives of the International Criminal Police Organization/Interpol (ICPO/Interpol), strongly emphasized the urgent need to respond more effectively to transnational criminality, as the legal tools available to governments were often not suitable for effectively combating new transnational manifestations of criminality. In addition, it adopted a number of recommendations covering national, regional and international action to contribute to closer international cooperation. In October 1991, an International Seminar on Organized Crime was held at Suzdal, which was attended by law enforcement officials and experts from 15 countries and ICPO/Interpol. The practical measures against organized crime formulated during the seminar included considerations concerning the nature, extent and impact of the problem and called for action in the fields of legislation, law enforcement methods, organizational structures, international cooperation and evaluation of the gravity of the threat.

In the meantime, in pursuance of General Assembly resolution 45/108 entitled: 'Review of the functioning and programme of work of the United Nations in crime prevention and criminal justice', the Ministerial Meeting on the Creation of an Effective United Nations Crime Prevention and Criminal Justice Programme was convened at Versailles from 21 to 23 November 1991. It was recognized that, in the fight against crime, even the most strenuous efforts by any individual state would have little success unless supported by international cooperative action. Only the United Nations could effectively coordinate such action, by developing and implementing a concerted and truly international strategy directed at providing practical help. Technical cooperation and assistance were thus of paramount importance in that context.

The General Assembly, in its resolution 46/152 of 18 December 1991, took note with appreciation of the report of the Ministerial Meeting and adopted the proposed statement of principles and programme of action, which, *inter alia*, called for the establishment of a commission on crime prevention and criminal justice. The Commission was established by resolution 1992/1 of the Economic and Social Council, as one of its functional commissions. At its first session, held from 21 to 30 April 1992, the Commission further underlined the importance of international cooperation to counteract crime and indicated that combating trans-national, organized and economic crime had to be priority themes for the United Nations crime prevention and criminal justice programme. An accompanying resolution requested the Secretary-General to continue the analysis of the impact of organized criminal activities upon society at large. The Commission, at its first session, also requested the Secretary-General, *inter alia*, to examine the possibility of coordinating efforts made at the multilateral level against laundering of proceeds of crime and related offenses, and to propose means for rendering technical assistance to requesting member states in drafting legislation, training law enforcement personnel, in developing regional, subregional and bilateral cooperation and in providing advice.[7]

In view of these activities and decisions, the General Assembly, in its resolution 47/87, requested the Commission on Crime Prevention and Criminal Justice to organize the ongoing review and analysis of the incidence of transnational organized criminal activity and the dissemination of information thereon, and called upon member states, international organizations and non-governmental organizations to cooperate with the United Nations in organizing practice-oriented workshops, research projects and training programmes to deal with organized criminal activities.

In 1993, the Economic and Social Council adopted three resolutions recommended to it by the Commission on Crime Prevention and Criminal Justice at its second session. In the first, the Secretary-General was requested to organize a World Ministerial Conference on Organized Transnational Crime, to be held in 1994 in Italy, the government of that country having offered to act as host. In the second resolution, the Council called, *inter alia*, for technical assistance to be provided for the prevention and control of the proceeds of crime. The crucial role of the United Nations crime prevention and criminal justice programme in promoting international cooperation in crime prevention and criminal justice and in responding to the needs of the international community in the face of both national and transnational criminality was then reaffirmed by the Council.

Organized transnational crime continued to be a topic for the Commission on Crime Prevention and Criminal Justice at its third session, where the discussion on this issue was reflected in three draft resolutions subsequently adopted by the Economic and Social Council. The first resolution highlighted the importance of the World Ministerial Conference on Organized Transnational Crime as a means of reaching agreement on the adoption of a series of measures against organized crime, including the establishment of a common perception of organized crime within the international community; the punishment, under national law, of participation in a criminal organization; confiscation of the proceeds of crime; the development of investigative methods to penetrate criminal organizations, including specialized investigative units; the development of international agreements for extradition, mutual legal assistance and the improvement of practical application of existing model treaties in these fields; technical cooperation, including the international exchange of intelligence and the training of law enforcement personnel; economic compensation for victims; and the feasibility of elaborating international instruments, including conventions, against organized transnational crime.

The second resolution was devoted to the control of the proceeds of crime, in which the Council recommended that the World Ministerial Conference should take into account the conclusions and recommendations of the International Conference on Preventing and Controlling Money-Laundering and the Use of the Proceeds of Crime: a Global Approach. The Council also requested the Secretary-General, taking into account the work already carried out by member states and intergovernmental organizations, to cooperate with them in the inclusion of anti-money-laundering provisions in national legislation and in the organization of training and assistance programmes.

In the third resolution, on criminal justice action to combat the organized smuggling of illegal migrants across national boundaries, the substantial role played by organized transnational crime in illegal migrants smuggling activities in many parts of the world was recognized. The Council also called upon member states and relevant specialized agencies and international organizations to cooperate, at the bilateral and multilateral levels, in tackling all aspects of the problem of the organized smuggling of illegal migrants, against which states should take prompt and effective countermeasures.

The involvement of organized transnational crime in an increasing range of activities was further stressed by the Commission on Crime Prevention and Criminal Justice through a resolution on international traffic in minors,[8] in which the Commission, being aware that this activity was carried out by criminal organizations that had transnational connections, and calling upon member states to consider ways of enacting legislation to combat this traffic and to promote cooperation amongst them, decided that international traffic in minors should be considered by the Commission at its fourth session in the context of its discussion on organized transnational crime.

In the field of drug abuse control, it should be recalled that in 1988, the United Nations Convention against Illicit Traffic in Narcotic Drugs and Psychotropic Substances was adopted. This Convention represented one of the first and most important international binding instruments drawn up to combat organized transnational organizations and one of their most lucrative activities. The Convention foresees, *inter alia,* criminalization of the laundering of the proceeds of drug trafficking and calls for international cooperation and assistance, including the development of means such as extradition, mutual legal assistance and transfer of proceedings. In 1990, the General Assembly adopted the Political Declaration and the Global Programme of Action against illicit production, supply, demand, trafficking and distribution of narcotic drugs and psychotropic substances, activities which strengthened transnational criminal organizations.

Regional initiatives enjoy a considerable advantage because of their two main characteristics. They are pursued in an environment where there are fewer cultural differences and fewer problems of compatibility between different juridical systems. In addition, such initiatives are designed to cope with specific problems and often complement other political and economic joint efforts and schemes. The results achieved in terms of convergence and compatibility of policies within regions can be considered as a very important first step in strengthening the process of worldwide action and more meaningful and effective international cooperation. The solutions selected to deal with common problems and to overcome obstacles, which still exist in spite of the prevailing homogeneity, can serve as useful examples of effective cooperation at the global level.

Regarding more effective forms of inter-state cooperation, examples can be found in a number of regional settings, like the Council of Europe and its network of conventions,[9] the European Union and its recent efforts to improve cooperation in criminal matters on the basis of the Maastricht Treaty, including the establishment of EUROPOL, the Organization of American States and its Inter-American Drug Abuse Control Commission (CICAD), the League of Arab States and the Commonwealth Secretariat, or in other groupings like the 'Schengen States',[10] the 'Nordic Scheme',[11] and the Benelux States.[12] Each regional group has developed different instruments responding to their needs, but these patterns of collaboration represent, simultaneously, a trend, as well as a way towards improved mutual cooperation.

The instruments so far developed were the outcome of the ever-growing concern of states about offenses with transnational aspects. While mutual assistance and extradition remain the backbone of regional cooperation, new arrangements have been elaborated, which include transfer of criminal proceedings, execution of foreign criminal judgements and transfer of prisoners. While the first, transfer of proceedings, was envisaged as a means of ensuring the prosecution of the accused where extradition was denied, the other two are based on the transfer of the last phase of a criminal case, and on the execution of a penalty on humanitarian grounds as well, since the convicted person is allowed to serve the sentence in his or her own country.

Regional initiatives have at least one common characteristic. Their origin lies in bilateral arrangements and cooperation schemes of a more or less informal nature but they have evolved into essential multilateral instruments of cooperation. In many instances, the multilateral arrangement is a framework for compatible and dynamic bilateral cooperation on various fronts. In others, multilateral instruments have built on the experience of bilateral arrangements and have advanced towards common and concerted action of specific proportions and against specific problems. In all cases, regional cooperation has evolved through the convergence of policies and a gradual confidence-building phase, reflecting the need of states to protect jointly their common interests and values. Another element of considerable importance is the realization by states in a given region that reliance not only on their own capacity but also on that of their neighbours is crucial in overcoming obstacles to their well-being. A direct consequence of this realization is that the concessions that are necessary in every type of cooperation and genuinely joint action are viewed as long-term gains rather than as losses.

In addition to the homogeneity of the countries involved, in historical, geopolitical and cultural terms, regional initiatives enjoy another advantage. More often than not, the divergences between the countries of the same region or at the same stage of development are not dramatic, and are effectively counterbalanced by other cohesive factors.

One of the most innovative aspects of regional instruments is the fact that the principle of territoriality is weakened and the question of sovereignty is approached in a new way. Serious obstacles to international cooperation result from the jurisdictional conflict between the courts of two states, when the territorial principle and the active personality principle are asserted. While the choice between the two principles would normally be based on the character of the offense, it is often suggested that obstacles are overcome, for example, by having simpler cases transferred at the stage of preparatory proceedings whereas other cases are transferred after sentencing.

In spite of their definite advantages and the inroads they have made, regional schemes are by no means a panacea. Transnational organized crime is known for its versatility and increasing sophistication, as well as its mobility. Regional arrangements and instruments deal with the problem in exactly the area they are designed to cover. It could be said that their effectiveness is simultaneously their limitation. While countries covered by a regional arrangement may enjoy relative security from, and score successes against, organized criminal groups located or operating within the region, it is inevitable that they will have to face the effects of these groups relocating outside the region and continuing to target that region as a whole. Eradicating the problem from a group of countries does not necessarily mean solving it. Relocation is a mechanism that does not entail much more than additional and unforeseen expenses for a well-organized criminal group. It may also imply an improvement of its operations and a more structured approach to its efforts to maximize opportunities. The effectiveness of a regional arrangement may also result in shifting the burden to other countries and regions less equipped to deal with it and less capable of doing so. The lack of a comprehensive mechanism based on such instruments, and intended to be the standard by which their usefulness is measured, becomes evident. These tools were often elaborated as a first response to criminal behaviour characterized by transboundary elements. Consequently, their creation was not followed by their systematization or by a mechanism extending their reach beyond certain limits. As a result, a general priority scale applicable to different situations in different settings does not exist.

The body of knowledge and expertise acquired in years of commitment may represent the benchmark for the international community when it has to identify the tasks that are to be accomplished to achieve the target of a world of peace, democracy and justice for all. They represent valuable tools for the international community at a time when international cooperation appears to be the only effective weapon against organized transnational crime.

**Basic Principles of International Cooperation**

Any discussion of international cooperation will necessarily involve a clear understanding of priorities and objectives. International cooperation on a particular issue, such as the ability of criminal justice systems to prevent and control organized crime, implies a thorough knowledge of the risks involved both in the short and long term. In addition, it requires an accurate assessment of the capacity of the criminal justice system to deal with complex forms of crime. A combination of these parameters, with the appropriate balance, would serve to put international cooperation into perspective. Only knowledge and careful evaluation can lead to the appropriate selection of priorities and objectives. Policy makers at the national level, those ultimately capable of and responsible for building, sustaining and advancing international cooperation, as well as setting its pace, need this knowledge to guide them towards rational decisions. Policy makers also have to be able to strike the appropriate balance between competing interests, both political and financial. The world today is characterized by limited resources. Balancing the multiple interests competing for these resources is difficult for every government, regardless of its level of development. International cooperation requires undivided attention and genuine commitment at all levels of government for the pooling and allocation of the resources commensurate to the risk posed to the international community by organized transnational crime.

Organized crime groups are becoming increasingly transnational, both in scope and activities. They achieve this by pursuing two main strategies: minimizing the 'law enforcement risk' and maximizing the opportunities available for illicit profit. Minimizing the law enforcement risk means calculating the sum of the probabilities of being identified, apprehended, prosecuted and convicted. Together with the exploitation of market opportunities and the creation of new ones, these are the essential components of what may be termed 'illegal enterprise's risk', the risk that organized criminal groups are prepared and willing to incur for carrying out their activities in more than one country. From the point of view of societies and governments, there is yet another risk, the 'transnational organized crime risk', which refers to the probability that organized crime groups will expand their structures and activities in countries other than those in which they were initially located. The two risks are related, the variables that are the main components of the one being the reverse image of the variables that make up the other.

The transnational organized crime risk tends to increase when the illegal enterprise's risk for the organized crime groups is unequally distributed among countries. Organized crime groups will tend to internationalize and expand in countries where the opportunities are greater and the law enforcement risk is lower. The more equally the risk is distributed among countries, the less the organized criminal groups will be tempted to displace their activities outside the countries where they are traditionally located. In other words, the greater the external risks for organized criminal groups, the lower the probability that they will internationalize their activities.

Controlling the international distribution of the illegal enterprise's risk should be the objective and indeed the rationale for cooperation among countries, especially in the area of law enforcement and criminal justice. As has already been emphasized, a more effective response to transnational criminality has become a matter or urgency, particularly in view of the growing exploitation by transnational criminals of traditional principles and the practice of sovereignty and territorial jurisdiction.

The legal tools available to governments are often found to be unequal to the task of effectively combating the new transnational manifestations of criminality and it is therefore through their attacks on traditional principles and sovereignty that organized criminals have succeeded in carrying out their illicit operations at a considerably lower risk to themselves.[13] If criminal organizations are attracted to the process of internationalization because they have found areas where the risk from the law enforcement authorities is minimal, then coordinated international action to equalize this risk in various countries will minimize or contain the process. Equalizing the risk means raising the quantity, quality and, more importantly, compatibility of preventive and control actions at an adequate level on a worldwide scale and putting in place mechanisms designed to maintain and improve that level in a consistent and coordinated fashion.

While controlling the illegal enterprise's risk means reducing illegal opportunities and vulnerability to a level sufficient to discourage, or at least not attract, transnational crime, controlling the distribution of the transnational organized crime risk is a matter of distributing the policies directed at the control of crimes and at authors of those crimes. The ultimate aim of this process would, therefore, be to secure an optimal distribution of risk among countries.

One of the fundamental objectives of international cooperation and technical assistance in this field would be to ensure that all countries reach some minimum common areas of preventive and control policies and constantly cooperate with others in order to maintain a minimum common level of reaction. This process implies, first of all, dealing with a series of questions that have to be answered to determine the most appropriate strategies and policies for increasing the risk for organized crime and, at the same time, equalizing it among countries.

The main questions concern the goals the international community wants to achieve; the degree and dimension of convergence and compatibility needed to counteract transnational crime; which policies need to be made compatible; the ways in which the goals can be achieved; what countries require to embark successfully on this task; and the mechanisms that could provide the impetus for convergence and compatibility, as well as coordination.

The preceding questions lie at the root of the philosophy of international cooperation and technical assistance in crime prevention and criminal justice matters. The discussion on the rationale for international cooperation and the factors inhibiting its effectiveness is bound to centre on an inherent difficulty. Experience has shown that there often appears to be a gap between the rhetoric and the substance of international cooperation.

There seems to be both a ritual and a practical approach to international cooperation. The former involves public declarations regarding the will of the international community to take action in criminal justice matters and an emphasis on a growing list of initiatives in international settings. At the practical level, what is at issue is the actual cooperation between one or more countries in compiling information, sharing intelligence, collecting and preserving evidence, arresting a fugitive, freezing or confiscating assets of criminal origin, and extraditing or prosecuting criminals.

These are two sides of the same coin. The political will and unwavering commitment behind international cooperation constitutes the framework for operations at the practical level. In some ways, they can be reconciled on the basis of a compromise between the collective interest and the individual interests countries have in criminal justice matters. International cooperation can be effective only if its efforts are producing more advantages for all countries - and consequently for the international community - than a single country can achieve through individual action.

This process of reconciliation will happen more easily when the effectiveness of international cooperation, and countries' individual interests become recurrent and reciprocal. The more countries become aware of the difficulties and costs of dealing individually with criminal justice matters, the more likely they are to regard international instruments and mechanisms as the solutions to their problem. Consequently, the more they legitimize international cooperation, and the more legitimized international cooperation is, the more effective it will become. Success will breed success and more countries will enter international agreements with greater enthusiasm, making international cooperation once again more and more effective. If this process is not primed, international cooperation will remain a rite, with little substance.

Another issue of central importance, and one directly linked to the fundamental concept of international cooperation, is technical assistance. Effective international cooperation often depends on the capacity of the criminal justice system of a given country. Raising the level of knowledge, expertise and professionalism of a criminal justice system requires resources that many countries lack. Technical assistance is then the only way of ensuring that structural difficulties are overcome. The provision of technical assistance can take many forms, depending on the needs of the recipient and on the availability of donor resources. Technical assistance can range from advisory services to the provision of equipment, and will almost invariably include specialized training. The planning and execution of technical assistance projects require constant cooperation and consultation with the competent authorities of the recipient country at every stage of the process. Particular attention should be given to ensuring that assistance is based on the actual needs of the country in question, to be determined by that country, if necessary in consultation with those providing the assistance. Assistance needs to be tailored not only to the specific needs but also to the political, cultural and legal traditions of the recipient country. It should be realized that measures and policies that have proved effective in dealing with a specific problem may need to be substantially modified to retain their effectiveness in different settings or systems. In many cases, the very basic principles or rationales of action are the only elements that can be retained, and new measures and policies have to be designed. A failure to structure and deliver technical assistance on these grounds risks not only rendering such assistance entirely ineffective but also creating an environment that is far from conducive to meaningful cooperation.

The overall capacity and stage of development of the criminal justice system are factors that should be taken into account in all technical assistance efforts, particularly when such assistance is intended to help the recipient country to deal with organized transnational crime. Because of the sophistication of this form of crime, assistance is often aimed at strengthening or improving legislative and law enforcement measures. Such interventions, however, need to be planned and developed on the basis of a thorough knowledge of the criminal justice system in question and its overall capacity, as well as on a careful evaluation of their impact on that particular criminal justice system. For example, the establishment of a special investigation unit for offences related to the laundering of the proceeds of crime may improve the detection and apprehension of money-launderers. Its successes may, however, be frustrated if the prosecuting and judicial authorities are not in a position to evaluate and use the evidence that the efforts of that unit have yielded.

Another issue that needs to be carefully considered is coordination. Multiple assistance projects are directed almost simultaneously at the same component of the criminal justice system, overlapping if not conflicting with each other. The result is an unnecessary duplication of effort, which may lead to confusion among recipients and thus render technical assistance ineffective. Coordination is necessary on the part of all concerned and should be viewed as an essential complement to the structured and thorough preparation and provision of technical assistance. Without it, the resources devoted to such assistance fail to achieve the intended goals.

The traditional rationale for technical assistance, either in drafting new legislation or in training criminal justice personnel, is to help countries to cope more effectively with their problems. The global situation has radically changed in the past few years, however, and so have the needs and goals of the international community. Technical assistance needs to be viewed in the context of the new political and economic realities and to be adapted to them, in terms of both concept and objectives. Technical assistance programmes should be designed to enable countries to equalize the organized crime risk and to do so in such a way as to contribute to the collective interest in deterring the expansion of organized crime.

If this objective is missed in planning and providing technical assistance, such assistance will remain a solidarity tax that developed countries pay directly or through multilateral mechanisms. It will be welcomed, but not enough, and the more countries are constrained by limited resources, the less technical assistance they will provide. It is essential, therefore, that technical assistance become more and more a productive investment for three different types of interests: those of the countries receiving assistance, those of the countries giving it and those of the international community.

## The Process of Convergence

### Goals

The main goal of convergence will be to reduce the transnational organized crime risk and equalize the illegal enterprise's risk. In doing this, an understanding of strategies and targets is vital.

The overall strategy of international cooperation should be to encourage and promote a gradual but consistent convergence of preventive and crime control policies among countries, in order to render them equally effective. Preventive policies are designed to reduce the opportunities for criminal activity and to minimize the vulnerability of legitimate businesses to the infiltration of organized crime. Crime control policies, in contrast, are intended to control the crimes committed by organized crime groups.

The targets of preventive policies are to build and maintain a consensus of public opinion, creating and strengthening conditions of legality and morality, and establishing and promoting the transparency of the financial systems. The targets of crime control policies are the criminals and their illicit assets. Both persons and assets are the key elements of the organizational structure of organized crime groups.

Once the goals of international cooperation have been identified, the scope of their convergence will have to be determined. The dangers posed by organized transnational crime and its effects point in the direction of a convergence of global scope. It should be kept in mind, however, that obtaining a worldwide consensus on an accepted set of policies against organized transnational crime is bound to be a process of increased involvement and integration among countries and regions. This process requires strong commitment on the part of the entire international community and a will to smooth out differences and overcome difficulties. The process has begun, however. Owing to the emergence of illicit drug trafficking as a global phenomenon, there are more similarities today in the policies of different countries to combat this form of crime than there were 10 years ago. The role of international and regional mechanisms in this area has been essential for nurturing and facilitating this process. Policies directed at the equalization of the law enforcement risk will require not only a similar realization on the part of the international community but also a more comprehensive approach.

The *strictu sensu* interpretation given to cooperation and assistance in the past limited such activity to a case-by-case relationship between the competent authorities of one state and those of another, supporting judicial or quasi-judicial proceedings. This form of cooperation, based on the needs of one country and on the requirement of reciprocity, began to reveal its limitations when it came face to face with the internationalization of organized crime. The characteristics of organized crime groups, namely secrecy, internal solidarity and structure, made it a peculiar phenomenon. It soon became self-evident that organized crime, particularly in its transnational forms, had dimensions that could not be dealt with by traditional law enforcement schemes.[14] Investigation, detection and prosecution were therefore seen to be critical issues in the fight against organized crime, in part because major problems arose from the lack of coordination between the legislative and law enforcement bodies in the countries concerned. It is thus clear that mechanisms are needed, covering all forms of cooperation and assistance, from police investigation to judicial proceedings, which will encourage the law enforcement authorities of countries affected by specific organized crime activities, to collaborate among themselves and work together effectively to deal with organized transnational crime.

The efforts of governments to secure more effective international cooperation may be used as a springboard for mechanisms that have already been tested, even if only as informal judicial assistance arrangements or collaborative transfrontier investigations. Admittedly, these arrangements often entail many more concessions on the part of governments than would be the case in more formal bilateral agreements. The successes scored by regional cooperation, however, constitute ample proof of the validity of this type of collaboration. 'Hot pursuit' and cross-border observation are examples of fruitful techniques implemented in a regional setting. Unlike traditional and more formal agreements of judicial assistance, no specific action is required by foreign authorities in terms of proceedings. The informal arrangements are primarily based on the mutual understanding that independent investigations by foreign law enforcement officers will be accepted and assisted.

While the basic premise of these arrangements is a working and often personal relationship between law enforcement officers, the process of confidence-building can serve as a model for arrangements of a broader scope and territorial coverage. Such confidence-building could be actively pursued, particularly under the present favourable political conditions, for example through the regular exchange of information and personnel. It is no doubt a slow process and may encounter certain obstacles. It can nevertheless make a significant contribution to establishing more formal arrangements and building an institutional framework for international cooperation. This contribution would consist in fostering and improving a better and more direct understanding of specific problems and methods of work, as well as cultural, political and legal traditions. The knowledge obtained would be crucial in modifying or designing policies that would be compatible and, therefore, conducive to international cooperation.

Governments may need to consider reviewing their criminal policies from both the substantive and the procedural perspective. From the substantive point of view, attention should be paid to the criminalization of certain forms of behaviour. The experience gained in the countries where organized crime is criminalized by comprehensive and appropriate legislation should encourage the elaboration and adoption of similar laws. This could be done in a concerted manner, thus avoiding discrepancies among the various countries and promoting the convergence of mechanisms and policies. The international debate on organized transnational crime has already reached some landmark points and this should testify both to the awareness and the willingness to fight it in a concerted and coordinated fashion. From the procedural point of view, governments need to consider issues related to traditional concepts of sovereignty and individual decision-making in the light of problems posed by new criminal activities. The realization at the political and decision-making level of the actual magnitude and complexity of organized transnational crime may serve as a basis for elaborating improved forms of international cooperation, drawing on the pool of knowledge and experience in the scientific community.

The differences between civil law and common law systems have not prevented international cooperation in the past. The long-standing tradition of bilateral treaties and multilateral conventions supports the idea that, where agreement is reached on a topic, mutual cooperation may run smoothly. The problem is how to develop strategies and techniques that will reduce the number of obstacles to international cooperation. The most recent instruments of international criminal law could provide useful suggestions to that end.

While there has been a trend towards progressive internationalization in the expansion of criminal organizations, experience has shown that organized crime groups have tended to begin extending their operations in countries close to their areas of origin, when these countries afforded better conditions for avoiding the law enforcement risk. This preference, stemming from migratory movements, greater knowledge of the economic and social systems and even familiarity with the language, is revealed by the dynamics of many organized groups now generally considered as transnational.

The Chinese Triads have expanded in Asia, as has the Sicilian Mafia in Europe, and the Colombian cartels have put out their tentacles in Latin and Central America, while the Russian criminal organizations have extended their activities to other countries of the Commonwealth of Independent States and to the countries of Eastern Europe. The process of internationalization that allows these well-established groups to operate in areas of the world far away from their traditional location originally began within the region. In order to prevent the development or expansion of other groups the regional dimension must be taken into account when policies and mechanisms are devised for the prevention and control of criminal activities.

Efforts in this direction will not begin to bear fruit until bilateral formal or informal cooperation has started to develop between countries of the same region. The convergence of policies and measures in the various regions of the world complements the promotion of wider international cooperation and the establishment of effective international mechanisms. International cooperation, however, also requires the active support of the international community not only in terms of resources but also through political commitment.

For regional and international cooperation to succeed, governments would have to interact with the international and regional organizations concerned and facilitate their work by providing expertise, information and resources; initiatives related to the provision of technical assistance would also require support.

At the international level, cooperation is to be sought, first of all, for the purposes of criminal investigations and proceedings aimed at confiscating the proceeds of crime. Assistance should be provided at the investigative level, either to identify and trace the proceeds, or to seize or freeze property. At the court level, foreign prosecutors may need assistance in enforcing a decision to confiscate. The question of handing over the confiscated property to the countries concerned, or sharing it with them, deserves particular attention, because it could well encourage these countries to become more involved in the fight against organized transnational crime.

An important issue in international cooperation in criminal matters is the consideration given to the basic rights and guarantees afforded to the prosecuted or convicted individual.[15] Significant results in international cooperation have been achieved by countries that share the same cultural and political values, while there is a reluctance to extend full cooperation to countries that do not guarantee the enforcement of the same ideals.[16] The issue of human rights is certainly one the international community must consistently pursue, but the protection of individual rights can surely be reconciled with the protection of the rights of society as a whole. Thus, bearing in mind the well-entrenched results of the democratic process, new strategies and techniques ought to be developed for improving international cooperation, while continuing to promote the universal protection of human rights.

*Compatibility of policies*

Combating organized crime involves a mechanism of strategies and policies that need to be strengthened inside a country. International cooperation must therefore be aimed at harmonizing those strategies and policies in different countries.

1. Preventive policies

One of the key issues is how to secure the compatibility of policies designed to reduce illegal opportunities for criminals. In the case of organized crime, a policy can be geared towards reducing the demand for illegal goods and services, or evaluating the impact that different approaches to that end may have.

Policies aimed at reducing illegal opportunities, decreasing the demand for illegal goods and services or attempting to regulate them would arguably be more effective if developed and applied at an international level. If there are territories where the demand is greater than in others, or if illegal goods are made legally available in some countries, organized crime groups will be attracted to the place where the difference in policies affords them better opportunities and they will develop their patterns of internationalization accordingly.

Markets are becoming global, and constant communication and growing interdependence increase both legal and illegal opportunities, making it more difficult to control them in the absence of international forms of regulation. Just as national enterprises look for opportunities in other countries, criminal enterprises exhibit the same attitudes and adopt the same behaviour in illegal but also in legal markets. As regulation of legitimate business is becoming more and more international and regional, similar policies are needed to counter the problems posed by organized crime.

One question of the utmost relevance and importance is how policies aimed at diminishing the vulnerability of legitimate industries to infiltration by organized crime groups can be made compatible. The convergence of policies that can produce the maximum level of transparency and competition in legitimate markets would be a step in the right direction. By promoting the flow of information and public scrutiny of legitimate business, transparency creates a shield against organized crime groups. Competition operates largely the same way by preventing an unlawful concentration of business power and by equalizing business opportunities. The European Union, for instance, has had considerable experience in these areas and has been engaged in regulating economic activity in the European market so as to reduce the risk of monopolies and tackle the problem of transparency of the financial systems through money-laundering legislation as well. Expanding the area of economic activity to encompass industries previously limited to one country and ensuring guarantees for open markets is a step towards minimizing the risk of infiltration of these activities and industries traditionally 'protected' from foreign competition by organized crimegroups.

The convergence of preventive policies in the area of corruption of public officials could be pursued and extended, *inter alia,* to corporate accounting and reporting procedures and tax examination policies that help to make it more difficult to generate illicit money for corruption purposes. The use of standardized codes of conduct for economic enterprises and public administration could also be promoted. The work of the United Nations and other intergovernmental organizations and the experiences in this area of particular countries may pave the way to a comprehensive process of convergence.

Money-laundering is an area in which the convergence of preventive policies has been developed more fully through a comprehensive set of measures, evolved in a number of countries and at the international level by intergovernmental entities. The starting point for equalizing the illegal enterprise's risk for organized crime groups is for all countries to begin to devise homogeneous policies for reporting suspicious transactions and to implement procedures for securing the identification of customers who use their banking and financial institutions. For non-banking financial institutions, licensing procedures may be necessary in order to prevent organized crime groups from using them as an alternative to the more regulated banking system. These preventive policies are strictly linked to criminal policies in the same area.

## 2. Crime control policies

The range of crime control policies is broad and includes substantive and procedural legislation, special programmes and law enforcement methods and their organization. Many of these policies for combating organized crime differ according to legal traditions and systems, the perception of the problem, the skills and capabilities of criminal justice system personnel, the level of organization of the criminal justice system and, more importantly, the level of resources available for the criminal justice system and its management.

In identifying policies that need to be made compatible, certain criteria have to be applied. In the present context, the need for compatibility is related to the equalization of the law enforcement risk in different countries in order to deter the internationalization of organized crime groups. Consequently, the maximum degree of compatibility among policies of different countries will be achieved when such policies are perceived by the organized crime groups themselves as having an equalizing effect. Compatibility is an important step towards achieving substantive international cooperation, because it helps to increase the capacity of different systems to work together.

The conditions for the convergence of domestic crime control policies are mainly two: the demonstrated effectiveness of these policies and some degree of flexibility in achieving compatibility with other policies of the same kind. On the basis of these criteria, the responsiveness of existing policies against organized crime to the need for compatibility of the law enforcement risk among different countries are to be analysed and evaluated.

The different legal traditions of civil and common law systems may account for many of the differences between countries. It is important that, beginning at the regional level and eventually extending to the international level, countries should achieve a common realization that crimes committed by an organized crime group represent a bigger threat than those committed by an individual or a casual organization.

The existence of organized crime groups is a threat *per se*. It is self-contained, because a criminal group is established with a view to committing any activity worth being exploited, striving to build it up and exercising the power that goes with it.

The increased risk to organized crime that crime control policies would be aiming at relates to the two targets mentioned earlier, persons and assets. Regarding the former, the core element of these policies would be the sanctions inflicted upon members of organized crime groups, when arrested, prosecuted and convicted, while for the latter it would be forfeiture and confiscation of the assets resulting from, or used in, criminal activity.

Reference should be made at this point to a set of policies involving a form of simultaneous prevention and control. These are policies traditionally used to interdict transnational movements of people. They have been concentrated on two main related issues: control of the borders and immigration laws. Although these policies are not specifically designed to equalize the law enforcement risk for organized crime groups, their adoption and implementation can have certain positive effects.

Traditionally, control at borders for the purpose of tracing criminals has not been a very effective tool against criminals who have a wide range of activities. Furthermore, even though some law enforcement operations have been helped by border checks, organized criminals have been accustomed to using fake documents or crossed uncontrolled borders. The usefulness of border checks for tracing criminals may have to be carefully evaluated in view of their heavy cost. In many cases, personal interdiction for criminals, in the sense of apprehension, may be less effectively achieved through border controls. The policy is much more effective in controlling migration flow, which is the main object of contemporary systems. The combination of border and immigration controls can be a very effective system for monitoring foreigners operating inside the countries and for collecting valuable intelligence.

Frequent analyses of the data on immigrants, categorized by nationality, place of birth, former place of residence, profession or work performed and new place of residence, can be useful in monitoring the migration of criminals and in some cases in alerting authorities to their infiltration of legitimate businesses. In a multi-ethnic world, these controls are difficult to maintain over a long period. For the purpose of controlling the organized crime risk, however, countries could plan to establish databases and implement some forms of immigrant monitoring and control for a short period, usually the time a criminal needs to settle down in the new society and begin to exploit its structures. These databases would be even more useful if they were shared on a regional basis.

Interdiction policies can work better against instrumentalities of crime through modern technology. Detection of illegal money, drugs, chemical precursors, weapons and other kinds of material supplied by organized groups is at present either haphazard, or managed through informants. Recent developments of computerized scanner technology can now monitor the movement and flow of goods much more effectively than in the past, making it more difficult for organized crime groups to smuggle illegal merchandise across the borders.

Interdiction policies need to be carefully structured and, where necessary, reshaped in accordance with present circumstances and realities, since the risk of organized crime is concurrent and linked with the worldwide trend of closer international relations, the opening of borders to free trade and the uninhibited circulation of persons, goods and capital. Global markets are becoming a reality and the risk of this trend being exploited by organized crime groups is clear and present.

The challenge is how to continue to pursue free trade and open border policies without compromising security and peace. The answer may lie in the increased use and development of new technologies. Admittedly, new technologies are expensive and require a substantial investment, which many countries may find difficult to make. However, a cost-benefit analysis should be made, in view of the efficiency and effectiveness of new technologies. In terms of management of criminal justice systems, international cooperation would stand to benefit from a rational approach to the issue in order to ensure that the most effective and appropriate technologies are applied at key points and possibly shared with other countries, at the same time keeping in mind the need for compatibility.

Legislation, both substantive and procedural, occupies a prominent place among policies to combat organized transnational crime. It remains one of the primary tools at the disposal of governments for the purpose of protecting the values and security of their societies and fostering growth and development. Legislation, however, needs to be dynamic and to adapt itself to, if not to foresee, developments. In the case of organized transnational crime, legislation should be developed with a view to fostering international cooperation and concerted action. Legislation should be structured and elaborated in such a way as to deal severe blows to organized crime groups at points where they would be most effective. One of these points is the organizational structure of criminal groups. Targeting this structure permits authorities to crack the shell of criminal groups and follow the thread leading to the top, effectively dismantling the organization. The offense of 'participation in an organized criminal association', as included in Italian law since 1982, and the offence of 'participation in the affairs of an enterprise through a pattern of racketeering', as described in the 1970 Racketeer Influenced and Corrupt Organizations (RICO) statute of the United States of America are intended to deal with the existence and the functioning of an organization devoted to committing crimes.

Creating such offences, or strengthening and adapting provisions that foresee similar offences in substantive legislation, will allow criminal law to attack the organizational structure of the organized crime groups perhaps even more than the crime of conspiracy alone could do. Experience in applying these two types of offense has had a very positive influence on the fight against organized crime in both Italy and the United States. In the Italian experience, the offense of participation in an 'organized crime association' has been decisive in successfully prosecuting and convicting many Mafia bosses in the first 'maxi-trial' against the Mafia in Sicily. In the United States, the RICO statute is generally considered to be the starting point of a new process of awareness of organized crime by the United States government and its criminal justice system. Its effectiveness has been demonstrated in the many indictments and convictions of members of organized crime groups that have resulted since the legislation was passed.

The Mutual Legal Assistance Treaty signed between Italy and the United States in 1984 has been, according to both sides, a powerful instrument for attacking the international expansion of Italian organized crime groups in the United States and their collusive relationships with the American Cosa Nostra. In the same way, mutual legal assistance treaties between Italy and other European countries owe a great deal of their effectiveness to the fact that they start from this typology of crime.

Legislation on control of the proceeds of crime is another issue that requires attention. The process initiated by the United Nations Convention against Illicit Traffic in Narcotic Drugs and Psychotropic Substances of 1988 has gone through a series of important international interventions, such as the 40 recommendations of the Financial Action Task Force on Money-Laundering and of other intergovernmental organizations such as the Council of Europe's 1991 Convention on Laundering, Search, Seizure and Confiscation of the Proceeds from Crime, the European Commission Directive of the same year and the Organization of American States' recommendations for Latin and Central America. International cooperation and concerted global actions would benefit greatly from the consolidation, extension and improvement of this process.

Harmonization of anti-money-laundering legislation is a powerful tool, which can equalize the risk among countries where criminals attempt to launder the proceeds of their crimes and to invest them. Once they find a loophole in the legislation of some country, they are quick to exploit it. Dealing with this requires not only the introduction of the crime of money-laundering, but also every possible effort, through the instruments of criminal law, to ensure that financial and non-financial institutions comply with the duties assigned to them by numerous regulations, especially regarding the reporting of suspicious transactions. If the legislation foreseeing sanctions for failure to report these transactions were more compatible, it would increase the protection offered to financial systems and would consequently foster more effective action while providing world financial markets with a safe environment in which to grow.

The introduction of money-laundering as an offence, however, may not, by itself, be enough. The experience of its implementation in countries that have linked the money-laundering crime to the predicate offence of drug trafficking reveals serious limitations. The exclusive link of money-laundering to drug offences has limited the capacity of financial institutions and law enforcement agencies to begin a greater number of investigations and to cooperate in cases transcending borders. Extending the predicate offence to 'all serious crimes' should be the starting point for equalizing law enforcement risk among countries and lend force to international cooperation.

Another area where it is essential that there be a consistent and strong commitment on the part of countries to make their legislation against transnational crime compatible is the internationalization of corruption. There is a growing realization of the need for more coherent and consistent international anti-corruption action. Recent recommendations by the Organisation for Economic Co-operation and Development provide guidelines for harmonizing national legislation for combating international corruption. Providing equal criminal treatment for domestic and international corruption is a matter of urgency. Therefore, countries should introduce into their domestic legislation measures such as the abolition of fiscal advantages that encourage domestic enterprises to corrupt foreign officials, and punishment for the corruption of foreign officials.[17]

Corruption is the bridge between economic and organized crime and it should be treated as a very serious threat. Corruption is usually accompanied by violence and these are the two methods organized crime groups use to penetrate legitimate activities. Corruption is often the substance of other crimes, such as fraud committed by an enterprise to pay bribes and money-laundering crimes.

The quantity and quality of sanctions are often used as criteria for quantifying the 'law enforcement risk'. As incarceration and confiscation of the assets are the two types of sanction that can disrupt a criminal organization, it is extremely important that the definition of these sanctions, their implementation and their perception by organized crime groups are as homogeneous as possible in different countries. Obstacles to convergence of the type and quantity of sanctions stem from divergent cultures and structures of criminal justice philosophies. The length of imprisonment, for example, may differ substantially from one country to another, as well as the balance between protection of human rights on the one hand and security considerations on the other.

In contrast, asset forfeiture and seizure are effective sanctions that could easily be made compatible. Legislation in this area is relatively new and its key provisions should not be difficult to harmonize. Laws that provide for asset-sharing among countries that have participated in the same law enforcement operation are a powerful instrument in the hands of the law enforcement system. Although these laws may have encountered some problems, the experience in drug cases has nevertheless been a positive one and has been successful in soliciting cooperation between law enforcement agencies of different countries, thereby demonstrating that those laws are powerful instruments of international cooperation.

The structural difference between the procedural law of countries where the inquisitorial or accusatory system prevails has not proved to be an obstacle to international cooperation between them. The experience of mutual legal assistance treaties between countries with different systems has shown that mutual legal assistance in criminal matters is possible despite such differences. The same could be said for the differences between systems characterized by mandatory criminal action on the one hand, and discretionary power on the other hand.

These differences, however, may be irrelevant in terms of law enforcement risk for crimes committed by organized crime groups. It is possible that, in cases where law enforcement capabilities are weak, the inquisitorial system can be more useful because it produces evidence before the trial takes place at which the evidence is going to be discussed. In this sense, it can be said that the system is more 'rigid', and there is no room for the criminals to influence the course of the proceedings.

The capacity of organized crime to intimidate those giving testimony can play a significant role in weakening the evidence discussed in trial. But this, and other side effects of the different systems that can be relevant in situations of threat against criminal justice systems, should be solved on a contingency basis without changing the principle of the parity of the parties in a trial.

The main problem in procedural law is that the methods for collecting evidence need to be made compatible in order to produce an equivalent quantity and quality of risk among countries. Domestic legislation, for example, may make use of modern techniques for tracing criminals and collecting evidence on their operations and on the organization itself. A reasonable balance can be found between the protection of privacy and the need of the law enforcement agencies to collect evidence through, for example, wiretapping and interceptions of telephone communication and electronic surveillance. Legislation providing for such methods, together with other law enforcement methods, such as undercover operations and controlled delivery, should be passed to enable law enforcement agencies to collect sufficient evidence to prove guilt beyond any reasonable doubt.

Another issue of high priority in the effectiveness of action against organized crime, and in the perception of organized crime groups of high risk, is the cooperation of witnesses and defendants with the law enforcement authorities. The experience of countries where the organized crime risk is high proves that intimidation and violence against witnesses and cooperative defendants is resorted to because these figures play an essential role in providing information on the structure of the group and its activities. Legislation and programmes for offering protection and assistance to cooperative witnesses and their relatives should therefore be an integral part of policies in each country that is having to deal with organized crime.

It is also essential to provide these people with a change of identity and to relocate them during and after the trial. Financial assistance, when possible, helps to overcome the difficulties they face as a result of cooperating with the criminal justice and law enforcement system.

As already mentioned, legislation allowing the use of new means of law enforcement, such as electronic surveillance and undercover operations, in order for the investigation to be effective and keep pace with the continuous evolution of technology, requires that these operations be conducted with a high level of professionalism, to equalize the risk among different countries. Professionalism among law enforcement agencies requires not only appropriate qualifications and training but also organization, coordination and resources.[18]

The question of resources, and whether they can ever converge (always in relation to their investment in the criminal justice system) is, of course, the most salient issue. The factors involved include budgetary problems and priorities in general and in the different areas of the criminal justice system. The same can be said for coordination among different law enforcement agencies. It is universally recognized that close coordination improves effectiveness, but it is part of the daily experience of many countries that coordination among law enforcement bodies is difficult to achieve and to maintain. Similarly with the issue of organization, centralized or decentralized patterns of organization respond to cultural, traditional and managerial criteria that cannot be harmonized. Each country should find the best organizational solution, based on its own pattern, trying to make its actions as efficient and effective as possible. The matter could, however, be approached from a different perspective. Technical assistance could assist greatly in securing the convergence of resources. The provision of expert knowledge and experience through advisory services and training to countries in need would raise the level of response to the problem of dealing with organized transnational crime. Even if the quantity of resources does not increase significantly, particularly in countries with severe budgetary problems, the quality of such resources, especially human resources, will rise to appropriate levels.

## Conclusions and Recommendations: An Agenda for International Cooperation

Having examined how, after bilateral cooperation, regional and international cooperation can, in turn, help to secure an effective convergence of national policies against organized crime, and having identified the cases in which compatibility of policies could increase the law enforcement risk for organized crime groups, thereby making it more difficult for them to internationalize their activities, the next step is to draw up an agenda for international cooperation.

The first step towards convergence should be achieved through regulatory and crime control legislation, establishing under domestic law, policies of demonstrated effectiveness that do not generate problems of compatibility where the legal systems differ, but that actually facilitate cooperation between countries. The second step should be the enhancement of law enforcement capabilities in terms of professionalism and technology.

In any agenda for international cooperation the regulatory measures necessary to obtain maximum transparency of financial systems and to prevent monopolies should not be neglected.

Consideration is to be given to specific offenses for crimes committed by criminal organizations. These could be membership in a criminal organization or participation in the affairs of a criminal enterprise, or other forms of conspiracy especially directed at the organizational aspects of the crimes committed.

Furthermore, measures should be addressed to the proceeds of crime, for example by enacting legislation that provides for forfeiture and confiscation of the assets of criminal origin, possibly including provisions for asset-sharing among countries participating in the same law enforcement operation. Introducing the criminal offence of money-laundering and extending it to the activities of laundering and investing proceeds of all serious crimes would be an essential step. Intentional omission or failure to report suspicious transactions on the part of banks and non-banking financial institutions could also be considered a criminal offense.

Other proposals that could be discussed and evaluated include increasing the severity of the offence in cases of crimes of domestic and international corruption, removing all financial and economic advantages of domestic enterprises obtained by corrupting public officials abroad, and extending the crime of corruption to the corruption of foreign public officials by national enterprises. This is particularly important in view of their great potential usefulness in mutual law enforcement assistance.

The agenda could also include the introduction of legislation allowing law enforcement agencies to conduct wiretapping, electronic surveillance and undercover operations. The ability of criminals to exploit high technology resources has to be matched by at least an equivalent law enforcement action. It is therefore essential to provide law enforcement agencies with the minimum required technology for wiretapping and electronic surveillance, together with standardized software for databases to be used for tactical and strategic intelligence.

The levels of sophistication reached by transnational criminal organizations in dealing with financial schemes means that the law enforcement agencies must be provided with specific training to deal with financial investigations.

The first and second steps require substantial international cooperation. Technical assistance programmes coordinated multilaterally and implemented both multilaterally and bilaterally, through different approaches, can provide the means of equalizing the law enforcement risk among countries as much as possible. These programmes must be coordinated if they are to produce effective results with greater cost efficiency. Regional or country-specific masterplans should be formulated, paying careful attention to the different needs of countries.

Any assessment of needs should not only consider the lack of policies and resources for achieving the points established in this agenda but should also assess the degree of flexibility of the juridical system where these policies are going to be applied. This would avoid possible rejection by the criminal justice system because of problems of internal compatibility. Convergence is a lengthy process and can only be achieved if there is a clear awareness of the initial differences that have to be decreased or accommodated.

International cooperation against organized transnational crime, which not only disregards the power and authority of the law but, as one of the main characteristics of its *modus operandi*, systematically breaches it, should be based on the collective feeling and understanding of the phenomenon from all those who belong to the community of nations.

In a certain sense, the pervasiveness of organized transnational crime may be compared to the threat from the deterioration of the environment or, even better, from the uncontrolled use of nuclear power. In 1986, at the time of the Chernobyl disaster, the world was forced to come to terms, for the first time ever, with the true extent of the dangers posed by a neglected activity, one which, because of its inherent volatility, might not be confined to borders that existed only on maps. Just as the repercussions of that explosion affected the people and environment of more than one country, the international community can no longer overlook the dangers of organized transnational crime, which is not hindered by national borders, and even profits from them because the borders may actually obstruct the rule of law.

To come to a common understanding and to collaborate in the fight against transnational organized crime does not mean that the distinct aptitudes and juridical cultures existing within the international community should be ignored. Nor does it mean endangering the sovereignty of states. On the contrary, since that sovereignty is challenged by criminals operating in a systemic fashion, the response to them needs to be structured and collectively shared.

The United Nations, because of its general mandate and international constituency, provides an appropriate forum in which a common understanding and global action can be promoted. Starting with the general need for exchanging information on organized crime patterns, on legislative provisions and on organizational structures of individual countries, the United Nations has been given a special responsibility to improve countries' capacities to combat this scourge, by enhancing the development of technical cooperation with countries in need of assistance.

Certainly, international cooperation will only be possible if the factors limiting it are eliminated. Among these factors, the lack of relevant cooperative arrangements emerges as the first problem, particularly in reference to extradition and mutual assistance in investigation and the gathering of evidence. The elaboration of new agreements providing for adequate assistance in combating organized crime, as well as the improvement and updating of existing treaties, would rapidly lead to the creation of a network of legal instruments that would make it possible to avoid delays or misinterpretation when assistance was sought. In this light, the United Nations model treaties could serve as a basis for the initial exercise. Of course, since the nature of organized crime is multiform and unpredictable, those models may have to be adapted to the various settings where they will be applied.

In cases in which transnational organized crime targets developing countries or countries in transition and their economic, political and social order, technical cooperation becomes essential for providing assistance in drafting penal laws appropriate for fighting organized crime, as well as in training law enforcement personnel, who will be called upon to apply new legislation and instruments and to cooperate with enforcers from other countries.

The higher the degree of consistency of these arrangements with both domestic realities and the tools available in other countries, the more effective international cooperation against transnational organized crime will be. Needs assessment may therefore be the preliminary step for further action by the United Nations, and other international organizations engaged in this area. Nevertheless, assistance also means financial and economic aid, with sufficient resources provided for technical cooperation activities.

Although there is no shortage of measures to be implemented, it is worth highlighting the importance of pursuing the goals step by step, without trying to target a prey that is unreachable. In other words, any discussion on sensitive issues, such as those concerning matters of domestic and international security, could be approached rationally and pragmatically.

The high-ranking participants in the World Ministerial Conference are well aware of the urgent needs and constraints of many countries, and have a unique opportunity to set up a programme for concerted action to strengthen regional and interregional cooperation. By taking into consideration national concerns regarding the consequences of organized crime, it is hoped that the Conference will be able to devise a more effective global strategy, building upon the statement of principles and programme of action adopted by the Ministerial Meeting on the Creation of an Effective United Nations Crime Prevention and Criminal Justice Programme, and adding a new decisive chapter to the history of international cooperation against organized transnational crime.

## NOTES

1. See Sixth United Nations Congress on the Prevention of Crime and the Treatment of Offenders, Caracas, Venezuela, 25 August-5 September 1980: *Report Prepared by the Secretariat* (United Nations publication, Sales No. E.81.IV.4).
2. See Seventh United Nations Congress on the Prevention of Crime and the Treatment of Offenders, Milan, 26 August-6 September 1985: *Report Prepared by the Secretariat* (United Nations publication, Sales No. E.86.IV.1), chap. IV, sect. A, para. 66.
3. Ibid., chap. I, sect. A.
4. Ibid., para. 6.
5. See Eighth United Nations Congress on the Prevention of Crime and the Treatment of Offenders, Havana, 27 August-7 September 1990: *Report Prepared by the Secretariat* (United Nations publication, Sales No. E.91.IV.2), chap. IV, sect. C.
6. Ibid., chap. I, sect. C.
7. *Official Records of the Economic and Social Council, 1992, Supplement No. 10* (E/1992/30), chap. I, sect. C, resolution 1/2.
8. *Official Records of the Economic and Social Council, 1994, Supplement No. 11* (E/1994/31), chap. I, sect. C, resolution 3/2.
9. See Muller-Rappard and Bassiouni, *European Inter-State Co-operation in Criminal Matters*, 2nd edition, 1993.
10. The Schengen Agreement between the Governments of the States of the Benelux Economic Union, the [then] Federal Republic of Germany and the French Republic [later joined by Italy, Portugal and Spain] on the Gradual Abolition of Checks at their Common Borders was signed on 14 June 1985 and led to the Convention of 19 June 1990 applying the Agreement.
11. Denmark, Finland, Iceland, Norway and Sweden have developed a system for harmonizing their domestic laws. This 'uniform' legislation is aimed at improving inter-state cooperation in criminal matters.
12. The Benelux Extradition Convention is one of the oldest regional mechanisms for cooperation, dating back to 1962.
13. Report of the Secretary-General on the strengthening of international cooperation in combating organized crime (A/47/381).
14. For an overview of the current state of development and needs in international cooperation against organized transnational crime, see Economic and Social Council resolution 1992/23, annex I, and the report of the Secretary-General on the impact of organized criminal activities upon society at large (E/CN.15/1993/3), submitted to the Commission on Crime Prevention and Criminal Justice at its second session.
15. C. Van den Wyngaert, 'The political offense exception to extradition', in *Acts of the International Seminar on Extradition (*Siracusa, Italy, 4-9 December 1989*)*; see also C. Van den Wyngaert, 'Rethinking the law of international criminal cooperation', in *Principles and Procedures for a New Transnational Criminal Law* (Eser & Lagodny, eds., 1992).
16. In the Council of Europe, for instance, 85 per cent of the extraditions are between member states.
17. P. Bernasconi, 'The necessity for an International Convention Preventing and Combating the Corruption of Public Officials', *Rivista Trimestrale di Diritto Penale dell'Economia*, Vol. VI, No. 4 (1993), p. 1138.
18. On the question of professionalism and the need for adequate coordination, see G. Falcone, *Cose di Cosa Nostra*, chap. VI, *Potere e Poteri* (Rizzoli, 1991).

# The Feasibility of Elaborating International Instruments, including Conventions, against Organized Transnational Crime

## Introduction

The present report is designed to afford an overall appraisal of prospects for international cooperation in the struggle against transnational organized crime - and in particular to consider whether it is feasible to elaborate international instruments, including a convention against transnational organized crime. It bears reiterating that the ultimate objectives of international cooperation are to ensure:

(a) that transnational criminal organizations encounter a high level of risk whatever home country they operate from and in whatever host countries they transact business;

(b) that legitimate industries can offer strong resistance to efforts at infiltration and takeover by transnational organized crime;

(c) that governments, the commercial sector, and the criminal justice system are resistant to corruption and violence by transnational criminal organizations; and

(d) that the activities of transnational criminal organizations are gradually circumscribed and ultimately eliminated.

Therefore, the overall goals are to make the environment for transnational criminal organizations hostile and inhospitable, to infiltrate, disrupt, and destroy the network structures on which many of these organizations are based, and to make continued transnational criminal activities as difficult and as costly as possible.

Other background documents submitted to the Ministerial Meeting have concentrated on the rationale for cooperation, the content of cooperation and the steps that have to be taken to promote greater harmonization of national legislation. The emphasis here, in contrast, is on the form of cooperation and, in particular, on the relative merits of bilateral and multilateral approaches in moving towards a regime that will be hostile to transnational organized crime.

Although each form of cooperation has its strengths and its weaknesses, bilateral and multilateral approaches are not mutually exclusive. While there are important differences of emphasis between them, each contributes in important ways to more vigorous criminal justice systems and a more effective law enforcement environment to deal with the threat from transnational criminal organizations. For the most part, bilateral, regional, and global approaches can be regarded as overlapping strategies that generally complement each other. Indeed, a multilevel approach of this kind tends to have a synergistic effect, especially when such cooperative ventures feed back into the national level and encourage states to develop domestic law that is consistent with the obligations they have accepted internationally.

There are rather different assumptions underlying bilateral cooperation on the one hand and multilateral cooperation on the other - especially when an effort is made to engage in global forms of multilateral cooperation. The bilateral approach is based on what might be termed an evolutionary model of cooperation, in which there is a gradually thickening web of bilateral linkages. The process is an incremental one, involving careful consolidation and gradual extension of the norms, mechanisms, and instruments of cooperation. The thickening web of bilateral cooperation works from the bottom up; the approach is deeply rooted in notions of the feasible and the practical. The ultimate goal is not ignored, but there is a clear recognition that it will take a long time to reach it. Underlying bilateral approaches is the belief that the best way to proceed is by building on convergent interests between two states with similar problems and a similar level of commitment to meeting them. Effectiveness is largely a matter of will and this is best manifested when states are determined to engage in intense and sustained cooperation to meet their common goals. At the same time, the existing bilateral mutual assistance and extradition treaties and various other forms of assistance offer a model of what might be done on a more ambitious scale.

At the other extreme, there is what might be termed a comprehensive approach to international cooperation. It is based on the logic that the challenge is a global one; consequently the best response is also one that is extensive in scope, multilateral in form and, as far as possible, global in reach. Moreover, there is an urgent need to bring a higher degree of order to a situation that may look like 'a rather untidy mix of global, regional, and bilateral arrangements, established without a great deal of thought given to the overall pattern'.[1] A multilateral approach would help to rectify this. Cooperation has grown up in incremental steps and without any overall design, but is now at a point at which the process requires some planning and regularization, in particular through more comprehensive and long-term approaches, such as the formulation and implementation of a convention against transnational organized crime. The key assumption of the multilateral approach is that drastic problems demand far-reaching responses. And like most attempts at international reform, this approach confronts the traditional emphasis on the concept of national sovereignty. The real issue, however, is not the loss of sovereignty but whether states are prepared to sacrifice some of the formalities of sovereignty in order to prevent the real erosion that is taking place as a result of the activities of transnational criminal organizations. Like most visionary schemes, the multilateral approach focuses upon the end result and proposes the shortest and most direct route for reaching it. It is, in effect, a top down approach that is aware of the problems and difficulties but acknowledges a compelling logic that provides the impetus to overcome these.[2]

Although the most ambitious multilateral schemes tend to have a sense of global vision, this is not invariably the case with multilateralism. Some multilateral schemes are regional in scope. Efforts to create a 'common judicial space' in regions such as Latin America and Western Europe, for example, offer an intermediate option. This more modest form of multilateralism attempts to extend bilateral cooperation to somewhat larger groups of like-minded states facing similar regional challenges from transnational organized crime. Although there is a recognition that the difficulties of cooperation often increase according to the number of states involved, this tends to be less of a problem where the states involved already have some kind of regional identity.

Against this background, the aim in this report is to examine the merits and shortcomings of bilateral and multilateral cooperative strategies in more depth. Section I looks at examples of bilateralism and offers an assessment of both the strengths and the weaknesses of this form of cooperation. Section II looks at multilateral approaches at the regional level, while in section III more ambitious forms of multilateral cooperation are considered, such as the elaboration of a possible convention against transnational organized crime. In section IV the main elements of such an international instrument are outlined, not as a definitive proposal, but rather as a basis for discussion and further thought. Section V sets out some concluding comments on international cooperation directed against transnational criminal organizations.

## A Thickening Web of Bilateral Efforts

Considerable progress has been made in the effort to internationalize and harmonize law enforcement efforts. Largely a reaction to the emergence of illicit drug trafficking as a global industry, this cooperation needs to be developed further in response to the increasingly diverse challenges posed by transnational criminal organizations.

One way to achieve this is through the more vigorous pursuit of bilateral cooperation. There are many examples of such cooperation already in place, and more agreements are being signed every year. In addition, states are attempting to broaden the scope of their mutual assistance treaties. In January 1994, for example, the United Kingdom of Great Britain and Northern Ireland and the United States of America signed a Mutual Legal Assistance Treaty enabling each side to ask the other to search for and seize the proceeds of serious crime, including drug trafficking, to take statements from witnesses, provide documents and records, and transfer prisoners temporarily when they are to give evidence.

Efforts have also been made to provide assistance to the states in transition in Eastern Europe. Germany has signed treaties with the Czech Republic, Poland and Slovakia on cooperation in the suppression of organized crime. Russia too has been the recipient of considerable assistance, much of it bilateral, but some of it multilateral and coordinated through the Crime Prevention and Criminal Justice Branch of the United Nations Secretariat. Indeed, one of the virtues of a bilateral forum is its flexibility: it is a form of cooperation which, even when it may be asymmetrical, could incorporate assistance to improve the balance between the countries concerned. It is also a form of cooperation in which there can be a very high degree of reciprocity.

A particularly good example of highly reciprocal bilateral cooperation - and one that has yielded very substantial dividends - is that between the United States and Italy. The United States-Italian Working Group on Organized Crime and Narcotics, formed in 1984 (extended to incorporate terrorism in 1986 and subsequently broadened to include Canada as an observer), is a model example of extensive bilateral cooperation. Indeed, 'because of the new instruments - particularly mutual assistance treaties - legal barriers to the exchange of investigative material, including grand jury information and information collected by foreign authorities otherwise covered by the secrecy of the investigating magistrate, were eliminated, and it became possible to work together in ongoing cases'.[3] This cooperation contributed to the disruption of the narcotics network established by the United States and Sicilian Mafias - the 'Pizza Connection' - through an operation 'in which law enforcement officers in Brazil, Canada, Germany, Italy, Spain, Switzerland and the United States all worked in concert for nearly a year, arrested more than a hundred individuals, and conducted an equal number of searches on a single day. In that same case, two Sicilian

Mafia members, Tommaso Buscetta and Salvatore Contorno, cooperated with both the United States and Italian authorities and provided testimony in trials in both countries. That joint testimony tested the limits of each system, which have very different rules regarding immunity agreements, pre-trial disclosures and cross examination. Because of the new treaties and a desire to work together, those differences were successfully bridged'.[4]

The case was indeed impressive for the degree of cooperation achieved not only at the prosecutorial level but also at the investigative level. Electronic surveillance was used to follow targets as they moved from one country to another. In addition, it proved possible to follow the money trail. More recent successes in a similar vein have included Operation Green Ice, an undercover money-laundering operation that revealed the links between the Sicilian Mafia and the Colombian drug cartels.

If law enforcement cooperation between Italy and the United States has been extremely successful, there are several factors that help to explain this:

(a) both states had very similar assessments of the drug trafficking and organized crime problem and gave it a high priority;

(b) both states had long experience in responding to organized crime at a domestic level and it was not too difficult to switch to a response at the international level;

(c) cooperation involved not just a formal agreement, but sustained cooperation to implement that agreement. This gave it a dynamic quality and provided an opportunity for the two countries to display their mutual commitment to overcoming the inevitable problems and difficulties that arose;

(d) it was a very tightly focused form of cooperation with specific aims and objectives and particular targets; and

(e) the Working Group was chaired by the United States Attorney General and the Italian Minister of the Interior, who has the responsibility for law enforcement in Italy. High-level involvement of this kind is crucial to keeping the group focused and to ensuring that agencies in both countries are receptive to the demands of cooperation.

These conditions are not always easy to replicate. Most other states have far less experience in dealing with organized crime at either the national or transnational level and therefore may not perceive the need for the depth of mutual commitment exhibited by Italian-United States cooperation. Consequently, not all bilateral agreements work so effectively or have such positive and beneficial results. In some cases, for example, asymmetry in law enforcement capabilities or asymmetrical commitments to cooperation can lead to a sense of frustration and disappointment.

These caveats notwithstanding, it is clear that bilateral cooperation can have very positive consequences in terms of law enforcement cooperation. If it does start to work effectively, however, bilateral cooperation can become a target for the transnational criminal organizations themselves. The Colombian cartels for example, did everything possible to disrupt bilateral cooperation between Colombia and the United States - especially after the 1979 Extradition Treaty. In effect, this Treaty meant that United States law enforcement capabilities could be used to compensate for the difficulties Colombia faced in prosecuting leading members of the cartels. The extradition of Carlos Lehder highlighted the dangers to other 'kingpins' of the drug trade being unable to find safe havens. The reaction by the cartels was ferocious largely because the instrument of cooperation was effective.

Bilateral cooperation, with its incremental approach, has some real strengths. In particular, it is a highly flexible strategy that can be tailored to what the states involved see as their specific needs and objectives. Furthermore, the commitment of states to implementing the accord is likely to be stronger: each state has a very clear obligation to its partner and the obligation is precise rather than diffuse. And so long as attention is given to implementation, then bilateral cooperation can be enormously effective.

At the same time, there are some limitations or shortcomings associated with bilateral extradition and mutual assistance treaties. In the first place, although the web of bilateralism is gradually thickening, major gaps remain. Furthermore, the whole could prove to be less than the sum of its parts: there is an *ad hoc* quality about this form of cooperation that produces inefficiencies, lacks of coordination and overlapping when looking at it from an overall perspective. Another problem is that bilateral cooperation is consuming of both time and resources. It is especially difficult for smaller states, which have neither the resources nor the expertise to engage in multiple bilateral negotiations, to develop the instruments of cooperation. Even though the provision of model treaties makes this task somewhat easier, the lack of resources is likely to remain a powerful inhibition. The implication is that, although the web of bilateral cooperation will continue to thicken, it needs to be complemented by multilateral forms of cooperation.

## Multilateral Cooperation and Regional Integration

Multilateral cooperation should not be seen simply as a compromise between various bilateral efforts. Rather, it is something that has significant benefits in its own right, as many regional arrangements have demonstrated. They can be understood as the criminal justice counterpart to the growth of economic and political integration in particular regions, such as Western Europe. Regional cooperation in judicial and criminal matters is the natural concomitant to efforts to achieve political and economic union, even though it involves some of the more sensitive and complex aspects of national sovereignty. In this sense, it can be understood as a spin-off (or spill-over) from broader political and economic processes - albeit based on the recognition that complete uniformity of national legislation is neither feasible nor desirable. As has been observed, 'The criminal law systems are all finely tuned to the specific characteristics of the different countries. This delicate equilibrium should not be disturbed, unless a substantial advantage is to be gained'.[5] At the same time, regional cooperation is also an acknowledgement that something needs to be done in response to the increased regional vulnerabilities accompanying the opening of internal borders and the development of the single market.

Regional cooperation is also based on the recognition that, although transnational organized crime is a global problem, it takes different forms in different regions and countries. Indeed, a strong argument can be made that regional problems demand regional responses. This does not mean that such a response is a substitute for national legislation or global approaches. It is simply that the states of a particular region may face a relatively homogeneous challenge, which provides the basis for a concerted approach.[6] This may be the case in Europe, where there is increasing awareness of the threat posed by various criminal organizations. Indeed, the more overt the threat, and the more widely shared the threat assessment, the greater the prospects for a vigorous programme of cooperation.

There have already been some very positive regional initiatives, which have extended the bounds of cooperation beyond the purely bilateral.[7] These include the Council of Europe's Convention on Laundering, Search, Seizure and Confiscation of the Proceeds from Crime.[8] This Convention contains far-reaching provisions allowing the signatories to criminalize laundering of the proceeds of non-drug-related crime. It was also extended beyond Europe to facilitate participation by countries such as the United States and Australia, which are not members of the Council but helped with the drafting of the Convention.

Another, more modest, regional initiative is the Caribbean Financial Action Task Force. As a result of the Caribbean Conference on Drug Money Laundering, held at Aruba from 8 to 10 June 1990, a series of recommendations for taking action against money-laundering was formulated. Some countries, however, have proved reluctant to take further action, not least because of the benefits they receive as tax havens, and progress has generally been slower than was initially anticipated.

More significant is the work of the Inter-American Drug Abuse Commission (CICAD) of the Organization of American States, which has initiated an action programme against the production and use of illicit substances and has adopted model legislation on money-laundering,[9] based largely on the recommendations of the Financial Action Task Force established by the Heads of State or Government of the Group of Seven major industrialized countries and the President of the European Commission of the European Union.

These efforts to achieve common judicial and security spaces, at least in relation to certain sectors of criminal activity such as drug trafficking and money-laundering, have their own logic.[10] At best, regional initiatives of this kind are relatively easy to formulate and implement, as the states in the region have a broad convergence of interest and relatively homogeneous needs and problems. On some occasions, however, as in the case of the Financial Action Task Force of the Group of Seven countries, the impulse for cooperation is evident in economic and political groupings that exceed the geographical contiguity of land borders. Once again, however, these states have similar needs and problems, which have enabled them successfully to develop a common approach in the area of international money-laundering.

These complementary, reinforcing initiatives provide an important supplement to bilateral cooperation. They are incremental exercises in multilateral cooperation, which in some cases seem to provide a useful framework for effective action against transnational criminal organizations. At the same time, under their influence, international cooperation against transnational organized crime takes on even more of the quality of a patchwork quilt, put together without any coherent design. Moreover, they only deal with particular segments of criminal activity and do not deal with the whole range of illicit actions and transactions perpetrated by transnational criminal organizations.

It is nevertheless clear that multilateral arrangements of this kind 'offer numerous advantages, not the least of which is that they may obviate the need to negotiate individual bilateral arrangements with large numbers of foreign governments'.[11] Negotiation is relatively easy for large states with highly developed administrative structures; but, as suggested above, for smaller states with limited resources and expertise, multilateral instruments or forms of cooperation are much more cost-effective. They are also particularly useful where governments are hostile or political relations inhibit direct bilateral cooperation. While political and ideological hostility is much less of a problem now that the cold war has ended, multilateral cooperation continues to offer opportunities for cooperation that simply would not be possible at the bilateral level. An additional advantage of multilateral cooperation is that it is less likely to be a target for counterattacks by organized criminal groups.

These advantages of multilateral cooperation should be viewed in conjunction with the patterns of *ad hoc* bilateral cooperation and what might be termed sectoral cooperation at the regional level.

## Towards a Convention Against Transnational Organized Crime: Desirability and Feasibility

In considering the prospects for a convention against transnational organized crime designed to go beyond a regional approach and encourage global application, several problems should be kept in mind.

The first difficulty with such a new instrument is its content. Similar conventions on terrorism and drug trafficking have been oriented toward a specific typology of crime. The question arises, therefore, whether a new international instrument on organized crime should cover the many crimes that transnational criminal organizations or domestic organized crime groups commit, or should focus on the way in which countries should respond to the threat posed by these organizations. The problem with concentrating on the crimes is that they are so extensive - and it is difficult to be all-embracing. The implication is that attention should be focused on the second aspect, that is the responsibility of governments to respond vigorously to the challenge, building upon the experience developed in the process of elaboration, ratification and implementation of the United Nations Convention against Illicit Traffic in Narcotic Drugs and Psychotropic Substances of 1988 and starting from the already existing proposals on legislation and law enforcement methods covered in the Convention itself. The extent of international support for the Convention is extraordinary: over 100 states are parties to it. This Convention, thanks to the commitment and political will of such a large number of countries, has had a major impact in bringing about concerted action against drug trafficking.

One of the inherent difficulties with multilateral cooperation, as manifested in the development of instruments of the kind being discussed here, is the achievement of consensus. In effect, breadth of participation must not be achieved at the expense of depth and intensity of cooperation and it is essential to ensure that negotiation does not result in a diluted convention that falls short of establishing the provisions necessary for an effective response to transnational criminal organizations. What is needed now, actually, is a framework for international cooperation, within which states could proceed with bilateral cooperation in a more systematized and effective way. Such a framework would make it possible to bridge the gaps inherent in bilateral cooperation. For example, the Vienna Convention has given rise to a wave of legislative activity at the national level, supported by the legal assistance programme of the United Nations International Drug Control Programme, as well as to the adoption of numerous bilateral and regional agreements that implement and further the Convention's provisions in fields of cooperation.

Another closely related problem inherent to multilateralism lies in the fact that it is far from clear precisely how multilateral the activities resulting from the convention would really be, especially where there are divergent assessments of the challenge. In one sense, a multilateral convention would provide a way of augmenting resources and mobilizing mutual support and assistance for what individual states are unable to do alone. It should however be emphasised that multilateral responses to global problems can only work if each party makes sacrifices commensurate with those of others.

Avoiding this kind of obstacle requires not only a broad consensus on what needs to be done to carry on the fight against transnational criminal organizations but also a commitment to take whatever action is necessary, despite the cost. In the context of a convention, there are two dimensions: if it is to be effective, it needs states to join and subsequently to exhibit the will and capability to meet their obligations under the convention.

Nonetheless, if the consolidation of various instruments into an international convention against transnational organized crime may not meet with universal approval, some of the reasons can be found in the obstacles to cooperation that have already been discussed, combined with an innate conservatism. As has been noted: 'Only if most countries were willing to re-examine some deeply entrenched legal procedures, and to recognize that their own traditional way of doing things was not necessarily the best or most effective approach to the problems in question, would the concepts of multilateral extradition and mutual assistance conventions become a reality'.[12]

The elaboration of a new instrument could be linked to the establishment of an effective and reliable system for collecting information, sharing it at the global level and analysing it as a guide for more decisive action. Transnational organized crime operates secretly because of the very nature of its illicit activities. As a consequence, collecting data becomes very difficult. International action against transnational criminal organizations based only on assumptions and reports cannot, however, suffice. Better and more reliable indicators, to be universally adopted and used in reporting, are urgently needed. The possibility of an international clearing-house to collect and share more reliable information should also be looked into as a very valuable means of complementing international action.

It is true that the exchange and processing of electronic data have recently created a potential for greater harmonization of data collection systems, but they have also highlighted the differences in national reporting systems. The necessary financial and human resources are not always available to comply with the various international reporting requirements. However, data collected through questionnaires are often not the most recent, as the gathering process is quite lengthy. As there is still a gap between the tasks that lie ahead and the goals that have been attained, the international community should make special efforts to provide the necessary feedback and support in the collection, analysis and dissemination of reliable and timely information on the incidence, expansion and effects of organized transnational crime.

The elaboration of an international convention against transnational organized crime would bring other advantages too, representing an invaluable potential for universal adherence. First, the very act of negotiating a convention would have certain benefits. For example, it would focus attention on the problem. Although specific criminal organizations, such as the Colombian cartels and, more recently, the Russian organized crime groups, have been given considerable attention, the emergence of transnational criminal organizations as a generic threat posing problems in many respects exceeding those of international terrorism has been relatively ignored. Indeed, there has been a paucity of both journalistic and scholarly analyses dealing with transnational criminal organizations and their activities as a problem faced not only by individual states but also by the international community as a whole. Negotiating a multilateral convention with global applicability would do much to rectify this. Indeed, a convention on transnational organized crime would be very important in symbolic terms, as it would represent the collective judgement of the international community that the problem has become sufficiently serious to demand concerted action in response. This could also have an important impact in terms of legitimizing national actions, including national legislation against the activities of transnational criminal organizations. In addition, the negotiation of a convention would lead to greater interaction among governments and particular ministries in ways that could themselves lead to enhanced cooperation. Developing a knowledge of other negotiators can be important, particularly if these negotiators also have some role in the subsequent implementation of policy. Lastly, the negotiation process itself would help to identify the areas of consensus on the problem, its dimensions, and the main strategies for responding to it.

Secondly, once the convention was in place, it would have several positive effects:

(a) it would provide a set of standards and expectations that the signatories would have an obligation to live up to. In a sense it would facilitate the exertion of peer pressure as a common effort of the international community in addressing the problem;

(b) it would have an important regularizing effect and provide for a more standardized form of cooperation than does the extension of bilateral accords, each of which has its own distinctive features;

(c) it would facilitate more systematic assistance in the areas of criminal justice and law enforcement, rather than the existing *ad hoc* approach;

(d) it would provide guidance for a programme of implementation that would assist in the dual objectives of harmonizing law enforcement risk and making it more difficult for transnational criminal organizations to infiltrate legitimate business.

It is clear from the above that there are both advantages and disadvantages to a multilateral convention against transnational organized crime. The issue is not clear cut. If governments do decide that the advantages outweigh the disadvantages, however, there are several other requirements that would have to be met to transform it from a theoretical possibility into a feasible and practical proposition. First, it would require a broad-based consensus on the seriousness of the challenge posed to nations and to the international community by transnational criminal organizations. A consensus of this kind appears to be developing - as is evident in the widespread (although still far from universal) adoption of regulations directed against money-laundering. The key to broadening this consensus is for governments that are affected by transnational criminal organizations to recognize that they are not alone, and for governments that are not currently the target of transnational organized criminal activity to understand that they are not immune, and that it may be only a matter of time before the problem impinges on them directly. Secondly, another crucial requirement is that the idea of elaborating a convention should have the unequivocal backing of most states. The more diverse this group of states is, the better, on the understanding that the convention should not be seen as an attempt by any particular grouping to impose required forms of behaviour on others with different levels of economic development or cultural traditions. The willingness of several highly committed states to give a high priority to successful implementation could create a bandwagon effect, encouraging others to join. A third requirement is that there should be a clear idea of the purpose and scope of the convention. It has to be carefully formulated in ways that specify the target (transnational criminal organizations and their members), the obligations that states incur (in terms of taking initiatives in their own national law, in positively responding to requests for assistance from others and in providing and exchanging information) and provisions for implementation (both procedural and substantive).

## Outline of Possible Elements for a New International Instrument

### General principles

An internationally binding instrument, such as a convention, against transnational criminal organizations and their activities could first of all express concern about the threat posed by transnational criminal organizations and the urgent need for international cooperation to respond to a phenomenon endangering stability and security, the integrity of financial institutions, the international order, as well as the processes of democratization and development. Secondly, it could establish the principles underlying cooperation among countries in responding to transnational organized crime,[13] as well as emphasizing that existing instruments of cooperation would be integrated into the convention.

It would also be important to have a clear understanding of the characteristics of transnational organized crime, paying particular attention to its structural features and *modus operandi*. These could include, for instance, the following: the grouping together of a number of individuals; the profit-making goal; the use of violence, intimidation and corruption; the hierarchical link or personal relationships that make it possible to control closely the activities of the group; the economic control of whole territories; the laundering of illicit profits in order not only to organize other criminal activities but also to set up businesses (with the consequent effect of corrupting them); the great potential of expansion beyond national boundaries; and the tendency to organize international operations together with other groups of different nationalities.[14]

To enumerate all the crimes that these organizations commit would be almost impossible and the list would need to be constantly updated. Organized crime groups are opportunistic and become involved in all sorts of crimes, as long as they are profitable. These crimes do not qualify *per se* as organized crime activity. It would, nevertheless, be possible to draw up a non-exhaustive list of the criminal acts most frequently committed by organized criminal groups operating across national borders, such as: the theft of cultural property; trafficking in arms; illegal gambling; smuggling of illegal migrants; trafficking in women and children for sexual slavery; extortion; violence against the judiciary and journalists; corruption of government and public officials; trafficking in radioactive material; illicit infiltration of licit business; trafficking in body parts; trafficking in endangered species; transnational auto-theft; money-laundering; computer-related crimes; and international fraud. Crimes such as drug trafficking and piracy, which are already the object of specific conventions, would be purposely excluded.

There should also be general principles related to modalities of cooperation. For example, the need to respond with as much diligence and as many resources as possible, within the limits of overall constraints on resources and the other demands on national policy, to the growth in transnational crime and the emergence of transnational criminal organizations as the major perpetrators of these crimes. Another general principle could be that states should take action unilaterally and in cooperation with each other to fight against transnational crime and to disrupt, dismantle and destroy the transnational organizations commonly engaging in these activities. In addition, it could be established that efforts to implement national initiatives and international cooperation against transnational criminal organizations should be consistent with - or governed by - respect for human rights.

*Specific provisions*

Some or all of the following specific and detailed provisions should be included in the instrument:

(a) Serious efforts should be made to develop both substantive and procedural national legislation against transnational criminal organizations and their activities, in convergence with the legislation of other signatories;

(b) All available arrangements of international cooperation against transnational criminal activities should be used and existing measures at the regional level implemented on a larger scale;

(c) Regulatory measures and administrative regulations should be developed that would make the commercial and banking sectors more transparent and accountable and therefore less susceptible

to infiltration by transnational criminal organizations;
(d) Concerted action should be taken against money-laundering[15] and the use of the proceeds of crime, including pressure on tax havens to tighten up their procedures and to cooperate in developing a higher level of transparency;
(e) Countries should assist each other by providing the persons, evidence and assets that are requested by a party to the convention, according to the principles contained in the United Nations Model Treaties on Extradition, on Mutual Assistance in Criminal Matters including its Optional Protocol concerning the proceeds of crime) and on the Transfer of Proceeding in Criminal Matters:[16]
(f) Uniform and effective techniques of investigation and prosecution should be developed against transnational criminal organizations, including more sophisticated means of information-gathering, collection of evidence and analysis of financial flows and/or investigation of suspicious transactions, and specialized national investigative units should be set up to deal specifically with organized crime;
(g) Information should be exchanged in order to assist other signatories in the investigation, apprehension and prosecution of those engaged in transnational crime;
(h) Requests for judicial and other forms of technical assistance should be given a positive response, with a view to strengthening national criminal justice and law enforcement systems against transnational criminal organizations;
(i) Modalities should be considered to encourage states to implement the convention fully;
(j) Collective measures should be taken to ensure that there are no safe havens, and to avoid either tacit support for, or collusion with, transnational criminal organizations.

As regards judicial assistance, the state parties to the convention should try to ensure that assistance is provided in the most efficient and cost-effective ways. It would be useful, for example, to develop a central clearing-house for information on legislative and other measures taken at the national level, their effectiveness and shortcomings. Furthermore, meeting of the state parties held periodically at a senior political level would play a key role in the search for donors to provide developing countries and countries in transition with technology, especially in the area of computerization, high-speed data exchange and other forms of information technology. Efforts could also be made to coordinate training programmemes to be conducted under the provisions of the convention.

Since the successful prosecution and adjudication of cases involving organized crime are hampered not only by the sophistication of this form of crime and by the fear of retribution for cooperating with the law enforcement agencies but also by divergent evidentiary rules in national laws, the convention could include standard guidelines in this field.[17]

The convention could also provide for the establishment, either at the national or the international levels, of special funds for economic compensation of victims of organized crime when compensation cannot be charged to the person responsible. Such funds would be partially subsidized by confiscated capital.

The possibility could be foreseen of establishing international machinery to implement the convention. If necessary, similar machinery could also abe established at the national level. The scope and ambitiousness of the machinery might vary, but it would probably include at least a designated point of contact for international cooperation under the terms of the convention.

State parties could also undertake to meet particular national reporting requirements for implementing the convention. In addition, they could be requested to produce annual assessments of trends in the development of transnational crime and transnational criminal organizations, calling upon outside specialists and national investigative bodies, as well as international agencies such as the International Criminal Police Organization (ICPO/Interpol). If resources permit, they could also engage in specific research analysis of particular areas of transnational crime.

The convention could establish a monitoring system, including provisions on periodic review and amendment procedures, to ensure that its provisions reflect changing patterns of transnational crime, as well as the reaction of transnational criminal organizations to international cooperation in criminal justice and law enforcement.

## Conclusions

The international community is becoming increasingly concerned about the impact that transnational organized crime produces on national economies, international relations, stability, security and peace. The decisive action taken against this form of crime in many countries, as well as the attention devoted to it by the Commission on Crime Prevention and Criminal Justice and the legislative bodies of the United Nations, in particular the General Assembly and the Economic and Social Council, demonstrate that the issue is a major priority for member states.[18]

The new responsibilities that governments have to take on because of the escalation of organized crime and the demand for global strategies to combat it, draw attention to the need for effective instruments, bearing in mind that what is most needed is a comprehensive, multi-layered approach to international cooperation in criminal justice and law enforcement in the fight against transnational organized crime. Ideally, a truly effective international approach would be composed of a web of bilateral, regional and multilateral agreements complementing and promoting one another. In fact, bilateral and multilateral forms of cooperation are complementary rather than mutually exclusive, but whether international cooperation can evolve in ways that allow a response to transnational criminal organizations commensurate with the threat depends on the capacity of states to understand that criminal justice and law enforcement systems can no longer be viewed as purely national concerns. Ultimately the prospects for cooperation depend on recognizing that a new kind of threat demands a new kind of response, in which international cooperation plays a central role. Experience has shown the importance of adopting international instruments in order to enact global strategies of action when dealing with issues of a transnational nature. A very successful example is found in the United Nations Convention against Illicit Traffic in Narcotic Drugs and Psychotropic Substances of 1988.

International cooperation is easier today than it was a few years ago. In fact, today there is a growing realization that states can only tackle the new forms and dimensions of crime effectively if they join forces. Many countries have explicitly recognized that they do not have sufficient capacity to face the new transnational forms of crime, particularly organized and economic crime, including corruption and money-laundering, environmental offences and increasing violence. The lack of qualified staff is a prevalent problem, and the training of criminal justice personnel a widely declared priority. There is a pressing need for expertise to deal with sophisticated new forms of criminality and for specialized personnel to handle criminal investigations and prosecutions. There have been requests for assistance in drafting legislation, in procuring equipment to enhance law enforcement capabilities, and in developing and applying bilateral or multilateral treaties and agreements.

There is also a growing awareness that the limited capabilities of many developing countries have been further taxed by the increasing demands on their criminal justice systems. They often operate under outdated legislation and imported procedures that are ill-suited to their conditions and the contemporary realities of crime. Economic crises and competing development priorities have worsened the crime problems in many countries, with serious effects on their law enforcement capacities. Furthermore, in countries in transition from a single-party to a multiparty political system, where protection of the state was formerly paramount, there is a move to institutionalize the observance of human rights and strike a balance between effective crime control and democratic principles. The goal of these countries is to ensure judicial independence to allow greater flexibility and build public confidence in the administration of justice. Since, however, the role and operation of the criminal justice system, including the police, prosecution, legal defence, courts and prisons, are in a process of change, organized crime finds fertile ground for expanding its activities.

A fundamental purpose of international cooperation is to contribute to the creation of self-reliant capacities in developing countries, as well as countries in transition. Strengthened technical cooperation in the fight against transnational organized crime should be viewed as a contribution to this end. Programme activities should be geared to developing expertise, especially in countries where it is scarce, and to promoting the highest standards of professionalism and specialization. Training and upgrading the skills of personnel working in the various areas of criminal justice is considered crucial. Adequate support of member states in this field would require that appropriate expertise be identified and material developed that would cater to the specific requirements of each region or each group of trainees. Furthermore, effective channels of communication are necessary in order to assess needs and prevailing circumstances, in order to tailor training activities to these needs.

While most technical cooperation activities rely on voluntary contributions from member states and funding agencies, the infrastructure for elaborating proposals, assessing needs, organizing and implementing projects and providing administrative support and the required follow-up should be developed and built into the basic framework of any global strategy. The new post-cold-war framework of international relations is relatively free of the impediments of the past that resulted from narrow political considerations. In this favourable environment, with the international community sharing the same values, the Conference represents the appropriate forum for member states to express all the commitment, political will and unwavering determination that are necessary to strengthen multilateral cooperation, taking global action against transnational organized crime a step further, with concrete and practical measures for implementation.[19]

ELABORATING INTERNATIONAL INSTRUMENTS

NOTES

1. The comment was made about police cooperation but has wider applicability. For the argument itself, see Malcolm Anderson, *Policing the World: Interpol and the Politics of International Police Cooperation* (Oxford: Clarendon Press, 1989), p.33.
2. Rainer Schmidt-Nothen, 'Der lange Marsch durch viele Konferenzen. Es gibt noch viel zu tun: Vertraege und Abkommen, die dem Kampf gegen das verbrechen dienen' [The long march through many conferences. There is still much to be done: treaties and agreements supporting the fight against crime], *Kriminalistik*, Vol.41, (1987), p.8-9.
3. Richard A. Martin, 'Problems in international law enforcement', *Fordham International Law Journal*, Vol.14, No. 3 (1990-1991), p.521.
4. Ibid. p. 522.
5. See Fleur Keyser-Ringnalda, 'European integration with regard to the confiscation of the proceeds of crime', paper compiled for the Tenth International Symposium on Economic Crime, Cambridge, July 1992.
6. See Reuters, 1993, 'Italy: Mafia looks forward to Europe without frontiers', *CJ Europe*, Vol. 3, No. 1 (January-February), p. 15.
7. See Bruce Zagaris and Sheila Castilla, 'Implementation of a worldwide anti-money laundering system: constructing an international financial regime' (Police Executive Research Forum, Washington, July 1993).
8. European Treaty Series No. 141 (1990).
9. Model regulations concerning laundering offences connected to illicit drug trafficking and related offences, adopted at the eleventh regular session of the Inter-American Drug Abuse Commission, held at Punta del Este from 10 to 13 March 1992.
10. See Cyrille Fijnaut, 'Policing Western Europe: Interpol, TREVI and Europol', *Police Studies*, Vol. 15, No.3, pp. 101-106, and H. F. Markus Mohler, 'A proposal for a European security space', *CJ Europe*, Vol.1, No. 1.
11. Ethan A. Nadelmann, *Cops Across Borders* (University Park, Pennsylvania: Pennsylvania State University Press, 1993), p.9.
12. See Eighth United Nations Congress on the Prevention of Crime and the Treatment of Offenders. Havana, 27 August-7 September, 1990: Report Prepared by the Secretariat (United Nations publication, Sales No. E.91.IV.2), chap. IV, sect. C, para. 253.
13. These principles are identified in the background documents on the most effective forms of international cooperation for the prevention and control of organized transnational crime at the investigative, prosecutorial and judicial levels (E/CONF.88/4) and on appropriate modalities and guidelines for the prevention and control of organized transnational crime at the regional and international levels (E/CONF.88/5).
14. Discussion document on the World Ministerial Conference on organized transnational crime (Economic and Social Council resolution 1994/12, annex) para. 9.
15. Among the most relevant measures against money-laundering taken at the regional and international levels are the following: The United Nations Convention against Illicit Traffic in Narcotic Drugs and Psychotropic Substances, adopted at Vienna on 19 December 1988 (E/CONF.82/15 and Corr.2); the 40 recommendations of the Financial Action Task Force, adopted at Aruba on 10 June 1990; the Council of Europe Convention on Laundering, Search and Confiscation of the Proceeds from Crime, adopted in Strasbourg on 8 November 1990 (European Treaty Series No. 141); the Council of the European Communities Directive on the Prevention of the Use of the Financial System for the Purpose of Money Laundering, adopted on 10 June 1991 (91/308/EEC); and the Inter-American Drug Abuse Control Commission (CICAD) Model Regulations concerning Laundering Offenses connected to Illicit Drug Trafficking and Related Offenses, adopted by CICAD in March 1992 and by the Organization of American States General Assembly in June 1992 (OEA/Ser.L/XIV.2; CICAD/INF.58/92).
16. See the annexes to General Assembly resolutions 45/116, 45/117 and 45/118. The Crime Prevention and Criminal Justice Branch is preparing manuals providing guidelines on how to implement these Model Treaties. For the advantages of using such instruments see the

report of the Secretary-General on the most effective forms of international cooperation for the prevention and control of organized transnational crime at the investigative, prosecutorial and judicial levels (E/CONF.88/4).
17. Official Records of the Economic and Social Council, 1994, Supplement No.11 (E/1994/31), chap. II, para. 25.
18. See General Assembly resolutions 44/71, 45/116, 45/117, 45/118, 45/119, 45/121, 46/152, 47/87, 48/102 and 48/103, and Economic and Social Council resolutions 1989/62, 1989/70, 1992/22 of 30 July 1992, 1993/29, 1993/30 and 1994/12.
19. See the report of the Secretary-General on the status of preparation of the World Ministerial Conference on Organized Transnational Crime (E/CN.15/1994/4/Add.3), paras. 26-27.

# Conclusions and Recommendations of the International Conference on Preventing and Controlling Money Laundering and the Use of the Proceeds of Crime: A Global Approach

**Introduction**

The Courmayeur Conference noted that money-laundering had acquired a global character and thus required a vigorous multi-disciplinary approach, and priority attention, at the international and national levels. In that connection, the Conference noted the need to enhance the efforts of the United Nations because of its global constituency, of the Financial Action Task Force (FATF) established by the Heads of State or Government of seven major industrialized countries (Group of Seven) and the President of the Commission of the European Communities at the fifteenth annual economic summit held in Paris in June 1989, and of other international and regional organizations, in the fight against money-laundering activities. Conference participants noted that there was an urgent need to strengthen international and national efforts and to expand the scope and application of measures which had already proved useful, such as the FATF recommendations.[1] There was also a need to coordinate the provision of technical assistance to governments, enabling them to design and apply their own strategies and strengthen their appropriate mechanisms for the prevention and control of money-laundering. It was recognized that it was necessary to involve all the relevant sectoral organizations in this operation, including law enforcement, judicial, banking and financial communities.

**An Increasingly and Undeniably Global Problem**

The Conference detailed numerous manifestations of the increased internationalization of criminal activities and of the globalization of money-laundering. The geographic expansion of the activities of the most notable transnational criminal organizations were described with respect to the accumulation of proceeds not only from drug trafficking but also from all serious crimes for profit, national and transnational, as well as from other methods of serious economic distortion such as usury. The increased professionalism of their activities and sophistication of the schemes used to launder the proceeds of those crimes were described, with particular attention to the progressive separation of money-laundering as an independent criminal service.

Trends in money-laundering techniques were increasing in sophistication and complexity. Organized criminal groups were, *inter alia*:

(a) taking advantage of weaknesses in national regulatory schemes;
(b) resorting to flexible and rapid transfers and movement of assets across national boundaries;
(c) exploiting the diversity of business regulations within and between national systems, particularly by using multiple business vehicles in different countries to conceal the origin of funds, ownership and control;
(d) benefiting from the assistance of professional categories which were unregulated and from those which were regulated but did not carry out effective self-control on matters of legal and ethical violations.

These trends demonstrated the global nature of the phenomenon and the need for developing effective means to remove or at least to reduce the opportunities available to money-launderers.

**Trends Emerging from Global Recognition of Necessary Prevention and Control Policies**

The trends in criminal money-laundering activity were a consequence of both the increasing demand for money-laundering services and the counter-pressures exerted by anti-money-laundering responses. Those responses had two principal goals. The first goal was to increase the risk of law enforcement, that was the risk of apprehension for the individual criminal or criminal enterprise and the risk of seizure of criminal assets. The seizure risk furnished the more effective deterrent against organized criminality, which could easily manage the apprehension risk by simple overstaffing and other personnel management practices. The second goal was the defensive one of protecting the legitimate economy and financial system from, *inter alia*, unfair competition from low-cost criminal proceeds against legitimate capital on which taxes had been paid.

Measures which had been recognized as effectively increasing the law-enforcement risk were the criminalization of money-laundering operations, forfeiture operations, restriction of bank secrecy in money-laundering inquiries, use of evidence-gathering techniques appropriate to overcoming the secrecy and the consensual nature of money-laundering offences, such as undercover operations and electronic surveillance, and international cooperation mechanisms which permitted virtually immediate communication and action by all the authorities concerned without obstructive formality.

A parallel trend was the recognition that preventive/regulatory mechanisms were an equally essential element of anti-money-laundering policies to defend the transparency of economic/financial systems and simultaneously to produce a complementary effect with control policies. The preventive/regulatory mechanisms were those made familiar to all by the Basel Declaration[2] and the FATF recommendations; among others were the 'know your customer' rule, recording and record-keeping requirements, reporting of suspicious transactions, immunity/indemnity for bank representatives reporting suspicious transactions, application of preventive/regulatory policies to non-bank institutions and businesses and professions which offered financial services. In that regard, it was necessary to recognize that regulatory schemes did burden banks and other supervised institutions, which should not be made to bear a disproportionate share of the costs of cooperation against money-laundering.

## Gaps in the Anti-Money Laundering Net: What Needed to be Done

The discussion and background documents revealed the absence of an effective and comprehensive global anti-money-laundering net which needed to be established in order to prevent money-launderers from simply moving their activities from one country to another or from one financial sector to another to avoid regulatory and control efforts. The failure of some countries to establish their own protective nets simply frustrated the efforts of neighbouring countries that had done so. Many countries had little established governance or experience in regulating complex state-of-the-art financial operations, and few had effective relations with the private financial (banking and non-banking) sector to ensure the coordination or cooperation needed to identify suspected activities. Gaps in the money-laundering net were geographic with the principal prevention or control efforts concentrated in western Europe, North America, Australia and in the more developed countries of Asia. Other gaps were sectoral, i.e. non-bank financial institutions; businesses and professions which furnished financial services but were largely unregulated; and offshore business and financial institutions which were inadequately regulated. Yet other gaps related to failure to implement recognized anti-money-laundering measures, such as the United Nations Convention against Illicit Traffic in Narcotic Drugs and Psychotropic Substances of 1988,[3] or to enact the necessary implementing legislation, failure effectively to implement the 40 recommendations drawn up by FATF; failure to effectively enforce anti-money-laundering regulations and legislation, once enacted; and finally, failure to control professions engaged in financial activities. Legislation was only the first step in the process of bringing the problem under control, and it might well be easier to get legislation enacted than to enforce it effectively in many countries.

**Implementation Priorities**

The Conference strongly urged that it would be counter-productive for a global approach to the prevention and control of money-laundering to recommend anything less than the full implementation of the 1988 Convention (regardless of any liberalization), the Basel Declaration and the 40 FATF recommendations. The challenge was to build a social defence system with administrative and regulatory tools, designed to make it difficult for services to be used for criminal purposes, buttressed by criminal law. As a credible deterrent, criminal law would continue to play an essential role. Anti-money-laundering measures were to be seen as a part of a coherent and global crime policy which should give priority to the fight against serious crime, especially against organized crime, which had a corrosive effect on economy and society. Nevertheless, certain needs commanded a worldwide degree of recognition as to the urgency of their implementation. Those priorities are discussed below.

*Criminalization of the laundering of drug and non-drug criminal proceeds*

Criminalization of drug money-laundering offences was required for states party to the 1988 Convention. Expansion of criminalization to the laundering of the proceeds of other serious crimes was the trend, as evidenced by, *inter alia*, the Council of Europe Convention on the Proceeds from Crime, the political declaration by Commonwealth Heads of State and Governments and the domestic legislation of a number of countries with substantial experience in the field. Such criminalization would also solve problems of dual criminality encountered in international cooperation procedures.

## Limitation of bank secrecy

Limitation of financial secrecy was a *sine qua non* of serious money-laundering control and of sincere international cooperation.

## 'Know your customer' rule

Application of the 'know your customer' rule of the Basel Declaration and the FATF recommendations, particularly with respect to abolishing anonymous bearer accounts and identification of the real party in interests being represented by a nominee, should be another basic test of the effectiveness of a country's money-laundering prevention policies.

## Identification and reporting of suspicious transactions

Identification and reporting of suspicious transactions needed to be permitted and encouraged by legislation fully protecting representatives of financial institutions from any liability for good-faith reporting of suspicious transactions. The expansion of at least the reporting requirements to cover the proceeds of all serious crime was one of the effective steps to preventing a situation in which a financial institution may not report a clearly suspicious transaction without knowing precisely what crime resulted in those proceeds. When reporting was permitted, it seemed self-evident that notice of that report, or of an official inquiry about a transaction, should not be given to the client.

## Improved regulation of businesses or professionals conducting financial operations

Improved regulation or other preventive measures were being found to be necessary to prevent money-laundering activity being displaced from tightly supervised banks and financial institutions to non-supervised businesses and professions which offered financial services. Such measures could be requirements that all transactions of a certain type or magnitude be conducted through an authorized financial intermediary (termed 'channelization'), or could impose certain identification, recording and/or reporting requirements on the offerer of financial services, but they must avoid the consequence whereby money-laundering was simply displaced from supervised banks to a wholly unregulated informal financial sector. Moreover, certain professions which have traditionally been unregulated or self-regulating could not be assumed to act effectively in implementing a self-regulating mandate. Therefore, legislative standard-setting might be necessary. It was, moreover, necessary to fight what was termed 'reputation laundering', i.e. the process of acquiring respectability in a new environment. It should therefore be appropriate that the professional groups concerned promoted behavioural codes, including a range of disciplinary sanctions up to the exclusion of those members who brought disrepute to their own group, in order to safeguard the reliability of that profession. Moreover, it was clear that the launderer was aware of the various directives, recommendations and conventions requiring banks and financial institutions to follow current standard requirements of identification and reporting. The launderer was turning to other businesses which did not necessarily offer financial services.

The Conference therefore recommends that research and studies should be carried out to identify those businesses which may well serve the launderer and to determine the feasibility of extending the application of current reporting and other requirements to possible areas other than banking and financial institutions with the objective of preventing rather than simply attempting to prosecute money-laundering, with all the difficulties that the latter course of action implies.

*Asset forfeiture*

Increased asset forfeiture and the availability of provisional measures, such as freezing or seizing of assets, contributed to a universally developing trend which could profitably be broadened beyond drug proceeds, always with due respect for the procedural guarantees for property rights established by national law. Asset forfeiture must be possible also for the proceeds of crimes committed abroad.[4]

*Workable international cooperation mechanisms*

Formal regulatory procedures, furnishing bank documents only after years of litigation and a lack of necessary legal instruments or administrative structures were obstacles which invited criminals to practice international money-laundering and to capitalize on collective governmental inertia and deficiencies. A further priority for implementation should be a rapid and uncomplicated mechanism for international cooperation in common administrative and legal matters. Mutual legal assistance arrangements which allowed the collection of admissible evidence were essential. Without such arrangements, national governments would tend not to devote the needed investigative resources to international cases.

The Conference therefore recommends that international organizations or mechanisms should reinforce common strategies to combat money-laundering; that ways and means should be found for taking expeditious action in that sphere; and, in particular, that a consensus on the basic substantive elements of cross-border crimes and on legal norms regulating the procedure for mutual assistance between states in respect of such crimes should be sought and achieved in order to expedite the giving and receiving of such assistance in an area where speed is of the utmost importance.

## A Global Strategy for a Global Problem

Implementation of anti-money-laundering policies by legislation and regulation was a function of national sovereignty, and not every country would move spontaneously towards such implementation. When a country did not, the global nature of the money-laundering problem and the demonstrated need for a consistent global response suggested a three-level strategy. At the bilateral level those countries most adversely affected and those most able to cooperate with the non-implementing country should help it to achieve international minimum standards. Simultaneously, at the regional level, relevant organizations (broadly understood to include not only geographic but also political and cultural groupings such as the Commonwealth) should give such assistance and encouragement necessary to bring all of their members up to appropriate regional standards, which might even go beyond the 1988 Convention and the FATF recommendations, as have the European Community Money-Laundering Directive and the Council of Europe Convention on the Proceeds from Crime. At the international level, the appropriate organizations could contribute to the processes going on at the bilateral and regional levels. For the country which wished to do its part for the global protective network, assistance and encouragement should be available from friends and neighbours, from regional groupings and from the international community. Effective coordination was needed at the regional and international levels for strategies and efforts to promote relevant action at the national level and cooperation between countries.

The seven areas described above as requiring immediate implementation were predicated on some assumptions about the presence of certain international and national enforcement mechanisms. Key among them was the concept that a net or web operated at three complementary levels - international, regional and national - and that the national level might be further divided into penal, cultural and administrative mechanisms. Political support and adequate resources, *inter alia*, were said to be essential conditions for effective action at all three levels, and government and multilateral, regional and international institutions must allocate adequate means and facilities for dealing efficaciously to successfully regulate or control activities which enjoyed the benefit of a high level of sophistication and which might exploit a high volume of legitimate transactions to achieve concealment, as might be the case with wire-transfer technology.

Those assumptions were not necessarily valid in all cases. If not, a variety of modalities of technical assistance might be necessary at the national level: needs assessment; legislative assistance; infrastructure development assistance; personnel development; and training in all relevant sectors, including national and interstate cooperation; comprehensive strategies for all involved government agencies, inter-agency coordination and functional cooperation; and transfer and sharing of technology, development and research.

At the international level, at least, the following modalities might be necessary: needs assessment; treaty development in extradition and mutual assistance matters; compatibility of treaty schemes and procedures; enhancing cooperation and information sharing, not only at the judicial level but also among regulators and law enforcement agencies; the same type of management rationalization of overlapping organizations at the level of regional and international organizations; and continuing applied research on the incentives and disincentives needed both to promote cooperation by the private sector with governments, and to consolidate coordination and cooperation between governments.

The overriding principle would be to establish effective operational mechanisms so that no person could place himself or herself above the law, and every person would be protected by the obligations of international, regional and domestic law for the protection of fundamental human rights.

### NOTES

1. In relation to this and all further references to the FATF recommendations, the delegation of China reserved its position on their acceptability.
2. See Statement of Principles of the Basel Committee on Banking Regulations and Supervisory Practices.
3. E/CONF.82/15 and Corr.2.
4. The delegation of Japan, in a letter addressed to the organizers of the Conference, expressed its reservation with respect to paragraph 21 because of insufficient time to study the text.

# Report of the Secretary-General

## Implementation of General Assembly Resolution 49/150 on the Naples Political Declaration and Global Action Plan against Organized Transnational Crime

**Action Taken Against Organized Transnational Crime: A Global Priority**

The 142 states present at the World Ministerial Conference on Organized Crime proclaimed their political will and strong determination, as well as their unequivocal commitment, to ensure the full and expeditious implementation of the Political Declaration and Global Action Plan, reflecting the urgency and priority attention attached to action against organized transnational crime. The Naples Conference was not the only forum in which the collective concern of states had been expressed, but was the culmination of efforts at the international level. The growth of organized transnational crime and its expansion both in terms of activities and across geographical borders brought about the realization that action against it could not be limited to the national level or to arrangements between a limited number of states. Efforts had to take into account the current political situation and the ease with which organized criminal groups crossed borders and took advantage of efforts designed to bring countries closer together and increase the free movement of goods, capital, services and people. Such efforts also had to be made in a manner tailored to the fact that organized transnational crime was making full use of modern technologies, thus increasing its sophistication and diversity and outpacing the capacity of many countries to deal with it. In their search for new opportunities and markets, organized criminal groups were ready to make sizeable investments in both equipment and human resources and were willing to bring their huge financial power to bear, in addition to using other more violent methods, for eliminating competition. In addition, the international community had realized that proceeds of crime directed at the legitimate economy posed a grave threat to financial stability and growth. The prospect of organized criminal groups infiltrating and attaining controlling interests in crucial sectors of the economies of developing countries and countries in transition had contributed to raising awareness and increasing concern among governments, particularly at a time of joint efforts towards economic restructuring on the basis of free market principles.

It was against this background that world leaders began placing concerted action against organized transnational crime high on their agenda. The seven major industrialized countries, at their summit meeting held at Naples in July 1994, gave special consideration to the response of the international community against organized transnational crime and money-laundering. In their summit communiqué, the Heads of State and Government of the seven major industrialized countries and the President of the European Commission expressed alarm about the growth of organized transnational crime and the use of illicit proceeds to take control of legitimate business. This was a world-wide problem, with countries in transition being increasingly targeted by criminal organizations. They also expressed their determination to strengthen international cooperation to address the situation and welcomed the World Ministerial Conference on Organized Transnational Crime, to be held at Naples. In the Chairman's statement, the Heads of State and Government of the Group of Seven stressed that organized crime and narcotics trafficking were a threat to political as well as economic and social life. Calling for increased international cooperation, they agreed that the World Ministerial Conference was a most important occasion to advance such cooperation.

At the United Nations fiftieth Anniversary Ceremony, held at San Francisco on 26 June 1995, the President of the United States of America called for agreement among the international community on a new agenda for the United Nations, to increase confidence and ensure support for the United Nations and to advance peace and prosperity for the next 50 years. In identifying the areas to which more attention should be paid on the part of the United Nations, President Clinton called for 'support through the United Nations for the fight against man-made and natural forces of disintegration, from crime syndicates and drug cartels to new diseases and disappearing forests. They cross borders at will. Nations can and must oppose them alone, but we know, and the Cairo Conference reaffirmed, that the most effective opposition requires strong international cooperation and mutual support'.

In the Chairman's statement of the summit meeting, held at Halifax in 1995, the Group of Seven declared that 'transnational criminal organizations are a growing threat to the security of our nations. They undermine the integrity of financial systems, breed corruption, and weaken emerging democracies and developing countries around the world. To counter their criminal activities effectively, we will work to reinforce existing institutions, strengthen our cooperation, exchange of information, and assistance to other nations'. The Heads of State and Government of the Group of Seven agreed to cooperate more closely together, and with others, to ensure that transnational criminal organizations cannot escape justice by crossing borders. They encouraged all governments to adhere to and implement relevant international conventions and the recommendations of the Financial Action Task Force. They recognized that ultimate success required all governments to provide for effective measures to prevent the laundering of proceeds from drug trafficking and other serious crimes. To implement their commitments in the fight against transnational organized crime, they established a group of senior experts, with a temporary mandate to look at existing arrangements for cooperation, both bilateral and multilateral, to identify significant gaps and options for improved coordination and to propose practical action to fill such gaps.

In the Naples Political Declaration and Global Action Plan, states proclaimed their determination to join forces and fight together against the expansion and diversification of organized transnational crime. Notwithstanding recent successes, they expressed their conviction that coordinated strategies and other forms of international cooperation should be further developed. States noted with concern that organized transnational crime threatened the social and economic growth of developing countries and countries in transition and their institutions; stressed that the international community should assist these countries in their efforts to enable their criminal justice institutions to adequately prevent and combat organized transnational crime; and observed that the fight against organized transnational crime should be accorded high priority by states and by all relevant global and regional organizations, with the necessary support of the general public, the media, business, institutions and non-governmental organizations. States arrived at these conclusions and proclaimed their determination to take the action specified in the Naples Political Declaration and Global Action Plan, while reaffirming the responsibility vested in the United Nations in crime prevention and criminal justice and recognizing the need to strengthen its role in the development of a comprehensive programme of action to prevent and control organized transnational crime.

The Naples Political Declaration and Global Action Plan was made possible by, but also attests to, a collective political will to deal with the problem at the global level and a consensus as to what needs to be done. This consensus is the result and culmination not only of the realization of the global effects of the problem, but also of a long process of convergence and balancing of national interests and perceptions, as well as the full recognition of varying needs and capacities. In the past, organized crime was considered one of the problems facing developed countries and, therefore, of little interest to developing countries which had other priorities and other more pressing needs. When organized crime began crossing borders and becoming a menace and a threat to developing countries, the scope of the problem was fundamentally altered. The changes in the political environment with the emergence of newly independent states, which entered a phase of economic and political transition, were soon perceived by organized criminal groups as increased opportunities for expansion and diversification, and added a new dimension to the issue. The interest and concern of developing countries and countries in transition grew and the issue of organized transnational crime became one of their priorities, also because its effects made it more difficult to pursue other standing development priorities.

A new situation was created for developed countries as well. Whereas in the not-too-distant past action against organized crime was to be planned and taken largely within their borders, or in cooperation with other countries of similar capacities and perceptions, increased transnationalization and expansion brought about imponderables as to activities of organized criminal groups, and difficulties with regard to effective law enforcement and judicial cooperation. The new dimensions of organized transnational crime require more resources not only for the expansion of cooperative arrangements, but also for new law enforcement techniques and capabilities. However, while developed countries already possess the infrastructure and crucial knowledge required in mustering the necessary resources and maximizing their efficiency and effectiveness, developing countries and countries in transition are in the very difficult position of easily being outpaced by organized criminal groups. Countering the onslaught of organized transnational crime requires diversion of scarce resources, delaying or even threatening the attainment of other objectives and development targets. In addition, developing countries and countries in transition are increasingly finding themselves in a quandary. Their drive towards development and growth in accordance with free market principles is under threat from the direct or indirect effects of organized transnational crime, while the limited effectiveness of their efforts, owing to the lack of the necessary resources, is often cited as a disincentive to the very much needed foreign investment and assistance.

The consensus and collective political will evidenced by the Naples Political Declaration and Global Action Plan, as well as the results of the other events mentioned above, are of great significance to future action by the international community against organized transnational crime. Of equal importance is the momentum built by the consistency and frequency with which the consensus and collective political will have been enunciated in the past two years. Such momentum and consensus are prerequisites for action to take a definitive shape and to have the desired effects in the shortest time possible, an element of importance in view of the rapid growth and expansion of organized transnational crime. The international community should begin taking decisive steps forward in the implementation of the policies and measures it decided upon in the Naples Political Declaration and Global Action Plan, building on but also sustaining this momentum.

Action against organized transnational crime would be more effective if it were collective, with its planning and implementation being the patrimony of all contributors to the consensus-building process and to the formulation of a strong collective political will. In the Naples Political Declaration and Global Action Plan, states recognized, while acknowledging its global implications, that prevention and control of organized transnational crime must necessarily vary from state to state and region to region and be based upon improvements in national capabilities, increased knowledge and shared experiences about organized criminal groups. Such variations at the national or regional levels are natural given the different manifestations and degrees of development of organized criminal groups and their activities. Further, differences in the degree of development of institutions and the financial capabilities of countries are bound to affect the responses to the problem. In situations of scarcity of funds and numerous competing priorities, the size and present effects of the problem of organized transnational crime are bound to guide the decisions of policy makers on the allocation of resources.

In addition to its recognized global implications, however, organized transnational crime has displayed the capacity to shift operations across borders, in order to minimize risk and maximize opportunities, and to take full advantage of gaps in national responses and of deficiencies in international cooperation. Further, organized transnational crime has shown the ability and readiness to benefit from economic growth and efforts towards economic reform and privatization in developing countries and countries in transition, mainly because of the variations in pace between such processes and the creation or strengthening of the appropriate institutions.

Consequently, current parameters may change too rapidly for existing mechanisms to respond adequately. In such a case, any opportunity for preventive action may be lost and control may become extremely difficult, placing limited resources and immature institutions under even more severe strain. It is, therefore, crucial to retain a global view and a long-term perspective in developing national policies and regional cooperation mechanisms against organized transnational crime. In addition, there needs to be a common denominator against which action can be measured, in order to ensure continuity and consistency, as well as the sustained pursuit of common objectives.

The significance of the Naples Political Declaration and Global Action Plan, viewed in the context of the initiatives that have been taken since their adoption, lies in having demonstrated that the international community has reached agreement on a basic set of common objectives and on the fundamental elements of the modalities required to attain them. Considerably more work is necessary, however, to operationalize this basic agreement by way of consistent and coordinated implementation. This agreement appears to be founded on the understanding that the problem is equally threatening for all countries of the world, and that those countries having difficulties in bringing their relevant mechanisms up to the required standard for effective action in preventing and controlling its effects will be assisted by those in a position to do so. In the face of a problem as pervasive and dangerous as organized transnational crime, however, a sense of anxiety about minimizing its impact at the national level often tends to prevail. This tendency becomes even more prevalent when considering some of the activities in which organized transnational crime is engaged, which involve violence and, consequently, capture the attention of the public through the media coverage that they receive. Further, governments are alarmed by the increasing involvement of organized transnational crime in legitimate business, coupled with the need of organized criminal groups to find ways of laundering their illicit proceeds.

One of the characteristics of this sense of anxiety is the tendency to disregard the benefits of building and sustaining consensus, and to rely on individual capacities in order to proceed forward at a presumably faster pace. Action taken in this context can be similar to action often taken at the regional level, in terms of homogeneity of perceptions, priorities, needs and immediate objectives, as well as relevant equivalency of the capacity of infrastructures. In the short term, the effectiveness of such action may be evident and may satisfy the urgency for measurable and visible results. In the case of organized transnational crime, however, the global nature of the problem ultimately demands a global approach and global solutions. Regional initiatives have been instrumental in meeting immediate needs and paving the way for global approaches on many issues. Such initiatives are, after all, based on the very same principles and the consensus which should characterize global action and can make it effective. In the regional context, however, consensus-building may be more easily attainable and sustainable, because of the reasons mentioned above.

Action taken in response to a sense of impatience with the global consensus-building process may appear to be breaking new ground and setting high standards of accomplishment. In this context, efforts to plan and implement such action may be useful in pointing to the ideal fashion of attaining the maximum objectives in the shortest time possible, thus serving as a guide and a yardstick by which to measure success. However, action proceeding at varying speeds may result in widening gaps instead of closing them and altogether eliminating them, particularly considering the flexibility and capacity for diversification of organized transnational crime. Differences in opinion and perspectives may present the risk of trivializing the matter and entangling it in long debates, ultimately slowing down the desired pace, if not placing the effectiveness of the action *per se* in jeopardy. While peer pressure in the context of an institutional framework is invaluable, the risk of misperceptions as to ultimate objectives and the ways to achieve them may be too great in view of the implications of organized transnational crime and the threat it poses to developed and developing countries alike.

Effective action at the global level would need to move forward at the same pace, the speed of which would need to be collectively agreed upon. Only in such a case can there be the commitment to meet goals and attain common objectives. In view of the divergent situations in which different countries are found, particularly in terms of capacity and infrastructure, this pace may not be as brisk as the international community would wish. There would be a need for a mechanism to identify in the shortest time possible cases in which there is a slow-down and attempt to rectify the situation by providing the appropriate technical assistance. When action is the result of consensus and collective commitment, the effectiveness of technical assistance would be greatly enhanced, since the objectives and modalities of such assistance would be the product of consent and overall agreement.

The effectiveness of global action against organized transnational crime would also depend on how well coordinated it is, particularly since such action is bound to involve technical cooperation. Coordination would ensure more efficient use of resources and would greatly enhance the impact of technical assistance, not only by directing it to those areas where it is most needed, but also by establishing and maintaining a constant relationship between the needs to be met and contributions towards common objectives and goals. Coordination, which should be viewed as an integral part of effective action, requires a constant flow of reliable information, the willingness of all parties concerned to rely on and contribute to the availability of such information, and the readiness in particular of donor countries and agencies to channel resources towards meeting needs as they arise.

## Implementation of the Naples Political Declaration and Global Action Plan Against Organized Transnational Crime: Programmatic Aspects and Modalities

Full implementation of the Naples Political Declaration and Global Action Plan will require considerable effort and investment on the part of states and the United Nations, as well as relevant intergovernmental and non-governmental organizations. In order to maximize the effect of appropriate action by the Commission on Crime Prevention and Criminal Justice, and also to assist states in directing their efforts and resources towards implementation more efficiently, it may be useful to chart a course by identifying areas on which attention should be concentrated and where the United Nations can make a useful contribution through planning and implementing operational activities.

At a time of limited resources, implementation would need to proceed in phases, which would be agreed upon by the international community. The foundation of this phased approach would need to be a sustained and concerted effort to maintain the momentum and increase the impetus created by the Naples Political Declaration and Global Action Plan and to further strengthen the consensus and political will that made them possible. In charting the course for full implementation, certain key factors would need to be kept in mind. The threat posed to the internal security and stability of sovereign states, as well as to international security, by the dramatic increase of organized transnational crime in the past decade is growing and will continue to grow and become more menacing if concerted and decisive action on the part of the international community is delayed. While energies have to be focused and action planned in the best and most efficient manner, the ultimate goals of effectively preventing and controlling organized transnational crime in all its forms and dimensions, and arresting its expansion at both the national and international levels, should be guiding the relevant efforts and should constitute the yardstick against which success is to be assessed.

Pursuant to the mandate entrusted to it by the General Assembly in resolution 49/159, the Commission on Crime Prevention and Criminal

Justice began moving in the direction of charting the course towards implementation at its fourth session. In Economic and Social Council resolution 1995/11, adopted on the recommendation of the Commission, certain areas of priority attention were identified. In addition to examining the opportunity and impact of international instruments such as a convention or conventions against organized transnational crime, and an indication of the issues and elements to be covered therein, priority attention was given to improving reliable knowledge on the structure and dynamics of organized transnational crime, legislative and regulatory measures, and technical cooperation.

*Strengthening international cooperation and the opportunity of a convention or conventions against organized transnational crime*

The new responsibilities that governments have to take on because of the escalation of organized transnational crime and the demand for global strategies to combat it, draw attention to the need for effective instruments, bearing in mind that what is most needed is a comprehensive, multi-layered approach to international cooperation in law enforcement and criminal justice in the fight against organized transnational crime. Ideally, a truly effective international approach would be composed of a web of bilateral, regional and multilateral arrangements complementing and promoting one another. In fact, bilateral and multilateral forms of cooperation are complementary rather than mutually exclusive. However, whether international cooperation can evolve in ways that allow a response to transnational criminal organizations commensurate with the threat depends on the capacity of states to understand that criminal justice and law enforcement systems can no longer be viewed as purely national concerns. Ultimately, the prospects of cooperation depend on recognizing that a new kind of threat demands a new kind of response, in which international cooperation plays a central role. Experience has shown the importance of adopting international instruments in order to enact global strategies of action when dealing with issues of a transnational nature. A very successful example is found in the United Nations Convention against Illicit Trafficking in Narcotic Drugs and Psychotropic Substances of 1988.

One of the major objectives of international cooperation must be to create greater harmonization in criminal justice systems, by improving the standards of countries with weaker criminal justice systems in general or by developing national legislation specifically directed against organized crime. It is crucial to eliminate 'sanctuary states' and ensure that national legislation against transnational organized crime is as compatible as possible. Complete harmonization is, of course, impossible, for some of the reasons identified above. Yet there is a level of harmonization, perhaps better described as inter-operability, that allows for continued national differences while still achieving the necessary degree of complementarity for effective concerted action against transnational crime. It has been emphasized that 'investigation of transnational crime, no less than its prosecution, will likewise involve multiple jurisdictions and cooperation among different governments. To be useful, the products of these investigations should be as nearly interchangeable as possible. Procedures need not necessarily be identical but they should incorporate rules to protect the accused, limit police power, ensure equitable tribunals and provide decent prisons'. Growing interchangeability and the capacity to use information and evidence across national jurisdictions are of major importance in the fight against transnational crime.

Multilateral cooperation should not be seen simply as a compromise between various bilateral efforts. Rather, it is something that has significant benefits in its own right, as many regional arrangements have demonstrated. They can be understood as the criminal justice counterpart to the growth of economic and political integration in many regions of the world, such as in western Europe. Regional cooperation in judicial and criminal matters is the natural concomitant to efforts to achieve political and economic union, even though it involves some of the more sensitive and complex aspects of national sovereignty. In this sense, multilateral cooperation can be understood as a spin-off from broader political and economic processes, which are proceeding with increasing frequency and speed - albeit based on the recognition that complete uniformity of national legislation is neither feasible nor desirable. As has been observed, 'the criminal law systems are all finely tuned to the specific characteristics of the different countries. This delicate equilibrium should not be disturbed, unless a substantial advantage is to be gained'.[1]

To be sure, the elaboration of an international instrument such as a convention is not obstacle-free. While a multilateral convention would provide a way of augmenting resources and mobilizing mutual support and assistance for what individual states are unable to do alone, it should be stressed that multilateral responses can only work if each party makes sacrifices commensurate with those of others. Avoiding this kind of obstacle requires a commitment to take whatever action is necessary despite the cost. If a convention is to be effective, it needs states to join and subsequently to exhibit the will and capability to meet their obligations under it. As has been noted: 'Only if most countries were willing to re-examine some deeply entrenched legal procedures, and to recognize that their own traditional way of doing things was not necessarily the best or most effective approach to the problems in question, would the concepts of multilateral ... conventions become a reality'.[2]

One of the difficulties with such a new instrument may be its content. Similar conventions on terrorism and drug trafficking have been oriented towards a specific type of crime. The question arises, therefore, whether a new international instrument on organized transnational crime should cover the many criminal activities in which organized criminal groups are engaging, or should focus on the way in which countries should respond to the threat posed by transnational criminal organizations. The problem with concentrating on the crimes is that they are so extensive - and it is difficult to be all embracing. The implication is that attention should be focused on the second aspect, that is the responsibility of governments to respond vigorously to the challenge, building upon the experience developed in the process of elaboration, ratification and implementation of the 1988 Vienna Convention and starting from the already existing proposals on legislation and law enforcement methods covered in the Convention itself. The extent of international support for the Vienna Convention is extraordinary: more than 100 states are parties to it. That Convention, thanks to the commitment and political will of such a large number of countries, has had a major impact in bringing about concerted action against drug trafficking.

Another difficulty lies in the fact that the elaboration of international conventions may be a long process that would require the achievement and maintenance of consensus at every stage. Breadth of participation should not be achieved at the expense of depth and intensity of cooperation. However, in the presence of a strong political will and broad consensus, as evidenced by the priority attached to action against organized transnational crime and the Naples Political Declaration and Global Action Plan, it would be possible to ensure that the negotiation process does not result in a diluted document that falls short of establishing the provisions necessary for an effective response to transnational criminal organizations. Effective action against organized transnational crime requires a framework within which states could pursue cooperation at all levels in a more systematic and effective way. Such a framework would make it possible to bridge the gaps that exist at present and are readily and fully exploited by organized transnational crime. For example, the Vienna Convention has given rise to a wave of legislative activity at the national level, supported by the legal assistance program of the United Nations International Drug Control Program, as well as to the adoption of numerous bilateral and regional agreements that implement and further the Convention's provisions.

In spite of its difficulties, the elaboration of an international convention against organized transnational crime could bring a number of advantages and may represent an invaluable potential for universal adherence. First, the very act of negotiating a convention would have certain benefits. For example, it would focus attention on the problem. Although specific criminal organizations have been given considerable attention, the emergence and expansion of transnational criminal organizations as a generic threat posing problems in many respects exceeding those of international terrorism has been relatively ignored. Indeed, there has been a paucity of both journalistic and scholarly analyses dealing with transnational criminal organizations and their activities as a problem faced not only by individual states but also by the international community as a whole. A convention on organized transnational crime would be very important in symbolic terms, as it would represent the collective judgement of the international community that the problem has become sufficiently serious to command a global response. This could also have an important impact in terms of legitimizing national actions, including national legislation against the activities of organized transnational crime. In addition, the negotiation of a convention would lead to greater interaction among governments and particular national agencies in ways that would themselves lead to enhanced international cooperation. Developing a knowledge of other negotiators can be important, particularly if these negotiators also have some role in the subsequent implementation of policy.

Secondly, once a convention was in place, it would have several positive effects:

(a) it would provide a set of standards and expectations that the signatories would have an obligation to live up to; in a sense it would facilitate the exertion of peer pressure as a common effort of the international community in addressing the problem;

(b) it would have an important regularizing effect and provide for a more standardized form of cooperation than does the extension of bilateral accords, each of which has its own distinctive features;

(c) it would facilitate more systematic assistance in the areas of criminal justice and law enforcement, rather than *ad hoc* approaches

(d) it would provide guidance for a program of implementation that would assist in the dual objectives of harmonizing law enforcement risk and making it more difficult for transnational criminal organizations to infiltrate legitimate business.

It is evident that there are both advantages and disadvantages to a multilateral convention against organized transnational crime. The issue is not clear-cut. If governments do decide that the advantages outweigh the disadvantages, however, there are several other requirements that would have to be met to transform it from a theoretical possibility into a feasible and practical proposition. First, it would necessitate the maintenance of the broad-based consensus on the seriousness of the challenge posed to nations and the international community by organized transnational crime. The key to maintaining and further broadening this consensus is for governments that are affected by organized transnational crime to recognize that they are not alone, and for governments that are not currently the target of organized transnational criminal activity to understand that they are not immune, and that it may only be a matter of time before the problem impinges on them directly. Secondly, another crucial requirement is that the idea of elaborating a convention should have the unequivocal backing of most states. The more diverse this group of states is, the better, on the understanding that a convention should not be seen as an attempt by any particular grouping to impose required reforms of behaviour on others with different levels of economic development or cultural traditions. The willingness of several highly committed states to give a high priority to successful implementation could create a bandwagon effect, encouraging others to join. A third requirement is that there should be a clear idea of the purpose and scope of a convention. It has to be carefully formulated in ways that specify the target (transnational criminal organizations and their members), the obligations that states would incur (in terms of taking initiatives in their own national law, in positively responding to requests for assistance from others and in providing and exchanging information) and provisions for implementation (both procedural and substantive).

*Increasing reliable knowledge*

Any discussion of international cooperation will necessarily involve a clear understanding of priorities and objectives. International cooperation on a particular issue, such as the ability of criminal justice systems to prevent and control organized crime, implies a thorough knowledge of the risks involved in both the short and long term. In addition, it requires an accurate assessment of the capacity of the criminal justice system to deal with complex forms of crime. A combination of these parameters, with the appropriate balance, would serve to put international cooperation into perspective. Only knowledge and careful evaluation can lead to the appropriate selection of priorities and objectives. Policy makers at the national level, those ultimately capable of and responsible for building, sustaining and advancing international cooperation, as well as setting its pace, need this knowledge to guide them towards rational decisions. Policy makers also have to be able to strike the appropriate balance between competing interests, both political and financial. Balancing the multiple interests competing for resources is difficult for every government, regardless of its level of development. International cooperation requires undivided attention and genuine commitment at all levels of government for the pooling and allocation of resources commensurate to the risk posed to the international community by organized transnational crime.

The tools available to governments are often found to be unequal to the task of effectively combating the new transnational manifestations of criminality and it is therefore through their attacks on traditional principles and sovereignty that organized criminals have succeeded in carrying out their illicit operations at a considerably lower risk to themselves. If criminal organizations are attracted to the process of internationalization because they have found areas in which the risk from law enforcement authorities is minimal, then coordinated international action to equalize this risk in various countries will minimize or contain the process. Equalizing the risk means raising the quantity, quality and, more importantly, compatibility of preventive and control action at an adequate level on a world-wide scale and putting in place mechanisms designed to maintain and improve that level in a consistent and coordinated fashion.

The capacity of states to prevent and control organized transnational crime depends largely on knowledge and the availability of reliable information about its characteristics, the structures of organized criminal groups, their methods of operation and their interests with respect to illicit activities. In many developed countries, the occurrence and growth of organized crime has led to considerable high-quality work with respect to accumulating knowledge and collecting reliable information. In spite of these advances, the task facing law enforcement agencies and the criminal justice system in general remains an arduous one, because of the increased diversification and expansion of organized crime across borders, as well as its tendency to become involved in activities characterized by high complexity. In most developing countries and countries in transition, however, various factors, ranging from lack of adequate resources to recent rapid political and economic developments and changes, have slowed down or inhibited the process of attaining a thorough understanding of the situation. Further, there are considerable difficulties in evaluating the threat posed by organized transnational crime and the capacity of law enforcement and criminal justice systems to respond to it. Compounding these difficulties are changes in the characteristics of organized transnational crime and an almost dramatic increase in the sophistication of its operations, as well as its mounting expansion in response to increased opportunities and weaknesses of national institutions.

The Naples Political Declaration and Global Action Plan emphasized the importance of adopting a generally agreed concept of organized crime as a basis for more compatible national responses and more effective international cooperation. In the absence of the comprehensive knowledge about organized crime referred to above, arriving at such a common concept may entail increased difficulties. Consequently, the full potential of international cooperation would be rather difficult to realize, leaving room for loopholes that have been, and continue to be, exploited by organized transnational crime. The lack of a common concept of organized crime can create considerable obstacles to the efforts of national law enforcement and judicial authorities to detect, prosecute and adjudicate cases of organized crime. One of the key areas affected would be the exchange and sharing of information and intelligence that is vital to these efforts. In many cases, even where bilateral or multilateral cooperation arrangements exist, there appears to be a lack of open channels of communication and information exchange between governments and between the competent national authorities. A reason often cited is the lack of understanding of a country's legal system and of the capacity of law enforcement and judicial authorities to produce the best possible results with the relevant information. Such concerns, which may also include apprehensions regarding the security of information or intelligence, have been known to hamper major investigations and cause long delays in judicial proceedings, sometimes resulting in the virtual impunity of the individuals apprehended, at a high financial and human cost.

The need to improve knowledge on organized crime and its transnational dimensions and activities has become more urgent at present, mainly because of the increased realization of its effects on national and international financial systems, as well as on institutions and society at large. There are two levels of knowledge required, which need to coexist and be developed concurrently.

The accumulation of theoretical knowledge has irreplaceable value for the purposes of educating younger generations and the public in general and for devising strategies and developing measures to counter the corrupting effects of organized crime on societal values. Theoretical knowledge, however, cannot substitute for the practical, operational knowledge that needs to be imparted to law enforcement and judicial personnel to enable them to prevent and control organized transnational crime at all levels. Each type of knowledge will stand to benefit greatly from the other, and a balanced development of both will go a long way towards achieving effective action against organized transnational crime. Academic institutions and professional associations have a major role to play in accumulating theoretical knowledge on organized transnational crime and in disseminating this knowledge, in close cooperation with governmental agencies and the education system, as well as in concert with the media, non-governmental organizations and the private sector.

The development of operational knowledge requires the capacity to process and evaluate information and intelligence derived from day-to-day operations and investigations, and from the experience of other countries in the field. While research is a major component of theoretical knowledge, experience and expertise acquired in field work form the basis of practical knowledge. Another essential element of practical knowledge is the ability of law enforcement and judicial personnel to evaluate the information collected and processed and the intelligence accumulated. This is particularly important in connection with the detection, investigation and adjudication of economic crimes and other illicit activities of organized criminal groups involving financial operations and business transactions.

The capacity to collect, process and evaluate information and intelligence not only at the national level, but also across borders, requires careful planning and consistent implementation of relevant strategies and policies, as well as emphasis on human resources development. In addition, the use of, and reliance on, modern telecommunications and data-processing equipment is of considerable importance, in view of their increasing utilization by organized transnational crime. Therefore, the accumulation of practical knowledge requires, in addition to commitment and determination, major and long-term investments by governments, often not only at the operational level but also at the institutional level.

For the purpose of the acquisition and dissemination of theoretical knowledge, academic institutions, professional associations and the media should be actively and tangibly encouraged and supported, and programmes should be put in place to enlist the involvement and participation of the private sector and non-governmental organizations. Comparative studies between practices and experiences in different countries would contribute to the accumulation of both types of knowledge, while the capacity to exchange and use information and intelligence would strengthen international cooperation and render action against organized transnational crime more effective.

In an effort to begin collecting information to facilitate the process of accumulating knowledge, the Crime Prevention and Criminal Justice Branch included the issue of transnational crime for the first time in the

Fourth United Nations Survey of Crime Trends and Operations of Criminal Justice Systems. The preliminary results of the Survey were submitted to the Ninth United Nations Congress on the Prevention of Crime and the Treatment of Offenders, and were made available to the Commission on Crime Prevention and Criminal Justice at its fourth session.[3]

One of the conclusions that can be drawn from the replies provided by governments is that there are considerable difficulties in many parts of the world in actually identifying activities that have a predominantly transnational character and in which organized criminal groups are engaged. While the potential effects of these activities are appreciated and there are indications of measures being devised to begin coming to terms with the problems created, in many cases there appears to be a lack of the necessary analysis that would focus on the specific characteristics of organized crime and the transnational dimensions of its activities. Consequently, there is a delay in legislative and regulatory action which, drawing on the results of such analysis, would prevent and control the further expansion and diversification of organized transnational crime, and promote more effective international cooperation.

Developed countries are generally in a position to devote the necessary resources for acquiring the body of both theoretical and practical knowledge that is required for the effective prevention and control of organized transnational crime and, as discussed earlier, considerable efforts in that direction are in progress.

However, the difficulties encountered by developing countries and countries with economies in transition make assistance crucial. The United Nations should be in a position to assist countries, through the provision of advisory services and training, in developing the means and techniques of gathering, processing and evaluating information and intelligence on the operations of organized transnational crime, on its methods and interests, as well as on the ways of laundering and using the proceeds of its activities. In collecting and processing information, emphasis should be placed on the expansion of organized crime across borders and on its increased levels of diversification and sophistication, which are elements that require particular attention since they differentiate this form of crime from other criminal activity. The accumulation of practical knowledge would largely depend on the studies that could be carried out at the national level, as well as on the comparative studies that could be carried out at the regional and international levels on the basis of reliable information.

In accordance with the Naples Political Declaration and Global Action Plan, the United Nations was mandated to assist states in the specific actions required for the increase and improvement of knowledge on organized transnational crime and its dynamics. Provision of the information and materials requested by the Secretary-General pursuant to Economic and Social Council resolution 1995/11 would permit the undertaking of a comprehensive and comparative study of the situation in the various regions of the world, thus contributing to the achievement of the goal of improving reliable knowledge on organized transnational crime, its structure and dynamics. According to the above-mentioned Council resolution, the collection and analysis of information should be carried out drawing on the contribution of states, which could include teamwork by highly qualified experts. This contribution would be invaluable, particularly given the need to take into account and build on work already done in this area, and considering the limited resources available to the United Nations crime prevention and criminal justice programme. The assistance of highly qualified experts, placed at the disposal of the Secretary-General by states and relevant international organizations, would greatly enhance the value, both scientific and practical, of the analysis and facilitate the work required for the necessary comparative study.

Through a global assessment of the transnational organized crime situation, the study would seek to contribute to a better understanding of the problems arising from differences that exist or emerge among various countries in the perception and evaluation of organized transnational crime, thus leading to the gradual development of a common perception of the phenomenon, and a global strategy for more effective international cooperation. The study should draw on national experiences, assisting, in the process, individual countries that lack the relevant capacity to identify the problem and begin collecting and processing reliable information. It should include an examination of specific types of criminality that are considered particularly dangerous or alarming and an examination of the problems arising from the expansion or reallocation of transnational criminal organizations to countries where defence mechanisms are weak. It should also consider conditions that are conducive to the rise and growth of criminal organizations, such as social, economic and political factors, structural characteristics of organized crime, as well as organizational shortcomings in the control agencies. It should include an analysis of the problems related to the different degrees of development of laws and regulations in individual countries, as well as an analysis of the activities and methods of operation of transnational criminal organizations. The results of the study would also be used for the development of special programmes, courses and curriculums for academic institutions, to ensure that theoretical knowledge is increased, improved and disseminated, and to create the basis for long-term and consistent action against organized transnational crime.

## Assistance in the legislative and regulatory fields

Legislation, both substantive and procedural, occupies a prominent place among policies to combat organized transnational crime. It remains one of the primary tools at the disposal of governments for the purpose of protecting the values and security of their societies and fostering growth and development. Legislation, however, needs to be dynamic and to adapt itself to, if not to foresee, developments. In the case of organized transnational crime, legislation should be developed with a view to fostering international cooperation and concerted action. Legislation should be structured and elaborated in such a way as to deal severe blows to organized crime groups at points where they would be most effective.

The Naples Political Declaration and Global Action Plan recognized the great importance of adequate legislative and regulatory measures for the prevention and control of organized transnational crime. In particular, it was recommended that states examine the experience of countries that have confronted organized crime and the intelligence derived from the analysis of its structures and criminal activities, as useful guiding principles concerning which substantive, procedural and regulatory legislation and organizational structures are necessary to combat the phenomenon. In addition, the regulatory measures recommended in the Naples Political Declaration and Global Action Plan with respect to money laundering and the proceeds of crime, and other law mechanisms to reinforce transparency and integrity in business and government, should be considered preventive measures of equal importance with penal law means of combating organized crime. It should be mentioned that attention was also paid to the possible need for substantive legislation that would address participation in criminal organizations or conspiracies, and imposing criminal liability on corporate bodies, as a means of strengthening capabilities to combat organized crime domestically and improve cooperation internationally.

As mentioned above, legislative and regulatory measures for the prevention and control of organized transnational crime are still lacking in a number of countries, in spite of the willingness to effectively address this form of crime. In the absence of specialized theoretical and practical knowledge, and in view of the difficulties faced in obtaining such knowledge, as well as the results of the experience accumulated in other countries, the elaboration of strategies and their implementation through legislative and regulatory measures are daunting tasks for many countries, particularly developing countries and those with economies in transition.

The Naples Political Declaration and Global Action Plan expressed the wish to strengthen and enhance the capability of states, as well as the United

Nations and other relevant global and regional organizations, to achieve more effective international cooperation against organized transnational crime, in relation, *inter alia*, to closer alignment of legislative texts concerning organized crime. In fact, divergences in legislative and regulatory measures have often been cited as among the principal difficulties encountered in bilateral and multilateral cooperation.

Governments may need to consider reviewing their criminal policies from both the substantive and the procedural perspective. From the substantive point of view, attention should be paid to the criminalization of certain forms of behaviour. The experience gained in the countries where organized crime is criminalized by comprehensive and appropriate legislation should encourage the elaboration and adoption of similar laws. This could be done in a concerted manner, thus avoiding discrepancies among the various countries and promoting the convergence of mechanisms and policies. The international debate on organized transnational crime has already reached some landmark points and this should testify to both the awareness and the willingness to fight it in a concerted and coordinated fashion. From the procedural point of view, governments would need to consider issues related to traditional concepts of sovereignty and individual decision-making in the light of problems posed by new criminal activities. The realization at the political and decision-making level of the actual magnitude and complexity of organized transnational crime may serve as a basis for elaborating improved forms of international cooperation, drawing on the pool of knowledge and experience in the scientific community.

The differences between civil law and common law systems have not prevented international cooperation in the past. The long-standing tradition of bilateral treaties and multilateral conventions supports the idea that, where agreement is reached on a topic, mutual cooperation may run smoothly. The problem is how to develop strategies and techniques that will reduce the number of obstacles to international cooperation. The most recent instruments of international criminal law could provide useful suggestions to that end.

The first step towards convergence, and eventual closer alignment of legislative and regulatory measures, would be through the adoption and promulgation of policies of demonstrated effectiveness that do not generate problems of compatibility where the legal systems differ, but that actually facilitate cooperation between countries. In the area of substantive legislation, efforts against organized transnational crime would be considerably strengthened through the introduction of reforms focused on criminalization of participation in a criminal organization, criminalization of conspiracy or similar forms of inchoate offences, prohibition of laundering of criminal proceeds, and sanctions and other measures, such as the confiscation of illicit proceeds, aimed at defeating the economic power of criminal organizations.

In any effort towards closer alignment of the legislative approach to organized transnational crime, the regulatory measures necessary to obtain maximum transparency of financial systems and to prevent monopolies should not be neglected.

In accordance with Economic and Social Council resolution 1995/11, the Secretary-General is to submit to member states for their consideration at the fifth session of the Commission on Crime Prevention and Criminal Justice a proposal on the creation of a central repository of existing legislative and regulatory measures, and information on organizational structures designed to combat organized crime, taking into account the capabilities of the United Nations Crime and Justice Information Network and the activities of other United Nations and relevant intergovernmental bodies. Should states deem it appropriate and desirable to proceed with the creation of such a repository, their continuous support and assistance would be a *sine qua non* for its usefulness and effectiveness. Such a repository would need to be continuously updated and complemented with comparative analyses and commentaries, as well as with information on the ways that measures are applied and on their contribution to the prevention and control of organized transnational crime. The material and information contained in the repository would be placed at the disposal of states and could be used in advisory services and training undertaken by the United Nations in response to requests for assistance in the field of prevention and control of organized transnational crime. The results of the comprehensive study on the organized transnational crime situation in the various regions of the world, mentioned above, would be combined with these comparative analyses to enhance the options available to states wishing to enact legislative and regulatory measures.

In Council resolution 1995/11, the Secretary-General was requested, as necessary, to submit concrete proposals to the Commission for approval, with a view to developing practical models and guidelines for substantive and procedural legislation, building on the experience and expertise of states and drawing on contributions from relevant organizations. Such models and guidelines would rely on information collected and analysed regarding best practices with respect to legislative and regulatory measures, as well as on the knowledge and experience accumulated through the comprehensive study. The United Nations could assist requesting states in tailoring these models and guidelines to their particular exigencies and their legal, cultural and social traditions, in order to facilitate integration of the relevant policies and measures within their specific systems, as well as their implementation. In specific areas that present particular difficulties, such as the laundering and use of the proceeds of crime, special attention could be given to assisting states not only in obtaining information on measures and developing the appropriate mechanisms, but also in assessing the needs of their systems in order to maximize the effectiveness of measures and in identifying the most appropriate mechanisms for their implementation.

*Technical cooperation*

Another issue of central importance, and one directly linked to the fundamental concept of international cooperation, is technical assistance. Effective international cooperation often depends on the capacity of the criminal justice system of a given country. Raising the level of knowledge, expertise and professionalism of a criminal justice system requires resources that many countries lack. Technical assistance is then the only way of ensuring that structural difficulties are overcome. The provision of technical assistance can take many forms, depending on the needs of the recipient and on the availability of donor resources. Technical assistance can range from advisory services to the provision of equipment, and will almost invariably include specialized training. The planning and execution of technical assistance projects require constant cooperation and consultation with the competent authorities of the recipient country at every stage of the process. Particular attention should be given to ensuring that assistance is based on the actual needs of the country in question, to be determined by that country, if necessary in consultation with those providing the assistance. Assistance needs to be tailored not only to the specific needs but also to the political, cultural and legal traditions of the recipient country. It should be realized that measures and policies that have proved effective in dealing with a specific problem may need to be substantially modified to retain their effectiveness in different settings or systems. In many cases, the very basic principles or rationale of action are the only elements that can be retained, and new measures and policies have to be designed. A failure to structure and deliver technical assistance on these grounds risks not only rendering such assistance entirely ineffective but also creating an environment that is far from conducive to meaningful cooperation.

The overall capacity and stage of development of the criminal justice system are factors that should be taken into account in all technical assistance efforts, particularly when such assistance is intended to help the recipient country to deal with organized transnational crime. Because of the sophistication of this form of crime, assistance is often aimed at strengthening or improving legislative and law enforcement measures. Such interventions, however, need to be planned and developed on the basis of a thorough knowledge of the criminal justice system in question and its overall capacity, as well as on a careful evaluation of their impact on that particular criminal justice system. For example, the establishment of a special investigation unit for offences related to the laundering of the proceeds of crime may improve the detection and apprehension of money launderers. Its successes may, however, be frustrated if the prosecuting and judicial authorities are not in a position to evaluate and use the evidence that the efforts of that unit have yielded.

Another issue that needs to be carefully considered is coordination. Multiple assistance projects are directed almost simultaneously at the same component of the criminal justice system, overlapping if not conflicting with each other. The result is an unnecessary duplication of effort, which may lead to confusion among recipients and thus render technical assistance ineffective. Coordination is necessary on the part of all concerned and should be viewed as an essential complement to the structured and thorough preparation and provision of technical assistance. Without it, the resources devoted to such assistance fail to achieve the intended goals.

The traditional rationale for technical assistance, either in drafting new legislation or in training criminal justice personnel, is to help countries to cope more effectively with their problems. The global situation has radically changed in the past few years, however, and so have the needs and goals of the international community. Technical assistance needs to be viewed in the context of the new political and economic realities and to be adapted to them, in terms of both concept and objectives. Technical assistance programmes should be designed to enable countries to equalize the organized crime risk and to do so in such a way as to contribute to the collective interest in deterring the expansion of organized crime.

If this objective is missed in planning and providing technical assistance, such assistance will remain a solidarity tax that developed countries pay directly or through multilateral mechanisms. It will be welcomed, but not enough, and the more countries are constrained by limited resources, the less technical assistance they will provide. It is essential, therefore, that technical assistance become more and more a productive investment for three different types of interests: those of the countries receiving assistance, those of the countries giving it and those of the international community.

A fundamental purpose of international cooperation is to contribute to the creation of self-reliant capacities in developing countries, as well as in countries with economies in transition. Strengthened technical cooperation in the fight against organized transnational crime should be viewed as a significant step in that direction. The operational activities of the United Nations crime prevention and criminal justice programme should be geared to developing expertise, especially in countries where it is scarce, and to promoting the highest standards of professionalism and specialization. Training and upgrading the skills of personnel working in the various areas of criminal justice is considered crucial, particularly with respect to the investigation, prosecution and adjudication of complex cases. For the purpose of maximizing resources and raising awareness, training seminars would be first organized at the regional level, concentrating on common exigencies and problems, with a view to eventually responding to requests for training courses at the national level. In order to achieve these aims, appropriate expertise would need to be identified and training material developed that would cater to the specific requirements of each region or each group of trainees. Furthermore, effective channels of communication are necessary in order to assess needs and prevailing circumstances, so that training activities can be tailored accordingly. The Commission may wish to identify the most appropriate ways of enabling the United Nations to respond to the requests of states and provide the assistance outlined above.

The accumulation of knowledge and expertise, and the development of the capacity to collect, process and analyse reliable information, will require efforts spanning a certain period of time. This would be necessary to put together the appropriate expertise and to carry out a study that would be truly comprehensive and constitute a major contribution to the common efforts of the international community against organized transnational crime. Capacity-building requires a long-term and consistent commitment to ensure that the benefits of assistance can be sustainable through the consolidation of mechanisms and procedures, and the creation of the necessary infrastructure. Organized transnational crime, however, continues to expand its reach and constitutes a growing threat to the international community. A well-balanced approach is, therefore, essential. The efforts to accumulate knowledge would need to be undertaken simultaneously with meeting the current and pressing needs of states in taking immediate measures to prevent and arrest the expansion of organized transnational crime, and mitigate its effects on their economies and institutions. Concurrently with building the capacity for pursuing common objectives, there is an urgent need to strengthen existing mechanisms and institutions to fight against the most immediate manifestations and threats posed by organized transnational crime.

In order to contribute to this balanced approach, the United Nations should assist requesting states in assessing their immediate needs, through the provision of advisory services. Such services should also be provided in reviewing existing measures, mechanisms and institutions in order to identify and put in place modalities for strengthening their capacity to respond to the problems created by the new manifestations of organized transnational crime. In response to requests from states, the United Nations should provide expert advice and options on the establishment of special investigative units and on developing reliable evidence-gathering techniques. For the purpose of strengthening the capacity of states to cooperate and exchange information, intelligence and experience, the United Nations should assist with the creation of special mechanisms and the implementation of appropriate measures. The pressing needs that currently exist are evidenced by the increase in requests for assistance which the Crime Prevention and Criminal Justice Branch has received in the past year. The Branch, often cooperating closely with the United Nations International Drug Control Program , has begun to respond to such requests from the governments of Belarus, Kyrgyzstan, Pakistan and the former Yugoslav Republic of Macedonia.

## Conclusions

States have attached high priority to the implementation of the Naples Political Declaration and Global Action Plan, as well as to the United Nations crime prevention and criminal justice program and its role in such implementation. This priority should soon be translated into practice if the momentum of the World Ministerial Conference on Organized Transnational Crime is to be sustained. The consensus on the threat posed by organized transnational crime and the urgency of effectively combating it, and the political will to take global action create the necessary foundations for implementation. Efforts by the international community and the United Nations should be guided by this consensus and political will and be geared towards sustaining and broadening them.

Building on the established consensus and taking full advantage of the present political climate, which is conducive to more meaningful international cooperation, states should specify the activities that need to be undertaken for implementation, agree on the pace of such implementation and devote their energies and undivided attention towards achieving the common goals identified in the Naples Political Declaration and Global Action Plan. Such action is essential to enable the Commission on Crime Prevention and Criminal Justice and the United Nations to undertake rational and effective planning.

In view of its general mandate and universal constituency, the United Nations provides an appropriate mechanism for the promotion of global action. The United Nations has been given a special responsibility to improve countries' capacities to combat organized transnational crime and can serve as global catalyst, bringing together divergent views, equalizing the burden and pace of implementation and encouraging efforts in that direction. While the United Nations is naturally held to austere standards of efficiency and effectiveness, it cannot move ahead without member states providing it with the means to do so. In the absence of these means, and in spite of its best efforts to use its limited resources with maximum efficiency, it becomes very difficult to make a real impact and produce measurable results. As with any other action on a global scale, resources are bound to be a central issue. The Secretary-General has begun translating into practice the priority attached to the fight against organized transnational crime in the context of the proposed programme budget for the biennium 1996-1997.[4] Regular budget resources, however, can only provide a minimum framework and, while they should be further increased, are not likely to be sufficient for the required action. They need to be supplemented by extrabudgetary resources through voluntary contributions from states, particularly in view of the vast needs of developing countries and countries in transition and the central role that the provision of practical assistance is bound to play in any efforts towards implementation of the Naples Political Declaration and Global Action Plan.

NOTES

1. *Testimony* of Philip B. Heymann, Deputy Attorney General, to the Foreign Affairs Committee, United States House of Representatives, 14 September 1993, p. 3.
2. See Fleur Keyser-Ringnalda, 'European integration with regard to the confiscation of the proceeds of crime', paper compiled for the Tenth International Symposium on Economic Crime, Cambridge, July 1992.
3. *Eighth United Nations Congress on the Prevention of Crime and the Treatment of Offenders, Havana, 27 August-7 September 1990* (United Nations publication, Sales No. E.91.IV.2), chap. IV, sect. C, para. 253.
4. See *Official Records of the General Assembly, Fiftieth Session, Supplement No. 6* (A/50/6/Rev.1), sect. 13.